ROS Robotics Projects

Build a variety of awesome robots that can see, sense, move, and do a lot more using the powerful Robot Operating System

Lentin Joseph

BIRMINGHAM - MUMBAI

ROS Robotics Projects

Copyright © 2017 Packt Publishing

First published: March 2017

Production reference: 1290317

Published by Packt Publishing Ltd.
Livery Place
35 Livery Street
Birmingham
B3 2PB, UK.
ISBN 978-1-78355-471-3

www.packtpub.com

Credits

Author
Lentin Joseph

Copy Editor
Madhusudan Uchil

Reviewer
Ruixiang Du

Project Coordinator
Judie Jose

Commissioning Editor
Kartikey Pandey

Proofreader
Safis Editing

Acquisition Editor
Namrata Patil

Indexer
Pratik Shirodkar

Content Development Editor
Amedh Pohad

Graphics
Kirk D'Penha

Technical Editor
Prashant Chaudhari

Production Coordinator
Shantanu Zagade

About the Author

Lentin Joseph is an author, entrepreneur, electronics engineer, robotics enthusiast, machine vision expert, embedded programmer, and the founder and CEO of Qbotics Labs (`http://www.qboticslabs.com`) from India.

He completed his bachelor's degree in electronics and communication engineering at the Federal Institute of Science and Technology (FISAT), Kerala. For his final year engineering project, he made a social robot that can interact with people. The project was a huge success and was mentioned in many forms of visual and print media. The main features of this robot were that it could communicate with people and reply intelligently and had some image processing capabilities such as face, motion, and color detection. The entire project was implemented using the Python programming language. His interest in robotics, image processing, and Python started with that project.

After his graduation, he worked for three years at a start-up company focusing on robotics and image processing. In the meantime, he learned to work with famous robotics software platforms such as Robot Operating System (ROS), V-REP, and Actin (a robotic simulation tool) and image processing libraries such as OpenCV, OpenNI, and PCL. He also knows about 3D robot design and embedded programming on Arduino and Tiva Launchpad.

After three years of work experience, he started a new company called Qbotics Labs, which mainly focuses on research into building some great products in domains such as robotics and machine vision. He maintains a personal website (`http://www.lentinjoseph.com`) and a technology blog called *technolabsz* (`http://www.technolabsz.com`). He publishes his works on his tech blog. He was also a speaker at PyCon2013, India, on the topic *Learning Robotics Using Python*.

Lentin is the author of the books *Learning Robotics Using Python* (`http://learn-robotics.com`) and *Mastering ROS for Robotics Programming* (`http://mastering-ros.com`), both by Packt Publishing. The first book was about building an autonomous mobile robot using ROS and OpenCV. This book was launched at ICRA 2015 and was featured on the ROS blog, Robohub, OpenCV, the Python website, and various other such forums. The second book is on mastering Robot Operating System, which was also launched at ICRA 2016, and is one of the bestselling books on ROS.

Lentin and his team were also winners of the HRATC 2016 challenge conducted as a part of ICRA 2016. He was also a finalist in the ICRA 2015 challenge, HRATC (`http://www.icra2016.org/conference/challenges/`).

Acknowledgements

I would like to express my gratitude to the readers of my previous two books on ROS (ROS). Actually, they encouraged me to write one more book on ROS itself.

I would like to thank the Packt Publishing team for giving support for publishing my books. It may have been a distant dream without you all.

I would especially like to thank Amedh Pohad and Namrata Patil of Packt Publishing, who guided me during the writing process. Thanks for all your suggestions.

A special thanks to Ruixiang Du and all other technical reviewers for improving the content and giving good suggestions. Without your suggestions, this book may not have become a good product.

The most important thing in my life is my family. Without their support, this would not have been possible. I would like to dedicate this book to my parents, who gave me the inspiration to write this book. This is my third book about ROS. Thanks for the constant support.

I would also like to mention my previous company, ASIMOV Robotics, who provided components for a few projects in this book. Thank you very much.

I thank all the readers who made by previous books successful. I hope you guys also like this book and make it successful.

About the Reviewer

Ruixiang Du is a PhD candidate in mechanical engineering at Worcester Polytechnic Institute (WPI). He currently works in the Systems and Robot Control laboratory with a research focus on the motion planning and control of autonomous mobile robots. He received a bachelor's degree in automation from North China Electric Power University in 2011 and a master's degree in robotics engineering from WPI in 2013.

Ruixiang has general interests in robotics and in real-time and embedded systems. He has worked on various robotic projects, with robot platforms ranging from medical robots and unmanned aerial/ground vehicles to humanoid robots. He was a member of Team WPI-CMU for the DARPA Robotics Challenge.

www.PacktPub.com

For support files and downloads related to your book, please visit www.PacktPub.com.

Did you know that Packt offers eBook versions of every book published, with PDF and ePub files available? You can upgrade to the eBook version at www.PacktPub.com and as a print book customer, you are entitled to a discount on the eBook copy. Get in touch with us at service@packtpub.com for more details.

At www.PacktPub.com, you can also read a collection of free technical articles, sign up for a range of free newsletters and receive exclusive discounts and offers on Packt books and eBooks.

https://www.packtpub.com/mapt

Get the most in-demand software skills with Mapt. Mapt gives you full access to all Packt books and video courses, as well as industry-leading tools to help you plan your personal development and advance your career.

Why subscribe?

- Fully searchable across every book published by Packt
- Copy and paste, print, and bookmark content
- On demand and accessible via a web browser

Customer Feedback

Thanks for purchasing this Packt book. At Packt, quality is at the heart of our editorial process. To help us improve, please leave us an honest review on this book's Amazon page at https://www.amazon.com/dp/1783554711.

If you'd like to join our team of regular reviewers, you can e-mail us at customerreviews@packtpub.com. We award our regular reviewers with free eBooks and videos in exchange for their valuable feedback. Help us be relentless in improving our products!

Table of Contents

Preface

ROS Robotics Projects is a practical guide to learning ROS by making interesting projects using it. The book assumes that you have some knowledge of ROS. However, if you do not have any experience with ROS, you can still learn from this book. The first chapter is dedicated to absolute beginners. ROS is widely used in robotics companies, universities, and robot research labs for designing and programming robots. If you would like to work in the robotics software domain or if you want to have a career as a robotics software engineer, this book is perfect for you.

The basic aim of this book is to teach ROS through interactive projects. The projects that we are discussing here can also be reused in your academic or industrial projects. This book handles a wide variety of new technology that can be interfaced with ROS. For example, you will see how to build a self-driving car prototype, how to build a deep-learning application using ROS, and how to build a VR application in ROS. These are only a few highlighted topics; in addition, you will find some 15 projects and applications using ROS and its libraries.

You can work with any project after meeting its prerequisites. Most of the projects can be completed without many dependencies. We are using popular and available hardware components to build most of the projects. So this will help us create almost all of these projects without much difficulty.

The book starts by discussing the basics of ROS and its variety of applications. This chapter will definitely be a starting point for absolute beginners. After this chapter, we will explore a wide variety of ROS projects.

Let's learn and make cool projects with ROS!

What this book covers

Chapter 1, *Getting Started with ROS Robotics Application Development*, is for absolute beginners to ROS. No need to worry if you don't have experience in ROS; this chapter will help you get an idea of the ROS software framework and its concepts.

Chapter 2, *Face Detection and Tracking Using ROS, OpenCV and Dynamixel Servos*, takes you through a cool project that you can make with ROS and the OpenCV library. This project basically creates a face tracker application in which your face will be tracked in such a way that the camera will always point to your face. We will use intelligent servos such as Dynamixel to rotate the robot on its axis.

Chapter 3, *Building a Siri-Like Chatbot in ROS*, is for those of you who want to make your robot interactive and intelligent without much hassle. This project creates a chatterbot in ROS that you can communicate with using text or speech. This project will be useful if you're going to create social or service robots.

Chapter 4, *Controlling Embedded Boards Using ROS*, helps you build a robot using Arduino, an embedded compatible board, Raspberry Pi, or Odroid and an interface to ROS. In this chapter, you will see a wide variety of embedded boards and interfacing projects made with them.

Chapter 5, *Teleoperate a Robot Using Hand Gestures*, will teach you how to build a gesture-control device using Arduino and IMU. The gestures are translated into motion commands by ROS nodes.

Chapter 6, *Object Detection and Recognition*, has interesting project for detecting objects. You will learn both 2D and 3D object recognition using powerful ROS packages.

Chapter 7, *Deep Learning Using ROS and TensorFlow*, is a project made using a trending technology in robotics. Using the TensorFlow library and ROS, we can implement interesting deep-learning applications. You can implement image recognition using deep learning, and an application using SVM can be found in this chapter.

Chapter 8, *ROS on MATLAB and Android*, is intended for building robot applications using ROS, MATLAB, and Android.

Chapter 9, *Building an Autonomous Mobile Robot*, is about creating an autonomous mobile robot with the help of ROS. You can see how to use packages such as navigation, gmapping, and AMCL to make a mobile robot autonomous.

Chapter 10, *Creating a Self-driving Car Using ROS*, is one of the more interesting projects in this book. In this chapter, we will build a simulation of self-driving car using ROS and Gazebo.

Chapter 11, *Teleoperating Robot Using VR Headset and Leap Motion*, shows you how to control a robot's actions using a VR headset and Leap Motion sensor. You can play around with virtual reality, a trending technology these days.

Chapter 12, *Controlling Your Robots over the Web*, we will see how to build interactive web applications using rosbridge in ROS.

What you need for this book

You should have a powerful PC running a Linux distribution, preferably Ubuntu 16.04 LTS.

You can use a laptop or desktop with a graphics card, and RAM of 4-8 GB is preferred. This is actually for running high-end simulations in Gazebo, as well as for processing point clouds and computer vision.

You should have the sensors, actuators, and I/O boards mentioned in the book and should be able to connect them all to your PC.

You also need Git installed to clone the package files.

If you are a Windows user, then it will be good to download VirtualBox and set up Ubuntu on it. You can have issues when you try to interface real hardware to ROS when working with VirtualBox. So, it is best if you can work from a real Linux system.

Who this book is for

If you are a robotics enthusiast or researcher who wants to learn more about building robot applications using ROS, this book is for you. In order to learn from this book, you should have a basic knowledge of ROS, GNU/Linux, and C++ programming concepts. The book is also good for programmers who want to explore the advanced features of ROS.

Conventions

In this book, you will find a number of text styles that distinguish between different kinds of information. Here are some examples of these styles and an explanation of their meaning.

Code words in text, database table names, folder names, filenames, file extensions, pathnames, dummy URLs, user input, and Twitter handles are shown as follows: "The next lines of code read the link and assign it to the to the `BeautifulSoup` function."

A block of code is set as follows:

```
ros::init(argc, argv,"face_tracker_controller");
ros::NodeHandle node_obj;
ros::Subscriber number_subscriber =
node_obj.subscribe("/face_centroid",10,face_callback);
dynamixel_control = node_obj.advertise<std_msgs::Float64>
("/pan_controller/command",10);
```

When we wish to draw your attention to a particular part of a code block, the relevant lines or items are set in bold:

```
ros::init(argc, argv,"face_tracker_controller");
ros::NodeHandle node_obj;
ros::Subscriber number_subscriber =
node_obj.subscribe("/face_centroid",10,face_callback);
dynamixel_control = node_obj.advertise<std_msgs::Float64>
("/pan_controller/command",10);
```

Any command-line input or output is written as follows:

```
$ git clone https://github.com/qboticslabs/ros_robotics_projects
```

New terms and **important words** are shown in bold. Words that you see on the screen, for example, in menus or dialog boxes, appear in the text like this: "In order to download new modules, we will go to **Files | Settings | Project Name | Project Interpreter**."

Warnings or important notes appear in a box like this.

Tips and tricks appear like this.

Reader feedback

Feedback from our readers is always welcome. Let us know what you think about this book-what you liked or disliked. Reader feedback is important for us as it helps us develop titles that you will really get the most out of. To send us general feedback, simply e-mail feedback@packtpub.com, and mention the book's title in the subject of your message. If there is a topic that you have expertise in and you are interested in either writing or contributing to a book, see our author guide at www.packtpub.com/authors.

Customer support

Now that you are the proud owner of a Packt book, we have a number of things to help you to get the most from your purchase.

Downloading the example code

You can download the example code files for this book from your account at http://www.packtpub.com. If you purchased this book elsewhere, you can visit http://www.packtpub.com/support and register to have the files e-mailed directly to you.

You can download the code files by following these steps:

1. Log in or register to our website using your e-mail address and password.
2. Hover the mouse pointer on the **SUPPORT** tab at the top.
3. Click on **Code Downloads & Errata**.
4. Enter the name of the book in the **Search** box.
5. Select the book for which you're looking to download the code files.
6. Choose from the drop-down menu where you purchased this book from.
7. Click on **Code Download**.

Once the file is downloaded, please make sure that you unzip or extract the folder using the latest version of:

- WinRAR / 7-Zip for Windows
- Zipeg / iZip / UnRarX for Mac
- 7-Zip / PeaZip for Linux

The code bundle for the book is also hosted on GitHub at https://github.com/PacktPubl ishing/ROS-Robotics-Projects. We also have other code bundles from our rich catalog of books and videos available at https://github.com/PacktPublishing/. Check them out!

Downloading the color images of this book

We also provide you with a PDF file that has color images of the screenshots/diagrams used in this book. The color images will help you better understand the changes in the output. You can download this file from https://www.packtpub.com/sites/default/files/down loads/ROSRoboticsProjects_ColorImages.pdf.

Errata

Although we have taken every care to ensure the accuracy of our content, mistakes do happen. If you find a mistake in one of our books-maybe a mistake in the text or the code- we would be grateful if you could report this to us. By doing so, you can save other readers from frustration and help us improve subsequent versions of this book. If you find any errata, please report them by visiting http://www.packtpub.com/submit-errata, selecting your book, clicking on the **Errata Submission Form** link, and entering the details of your errata. Once your errata are verified, your submission will be accepted and the errata will be uploaded to our website or added to any list of existing errata under the Errata section of that title.

To view the previously submitted errata, go to https://www.packtpub.com/books/conten t/supportand enter the name of the book in the search field. The required information will appear under the **Errata** section.

Piracy

Piracy of copyrighted material on the Internet is an ongoing problem across all media. At Packt, we take the protection of our copyright and licenses very seriously. If you come across any illegal copies of our works in any form on the Internet, please provide us with the location address or website name immediately so that we can pursue a remedy.

Please contact us at copyright@packtpub.com with a link to the suspected pirated material.

We appreciate your help in protecting our authors and our ability to bring you valuable content.

Questions

If you have a problem with any aspect of this book, you can contact us at `questions@packtpub.com`, and we will do our best to address the problem.

1
Getting Started with ROS Robotics Application Development

Robotics is one of the upcoming technologies that can change the world. Robots can replace people in many ways, and we are all afraid of them stealing our jobs. One thing is for sure: robotics will be one of the influential technologies in the future. When a new technology gains momentum, the opportunities in that field also increase. This means that robotics and automation can generate lot of job opportunities in the future.

One of the main areas in robotics that can provide mass job opportunities is robotics software development. As we all know, software gives life to a robot or any machine. We can expand a robot's capabilities through software. If a robot exists, its capabilities such as control, sensing, and intelligence are realized using software.

Robotics software involves a combination of related technologies, such as computer vision, artificial intelligence, and control theory. In short, developing software for a robot is not a simple task; it may require expertise in many fields.

If you're looking for mobile application development in iOS or Android, there is a **software development kit (SDK)** available to build applications in it, but what about robots? Is there any generic software framework available? Yes. One of the more popular robotics software frameworks is called **Robot Operating System (ROS)**.

In this chapter, we will take a look at an abstract concept of ROS and how to install it. The entire book is dedicated to ROS projects, so this chapter will be a kick-start guide for those projects.

The following topics are going to be covered in this chapter:

- Getting started with ROS
- Why we use ROS
- Basic concepts of ROS
- Robot, sensors, and actuators supporting ROS
- Installing ROS
- ROS in industries and research

So let's get started discussing ROS.

Getting started with ROS

ROS is an open source, flexible software framework for programming robots. ROS provides a hardware abstraction layer, in which developers can build robotics applications without worrying about the underlying hardware. ROS also provides different software tools to visualize and debug robot data. The core of the ROS framework is a message-passing middleware in which processes can communicate and exchange data with each other even when running from different machines. ROS message passing can be synchronous or asynchronous.

Software in ROS is organized as packages, and it offers good modularity and reusability. Using the ROS message-passing middleware and hardware abstraction layer, developers can create tons of robotic capabilities, such as mapping and navigation (in mobile robots). Almost all capabilities in ROS will be robot agnostic so that all kinds of robots can use it. New robots can directly use this capability package without modifying any code inside the package.

ROS has widespread collaborations in universities, and lots of developers contribute to it. We can say that ROS is a community-driven project supported by developers worldwide. The active developer ecosystem distinguishes ROS from other robotic frameworks.

In short, ROS is the combination of **Plumbing** (or communication), **Tools**, **Capabilities** and **Ecosystem**. These capabilities are demonstrated in the following figure:

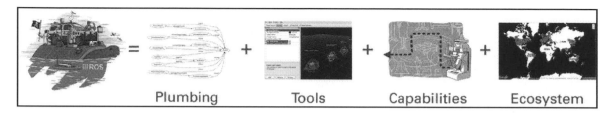

Figure 1: The ROS equation

The ROS project was started in 2007 in Stanford University under the name Switchyard. Later on, in 2008, the development was undertaken by a robotic research start-up called **Willow Garage**. The major development in ROS happened in Willow Garage. In 2013, the Willow Garage researchers formed the **Open Source Robotics Foundation (OSRF)**. ROS is actively maintained by OSRF now.

Here are links to their websites:

- Willow Garage: http://www.willowgarage.com/
- OSRF: http://www.osrfoundation.org/

ROS distributions

The ROS distributions are very similar to Linux distributions, that is, a versioned set of ROS packages. Each distribution maintains a stable set of core packages up to the **end of life (EOL)** of the distribution.

The ROS distributions are fully compatible with Ubuntu, and most of the ROS distributions are planned according to the respective Ubuntu versions.

Given here are some of latest ROS distributions recommended for use from the ROS website (http://wiki.ros.org/Distributions):

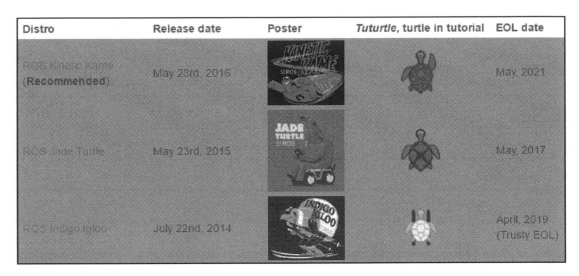

Distro	Release date	Poster	*Tuturtle*, turtle in tutorial	EOL date
ROS Kinetic Kame (Recommended)	May 23rd, 2016			May, 2021
ROS Jade Turtle	May 23rd, 2015			May, 2017
ROS Indigo Igloo	July 22nd, 2014			April, 2019 (Trusty EOL)

Figure 2: Latest ROS distributions

The latest ROS distribution is Kinect Kame. We will get support for this distribution up to May 2021. One of the problems with this latest ROS distribution is that most of the packages will not be available on it because it will take time to migrate them from the previous distribution. If you are looking for a stable distribution, you can go for **ROS Indigo Igloo**, because the distribution started in 2015, and most of the packages are available on this distribution. The **ROS Jade Turtle** distribution will stop being supported on May 2017, so I do not recommend you use it.

Supported operating systems

The main operating system ROS is tuned for is Ubuntu. ROS distributions are planned according to Ubuntu releases. Other than Ubuntu, it is partially supported by Ubuntu ARM, Debian, Gentoo, Mac OS X, Arch Linux, Android, Windows, and Open Embedded:

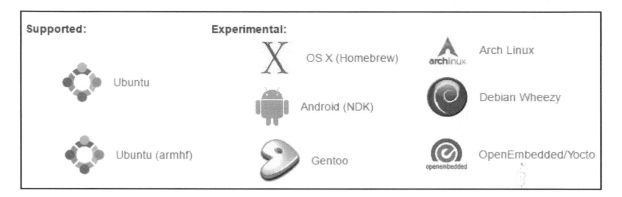

Figure 3: OSes supporting ROS

This table shows new ROS distributions and the specific versions of the supporting OSes:

ROS distribution	Supporting OSes
Kinetic Kame (LTS)	Ubuntu 16.04 (LTS) and 15.10, Debian 8, OS X (Homebrew), Gentoo, and Ubuntu ARM
Jade Turtle	Ubuntu 15.04, 14.10, and 14.04, Ubuntu ARM, OS X (Homebrew), Gentoo, Arch Linux, Android NDK, and Debian 8
Indigo Igloo (LTS)	Ubuntu 14.04 (LTS) and 13.10, Ubuntu ARM, OS X (Homebrew), Gentoo, Arch Linux, Android NDK, and Debian 7

ROS Indigo and Kinetic are **long-term support** (**LTS**) distributions, coming with the LTS version of Ubuntu. The advantage of using LTS distribution is that we will get maximum lifespan and support.

Robots and sensors supported by ROS

The ROS framework is one of the successful robotics frameworks, and universities around the globe contribute to it. Because of the active ecosystem and open source nature, ROS is being used in a majority of robots and is compatible with major robotic hardware and software. Here are some of the famous robots completely running on ROS:

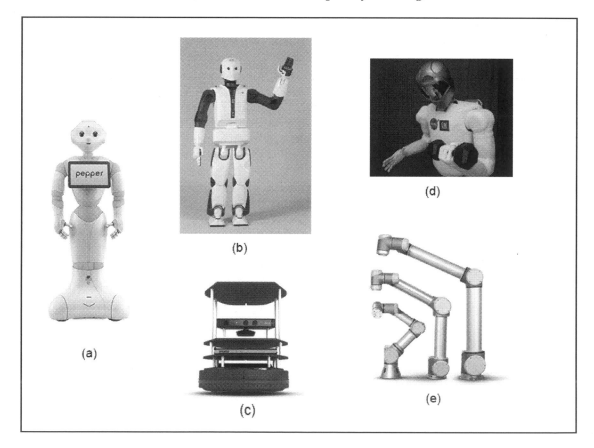

Figure 4: Popular robots supported by ROS

The names of the robots listed in the images are Pepper **(a)**, REEM-C **(b)**, TurtleBot **(c)**, Robonaut **(d)**, Universal Robots **(e)**.

The robots supported by ROS are listed at the following link:

```
http://wiki.ros.org/Robots.
```

The following are links to get ROS packages of robots from:

- **Pepper:** http://wiki.ros.org/Robots/Pepper
- **REEM-C:** http://wiki.ros.org/Robots/Robonaut2
- **TurtleBot 2:** http://wiki.ros.org/Robots/TurtleBot
- **Robonaut:** http://wiki.ros.org/Robots/Robonaut2
- **Universal Robotic arms:** http://wiki.ros.org/universal_robot

Some popular sensors supporting ROS are as follows:

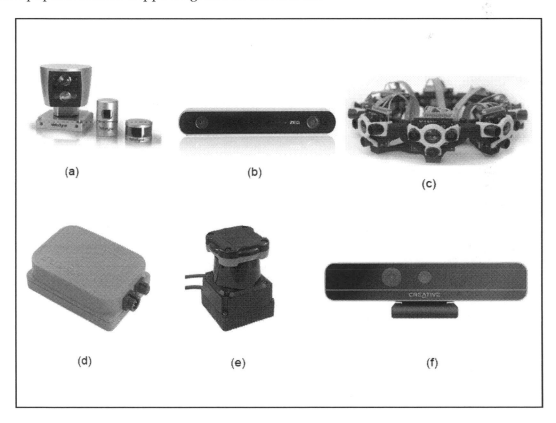

Figure 5: Popular robot sensors supported in ROS

The names of the sensors listed in the image are Velodyne **(a)**, ZED Camera **(b)**, Teraranger **(c)**, Xsens **(d)**, Hokuyo Laser range finder **(e)**, and Intel RealSense **(f)**.

The list of sensors supported by ROS is available at the following link:

`http://wiki.ros.org/Sensors`

These are the links to the ROS wiki pages of these sensors:

- **Velodyne(a)**: `http://wiki.ros.org/Velodyne`
- **ZED Camera(b)**: `http://wiki.ros.org/zed-ros-wrapper`
- **Teraranger(c)**: `http://wiki.ros.org/terarangerone`
- **Xsens(d)**: `http://wiki.ros.org/terarangerone`
- **Hokuyo Laser range finder(e)**: `http://wiki.ros.org/hokuyo_node`
- **Intel real sense(f)**: `http://wiki.ros.org/realsense_camera`

Why ROS

The main intention behind building the ROS framework is to become a generic software framework for robots. Even though there was robotics research happening before ROS, most of the software was exclusive to their own robots. Their software may be open source, but it is very difficult to reuse.

Compared to existing robotic frameworks, ROS is outperforming in the following aspects:

- **Collaborative development**: As we discussed, ROS is open source and free to use for industries and research. Developers can expand the functionalities of ROS by adding packages. Almost all the packages of ROS work on a hardware abstraction layer, so it can be reused easily for other robots. So if one university is good in mobile navigation and other in robotic manipulators, they can contribute that to the ROS community and other developers can reuse their packages and build new applications.
- **Language support**: The ROS communication framework can be easily implemented in any modern language. It already supports popular languages such as C++, Python, and Lisp, and it has experimental libraries for Java and Lua.
- **Library integration**: ROS has an interface to many third-party robotics libraries, such as **Open Source Computer Vision (Open-CV)**, **Point Cloud Library (PCL)**, Open-NI, Open-Rave, and Orocos. Developers can work with any of these libraries without much hassle.

- **Simulator integration**: ROS also has ties to open source simulators such as Gazebo and has a good interface with proprietary simulators such as Webots and V-REP.

- **Code testing**: ROS offers an inbuilt testing framework called **rostest** to check code quality and bugs.

- **Scalability**: The ROS framework is designed to be scalable. We can perform heavy computation tasks with robots using ROS, which can either be placed on the cloud or on heterogeneous clusters.

- **Customizability**: As we have discussed, ROS is completely open source and free, so one can customize this framework as per the robot's requirement. If we only want to work with the ROS messaging platform, we can remove all the other components and use only that. One can even customize ROS for a specific robot for better performance.

- **Community**: ROS is a community-driven project, and it is mainly led by OSRF. The large community support is a great plus for ROS, and one can easily start robotics application development.

Given here are the URLs of libraries and simulators integrated with ROS:

- Open-CV: http://wiki.ros.org/vision_opencv
- PCL: http://wiki.ros.org/pcl_ros
- Open-NI: http://wiki.ros.org/openni_launch
- Open-Rave: http://openrave.org/
- Orocos: http://www.orocos.org/
- Webots: https://www.cyberbotics.com/overview
- V-REP: http://www.coppeliarobotics.com/

Let's go through some of the basic concepts of ROS; they can help you get started with ROS projects.

Fundamentals of ROS

Understanding the basic working of ROS and its terminology can help you understand existing ROS applications and build your own. This section will teach you important concepts that we are going to use in the upcoming chapters. If you find a topic missed in this chapter, it will be covered in a corresponding later chapter.

There are three different concepts in ROS. Let's take a look at them.

The filesystem level

The filesystem level explains how ROS files are organized on the hard disk:

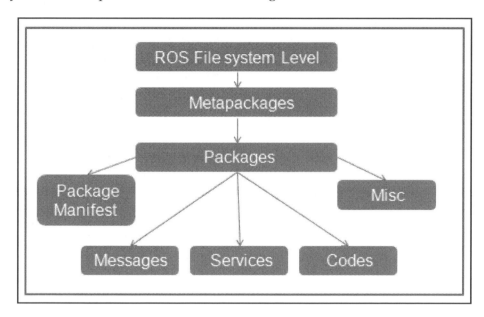

Figure 6: The ROS filesystem level

As you can see from the figure, the filesystem in ROS can be categorized mainly as metapackages, packages, package manifest, messages, services, codes and miscellaneous files. The following is a short description of each component:

- **Metapackages**: Metapackages group together a list of packages for a specific application. For example, in ROS, there is a metapackage called **navigation** for mobile robot navigation. It can hold the information on related packages and helps install those packages during its own installation.
- **Packages**: The software in ROS is mainly organized as ROS packages. We can say that ROS packages are the atomic build unit of ROS. A package may consist of ROS nodes/processes, datasets, and configuration files, organized in a single module.

- **Package manifest**: Inside every package will be a manifest file called `package.xml`. This file consists of information such as the name, version, author, license, and dependencies required of the package. The `package.xml` file of a metapackage consists of the names of related packages.
- **Messages (msg)**: ROS communicates by sending ROS messages. The type of message data can be defined inside a file with the `.msg` extension. These files are called message files. We are following a convention that the message files are kept under `our_package/msg/message_files.msg`.
- **Service (srv)**: One of the computation graph level concepts is services. Similar to ROS messages, the convention is to put service definitions under `our_package/srv/service_files.srv`.

The computation graph level

The ROS computation graph is the peer-to-peer network of the ROS process, and it processes the data together. The ROS computation graph concepts are nodes, topics, messages, master, parameter server, services, and bags:

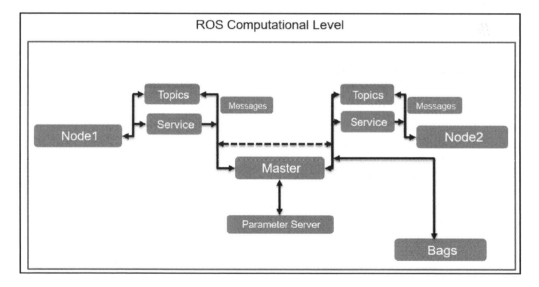

Figure 7: The ROS computational graph concept diagram

The preceding figure shows the various concepts in the ROS computational graph. Here is a short description of each concept:

- **Nodes**: ROS nodes are simply a process that is using ROS APIs to communicate with each other. A robot may have many nodes to perform its computations. For example, an autonomous mobile robot may have a node each for hardware interfacing, reading laser scans, and localization and mapping. We can create ROS nodes using ROS client libraries such as `roscpp` and `rospy`, which we will be discussing in the upcoming sections.

- **Master**: The ROS master works as an intermediate node that aids connections between different ROS nodes. The master has all the details about all nodes running in the ROS environment. It will exchange details of one node with another in order to establish a connection between them. After exchanging the information, communication will start between the two ROS nodes.

- **Parameter server**: The parameter server is a pretty useful thing in ROS. A node can store a variable in the parameter server and set its privacy too. If the parameter has a global scope, it can be accessed by all other nodes. The ROS parameter runs along with the ROS master.

- **Messages**: ROS nodes can communicate with each other in many ways. In all methods, nodes send and receive data in the form of ROS messages. The ROS message is a data structure used by ROS nodes to exchange data.

- **Topics**: One of the methods to communicate and exchange ROS messages between two ROS nodes is called **ROS topics**. Topics are named buses, in which data is exchanged using ROS messages. Each topic will have a specific name, and one node will publish data to a topic and an other node can read from the topic by subscribing to it.

- **Services**: Services are another kind of communication method, like topics. Topics use publish or subscribe interaction, but in services, a request or reply method is used. One node will act as the service provider, which has a service routine running, and a client node requests a service from the server. The server will execute the service routine and send the result to the client. The client node should wait until the server responds with the results.

- **Bags**: Bags are a useful utility in ROS for the recording and playback of ROS topics. While working on robots, there may be some situations where we need to work without actual hardware. Using `rosbag`, we can record sensor data and can copy the bag file to other computers to inspect data by playing it back.

The ROS community level

The community level comprises the ROS resources for sharing software and knowledge:

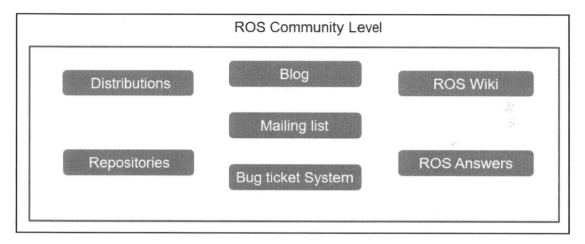

Figure 8: ROS community level diagram

Here is a brief description of each section:

- **Distributions**: ROS distributions are versioned collections of ROS packages, like Linux distribution.
- **Repositories**: ROS-related packages and files depend on a **version-control system (VCS)** such as Git, SVN, and Mercurial, using which developers around the world can contribute to the packages.
- The **ROS Wiki**: The ROS community wiki is the knowledge center of ROS, in which anyone can create documentation for their packages. You can find standard documentation and tutorials about ROS from the ROS wiki.
- **Mailing lists**: Subscribing to the ROS mailing lists enables users to get new updates regarding ROS packages and gives them a place to ask questions about ROS (http://wiki.ros.org/Mailing%20Lists).
- **ROS Answers**: The ROS Answers website is the Stack Overflow of ROS. Users can ask questions regarding ROS and related areas (http://answers.ros.org/questions/).
- **Blog**: The ROS blog provides regular updates about the ROS community with photos and videos (http://www.ros.org/news).

Communication in ROS

Let's see how two nodes communicate with each other using ROS topics. The following diagram shows how it happens:

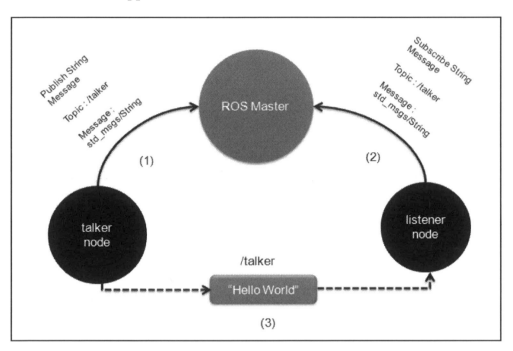

Figure 9: Communication between ROS nodes using topics

As you can see, there are two nodes, named *talker* and *listener*. The **talker node** publishes a string message called **Hello World** into a topic called **/talker**, and the **listener node** is subscribed to this topic. Let's see what happens at each stage, marked **(1)**, **(2)**, and **(3)**:

1. Before running any nodes in ROS, we should start the **ROS Master**. After it has been started, it will wait for nodes. When the **talker node** (publisher) starts running, it will first connect to the **ROS Master** and exchange the publishing topic details with the master. This includes topic name, message type, and publishing node URI. The URI of the master is a global value, and all nodes can connect to it. The master maintains tables of the publisher connected to it. Whenever a publisher's details change, the table updates automatically.

2. When we start the **listener node** (subscriber), it will connect to the master and exchange the details of the node, such as the topic going to be subscribed to, its message type, and the node URI. The master also maintains a table of subscribers, similar to the publisher.
3. Whenever there is a subscriber and publisher for the same topic, the master node will exchange the publisher URI with the subscriber. This will help both nodes connect with each other and exchange data. After they've connected with each other, there is no role for the master. The data is not flowing through the master; instead, the nodes are interconnected and exchange messages.

ROS client libraries

The ROS client libraries are used to write ROS nodes. All the ROS concepts are implemented in client libraries. So we can just use it without implementing everything from scratch. We can implement ROS nodes with a publisher and subscriber, we can write service callbacks, and so on using client libraries.

The main ROS client libraries are in C++ and Python. Here is a list of popular ROS client libraries:

- `roscpp`: This is one of the most recommended and widely used ROS client libraries for building ROS nodes. This client library has most of the ROS concepts implemented and can be used in high-performance applications.
- `rospy`: This is a pure implementation of the ROS client library in Python. The advantage of this library is the ease of prototyping, so development time is shorter. It is not recommended for high-performance applications, but it is perfect for non-critical tasks.
- `roslisp`: This is the client library for LISP and is commonly used to build robot planning libraries.

Details of all client ROS libraries are given in the following link:
`http://wiki.ros.org/Client%20Libraries`.

ROS tools

ROS has a variety of GUI and command-line tools to inspect and debug messages. Let's look at some commonly used ones.

Rviz (ROS Visualizer)

Rviz (`http://wiki.ros.org/rviz`) is one of the 3D visualizers available in ROS to visualize 2D and 3D values from ROS topics and parameters. Rviz helps visualize data such as robot models, robot 3D transform data (TF), point cloud, laser and image data, and a variety of different sensor data.

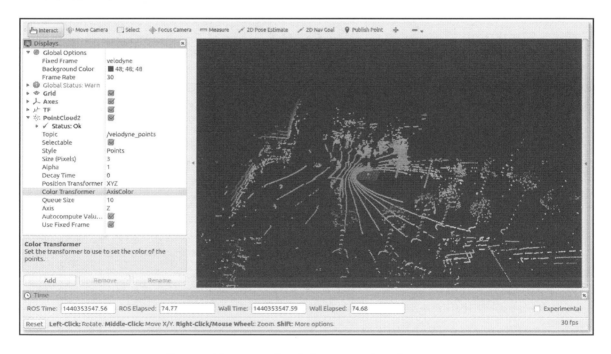

Figure 10: Point cloud data visualized in Rviz

rqt_plot

The **rqt_plot** program (`http://wiki.ros.org/rqt_plot`) is a tool for plotting scalar values that are in the form of ROS topics. We can provide a topic name in the **Topic** box.

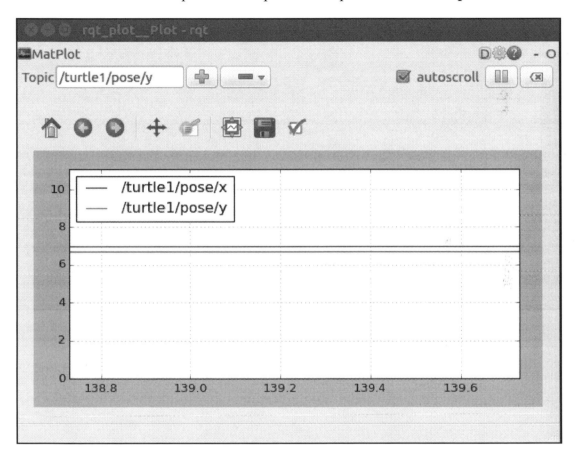

Figure 11: rqt_plot

rqt_graph

The **rqt_graph** (http://wiki.ros.org/rqt_graph) ROS GUI tool can visualize the graph of interconnection between ROS nodes.

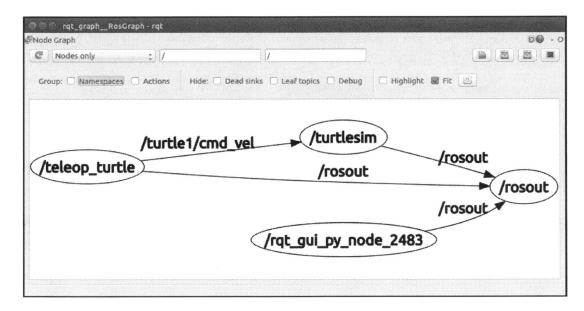

Figure 12: rqt_graph

 The complete list of ROS tools is available at the following link: http://wiki.ros.org/Tools

Simulators of ROS

One of the open source robotic simulators tightly integrated with ROS is Gazebo (http://gazebosim.org). Gazebo is a dynamic robotic simulator with a wide variety the robot models and extensive sensor support The functionalities of Gazebo can be added via plugins. The sensor values can be accessed to ROS through topics, parameters and services. Gazebo can use when your simulation needs full compatibility with ROS. Most of the robotics simulators are proprietary and expensive; if you can't afford it, you can directly use Gazebo without any doubt.

The ROS interface of Gazebo is available at the following link: http://wiki.ros.org/gazebo

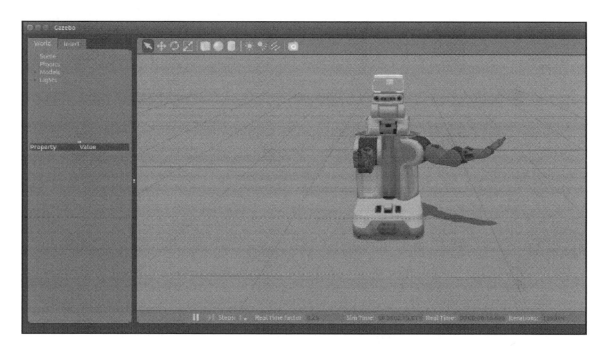

Figure 13: Gazebo simulator

Installing ROS kinetic on Ubuntu 16.04 LTS

As we have discussed, there are a variety of ROS distributions available to download and install, so choosing the exact distribution for our needs may be confusing. Following are answers to some of the frequently asked questions while choosing a distribution:

- Which distribution should I choose to get maximum support?
    - **Answer**: If you are interested in getting maximum support, choose an LTS release. It will be good if you choose the second most recent LTS distribution.

- I need the latest features of ROS; which should I choose?

  - **Answer**: Go for the latest version then; you may not get the latest complete packages immediately after the release. You may have to wait for a few months after the release. This is because of the migration period from one distribution to other.

In this book, we are dealing with two LTS distributions: ROS Indigo, which is a stable release, and ROS Kinetic, the latest one.

Getting started with the installation

Go to the ROS website (`http://www.ros.org/`), and navigate to **Getting Started** | **Install**.

You will get a screen listing the latest ROS distributions:

Figure 14: Latest ROS distributions on the website

You can get the complete installation instructions for each distribution if you click on the **Install** button.

We'll now step through the instructions to install the latest ROS distribution.

Configuring Ubuntu repositories

We are going to install ROS on Ubuntu from the ROS package repository. The repository will have prebuilt binaries of ROS in .deb format. To be able to use packages from the ROS repository, we have to configure the repository options of Ubuntu first.

 Here are the details of the different kinds of Ubuntu repositories:
(https://help.ubuntu.com/community/Repositories/Ubuntu)

To configure the repository, first search for **Software & Updates** in the Ubuntu search bar.

Figure 15: Ubuntu Software & Updates

Click on **Software and & Updates** and enable all the Ubuntu repositories, as shown in the following screenshot:

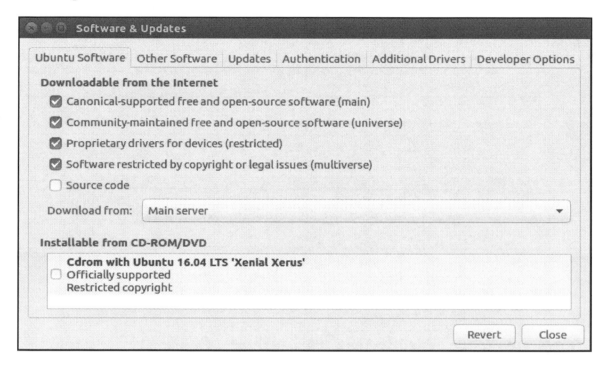

Figure 16: The Ubuntu Software & Updates centre

Setting up source.list

The next step is to allow ROS packages from the ROS repository server, called packages.ros.org. The ROS repository server details have to be fed into source.list, which is in the /etc/apt/.

The following command will do this job for ROS Kinetic, Jade, and Indigo:

```
sudo sh -c 'echo "deb http://packages.ros.org/ros/ubuntu $(lsb_release
-sc) main" > /etc/apt/sources.list.d/ros-latest.list'
```

Setting up keys

When a new repository is added to Ubuntu, we should add the keys to make it trusted and to be able to validate the origin of the packages. The following key should be added to Ubuntu before starting installation:

```
sudo apt-key adv --keyserver hkp://ha.pool.sks-keyservers.net:80 --
recv-key 0xB01FA116
```

Now we are sure that we are downloading from an authorized server.

Installing ROS

Now, we are ready to install ROS packages on Ubuntu. The first step is to update the list of packages on Ubuntu. You can use the following command to update the list:

```
$ sudo apt-get update
```

This will fetch all packages from the servers that are in source.list.

After getting the package list, we have to install the entire ROS package suite using the following command:

- ROS Kinect:

```
$ sudo apt-get install ros-kinetic-desktop-full
```

- ROS Jade:

```
$ sudo apt-get install ros-jade-desktop-full
```

- ROS Indigo:

```
$ sudo apt-get install ros-indigo-desktop-full
```

This will install most of the important packages in ROS. You will need at least 15 GB of space in your root Ubuntu partition to install and work with ROS.

Initializing rosdep

The rosdep tool in ROS helps us easily install dependencies of packages that we are going to compile. This tool is also necessary for some core components of ROS.

This command launches `rosdep`:

```
$ sudo rosdep init
$ rosdep update
```

Setting the ROS environment

Congratulations! We are done with the ROS installation, but what next?

The ROS installation mainly consists of scripts and executables, which are mostly installed to `/opt/ros/<ros_version>`.

To get access to these commands and scripts, we should add ROS environment variables to the Ubuntu Terminal. It's easy to do this. To access ROS commands from inside the Terminal, we have to source the following bash file:

`/opt/ros/<ros_version>/setup.bash`

Here's the command to do so:

```
$ source /opt/ros/kinetic/setup.bash
```

But in order to get the ROS environment in multiple Terminals, we should add the command to the `.bashrc` script, which is in the home folder. The `.bashrc` script will be sourced whenever a new Terminal opens.

```
$ echo "source /opt/ros/kinetic/setup.bash" >> ~/.bashrc
$ source ~/.bashrc
```

We can install multiple ROS distributions on Ubuntu. If there are multiple distributions, we can switch to each ROS distribution by changing the distribution name in the preceding command.

Getting rosinstall

Last but not least, there is the ROS command-line tool, called `rosinstall`, for installing source trees for particular ROS packages. The tool is based on Python, and you can install it using the following command:

```
$ sudo apt-get install python-rosinstall
```

We are done with the ROS installation. Just check whether the installation is proper, by running the following commands.

Open a Terminal window and run the `roscore` command:

```
$ roscore
```

Run a `turtlesim` node in another Terminal:

```
$ rosrun turtlesim turtlesim_node
```

If everything is proper, you will get this:

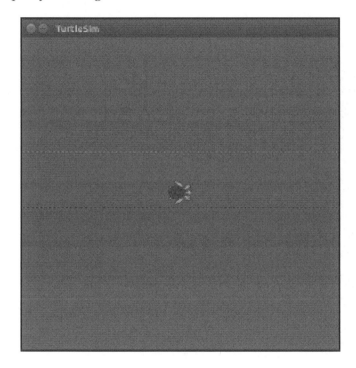

Figure 17: The turtlesim node

Setting ROS on VirtualBox

As you know, complete ROS support is only present on Ubuntu. So what about Windows and Mac OS X users? Can't they use ROS? Yes, they can, using a tool called **VirtualBox** (https://www.virtualbox.org/). VirtualBox allows us to install a guest OS without affecting the host OS. The virtual OS can work along with the host OS in a given specification of a virtual computer, such as the number of processors and RAM and hard disk size.

You can download VirtualBox for popular OSes from the following link:
`https://www.virtualbox.org/wiki/Downloads`
The complete installation procedure for Ubuntu on VirtualBox is shown in the following tutorial video on YouTube:
`https://www.youtube.com/watch?v=DPIPC25xzUM`

The Following shows the screenshot of the VirtualBox GUI. You can see the virtual OS list on the left side and the virtual PC configuration on the right side. The buttons for creating a new virtual OS and starting the existing VirtualBox can be seen on the top panel. The optimal virtual PC configuration is shown in the following screenshot:

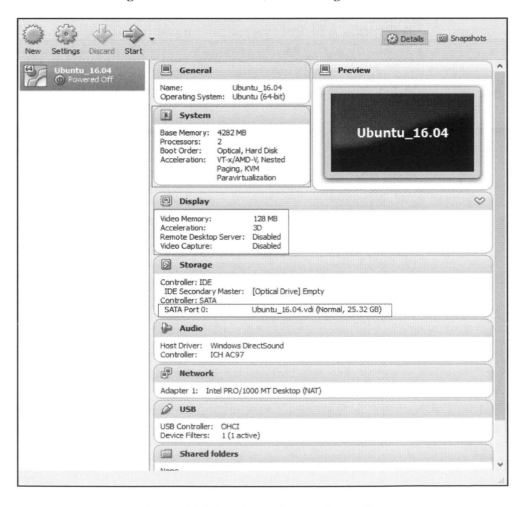

Figure 18: The VirtualBox configuration

Here are the main specifications of the virtual PC:

- **Number of CPUs**: 1
- **RAM**: 4 GB
- **Display | Video Memory**: 128 MB
- **Acceleration**: 3D
- **Storage**: 20 GB to 30 GB
- Network adapter on NAT

In order to have hardware acceleration, you should install drivers from the VirtualBox Guest add-ons disc. After booting into the Ubuntu desktop, navigate to **Devices | Insert Guest Addition CD Image**. This will mount the CD image in Ubuntu and ask the user to run the script to install drivers. If we allow it, it will automatically install all the drivers. After a reboot, you will get full acceleration on the Ubuntu guest.

There is no difference in ROS installation on VirtualBox .If the virtual network adapter is in NAT mode, the Internet connection of the host OS will be shared with the guest OS. So the guest can work the same as the real OS.

Setting the ROS workspace

After setting ROS on a real PC or VirtualBox, the next step is to create a workspace in ROS. The ROS workspace is a place where we keep ROS packages. In the latest ROS distribution, we use a catkin-based workspace to build and install ROS packages. The catkin system (http://wiki.ros.org/catkin) is the official build system of ROS, which helps us build the source code into a target executable or libraries inside the ROS workspace.

Building an ROS workspace is an easy task; just open a Terminal and follow these instructions:

1. The first step is to create an empty workspace folder and another folder called src to store the ROS package in. The following command will do this job. The workspace folder name here is catkin_ws.

   ```
   $ mkdir -p ~/catkin_ws/src
   ```

2. Switch to the src folder and execute the catkin_init_workspace command. This command will initialize a catkin workspace in the current src folder. We can now start creating packages inside the src folder.

```
$ cd ~/catkin_ws/src
$ catkin_init_workspace
```

3. After initializing the catkin workspace, we can build the packages inside the workspace using the following command, catkin_make. We can build the workspace even without any packages.

```
$ cd ~/catkin_ws/
$ catkin_make
```

4. This will create additional folders called build and devel inside the ROS workspace:

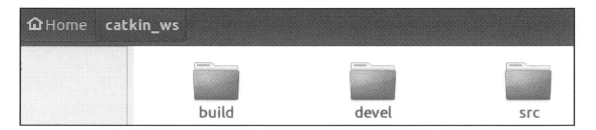

Figure 19: The catkin workspace folders

5. Once you've built the workspace, in order to access packages inside the workspace we should add the workspace environment to our .bashrc file using the following command:

```
$ echo "source ~/catkin_ws/devel/setup.bash" >>
~/.bashrc
$ source ~/.bashrc
```

6. If everything is done, you can verify it by executing the following command. This command will print the entire ROS package path. If your workspace path is in the output, you are done!

```
$ echo $ROS_PACKAGE_PATH
```

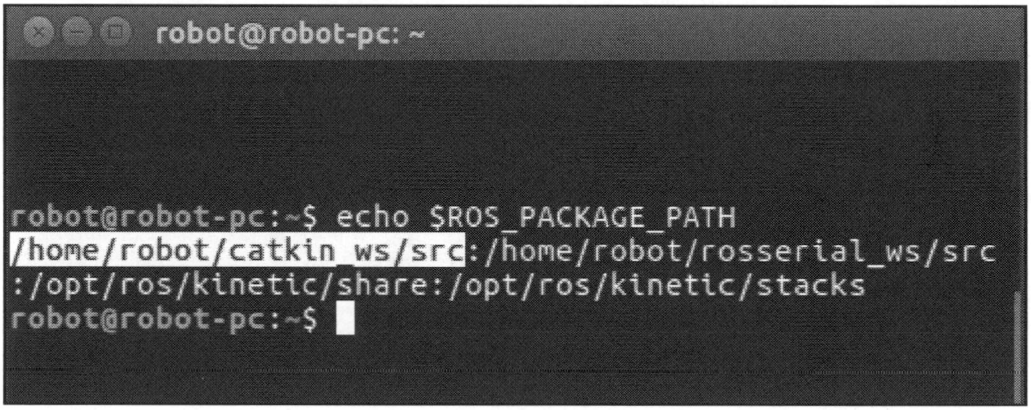

Figure 20: The ROS package path

Opportunities for ROS in industries and research

Now that we've installed ROS and set up our ROS workspace, we can discuss the advantages of using it. Why is learning ROS so important for robotics researchers? The reason is that ROS is becoming a generic framework to program all kinds of robots. So robots in universities and industries mainly use ROS.

Here are some famous robotics companies using ROS for their robots:

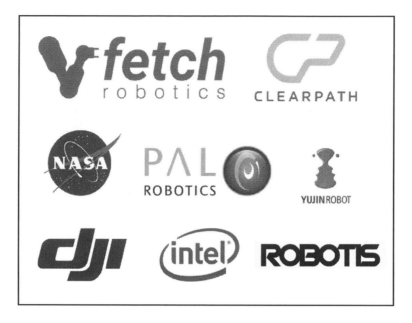

Figure 21: The companies using ROS

You can find them here:

- **Fetch Robotics**: http://fetchrobotics.com/
- **Clearpath Robotics**: https://www.clearpathrobotics.com/
- **PAL Robotics**: http://www.pal-robotics.com/en/home/
- **Yujin Robot**: http://en.yujinrobot.com/
- **DJI**: http://www.dji.com/
- **ROBOTIS**: http://www.robotis.com/html/en.php

The following is one of the job listings on Fetch Robotics for a robotics application development engineer (http://fetchrobotics.com/careers/):

Required Skills:

- BS or MS in Computer Science, Robotics, or a related field.

- 3+ year of software engineering experience.

- Experience with C++ and/or Python in a Linux Environment.

- Experience with Software Development on/with Robotic Platforms.

- Experience with Robot Operating System (ROS).

- Love of robots is a must as you will be surrounded by them.

Nice To Haves:

- Experience with MoveIt, SBPL and/or OMPL.

- Experience with OpenCV or PCL.

Figure 22: A typical job requirement for an ROS application engineer

Knowledge of ROS will help you land a robotics application engineering job easily. If you go through the skill set of any job related to robotics, you're bound to find ROS on it.

There are independent courses and workshops in universities and industries to teach ROS development in robots. Knowing ROS will help you get an internship and MS, PhD, and postdoc opportunities from prestigious robotic institutions such as CMU's Robotics Institute (http://www.ri.cmu.edu/) and UPenn's GRAP Lab (https://www.grasp.upenn.edu/).

The following chapters will help you build a practical foundation of and core skills in ROS.

Questions

- What are the main components of ROS?
- What are the advantages of using ROS over other robotics frameworks?
- What are the different concepts of ROS?
- What are the different concepts of the ROS computation graph?

Summary

This chapter was an introductory chapter for starting with robotics application development using ROS. The main aim of this chapter was to get started with ROS by installing and understanding it. This chapter can be used as a kick-start guide for ROS application development and can help you understand the following chapters, which mainly demonstrate ROS-based applications. At the end of this chapter, we saw job and research opportunities related to ROS and also saw that lot of companies and universities are looking for ROS developers for different robotics applications. From the next chapter onward, we can discuss different ROS-based projects.

2
Face Detection and Tracking Using ROS, OpenCV and Dynamixel Servos

One of the capabilities of most service and social robots is face detection and tracking. These robots can identify faces and can move their heads according to the human face that moves around it. There are numerous implementations of face detection and tracking systems on the Web. Most trackers have a pan-and-tilt mechanism, and a camera is mounted on the top of the servos. In this chapter, we will see a simple tracker that only has a pan mechanism. We are going to use a USB webcam mounted on an AX-12 Dynamixel servo. The controlling of Dynamixel servo and image processing are done in ROS.

The following topics will be covered in this chapter:

- An overview of the project
- Hardware and software prerequisites
- Configuring Dynamixel AX-12 servos
- The connection diagram of the project
- Interfacing Dynamixel with ROS
- Creating ROS packages for a face tracker and controller
- The ROS-OpenCV interface
- Implementing a face tracker and face tracker controller
- The final run

Overview of the project

The aim of the project is to build a simple face tracker that can track face only along the horizontal axis of the camera. The face tracker hardware consists of a webcam, Dynamixel servo called AX-12, and a supporting bracket to mount the camera on the servo. The servo tracker will follow the face until it aligns to the center of the image from the webcam. Once it reaches the center, it will stop and wait for face movement. The face detection is done using an OpenCV and ROS interface, and the controlling of the servo is done using a Dynamixel motor driver in ROS.

We are going to create two ROS packages for this complete tracking system; one is for face detection and finding the centroid of the face, and the other is for sending commands to the servo to track the face using the centroid values.

Okay! Let's start discussing the hardware and software prerequisites of this project.

 The complete source code of this project can be cloned from the following Git repository. The following command will clone the project repo:
```
$ git clone
https://github.com/qboticslabs/ros_robotics_projects
```

Hardware and software prerequisites

The following is a table of the hardware components that can be used for building this project. You can also see the rough price and a purchase link for each component.

List of hardware components:

No	Component name	Estimated price (USD)	Purchase link
1	Webcam	32	https://amzn.com/B003LVZO8S
2	Dynamixel AX-12A servo with mounting bracket	76	https://amzn.com/B0051OXJXU
3	USB-to-Dynamixel Adapter	50	http://www.robotshop.com/en/robotis-usb-to-dynamixel-adapter.html
4	Extra 3-pin cables for AX-12 servos	12	http://www.trossenrobotics.com/p/100mm-3-Pin-DYNAMIXEL-Compatible-Cable-10-Pack
5	Power adapter	5	https://amzn.com/B005JRGOCM
6	6-port AX/MX power hub	5	http://www.trossenrobotics.com/6-port-ax-mx-power-hub

7	USB extension cable	1	https://amzn.com/B00YBKA5Z0
	Total cost with shipping and tax	Around 190-200	

 The URLs and prices can vary. If the links are not available, a Google search might do the job. The shipping charges and tax are excluded from the prices.

If you are thinking that the total cost is not affordable, then there are cheap alternatives to do this project too. The main heart of this project is the Dynamixel servo. We can replace this servo with RC servos, which only cost around $10, and an Arduino board costing around $20 can be used to control the servo too. The ROS and Arduino interfacing will be discussed in the upcoming chapters, so you can think about porting the face tracker project using an Arduino and RC servo.

Okay, let's look at the software prerequisites of the project. The prerequisites include the ROS framework, OS version, and ROS packages:

No	Name of the software	Estimated price (USD)	Download link
1	Ubuntu 16.04 LTS	Free	http://releases.ubuntu.com/16.04/
2	ROS Kinetic LTS	Free	http://wiki.ros.org/kinetic/Installation/Ubuntu
3	ROS usb_cam package	Free	http://wiki.ros.org/usb_cam
4	ROS cv_bridge package	Free	http://wiki.ros.org/cv_bridge
5	ROS Dynamixel controller	Free	https://github.com/arebgun/dynamixel_motor
6	Windows 7 or higher	Around $120	https://www.microsoft.com/en-in/software-download/windows7
7	RoboPlus (Windows application)	Free	http://www.robotis.com/download/software/RoboPlusWeb%28v1.1.3.0%29.exe

This table gives you an idea of the software we are going to be using for this project. We may need both Windows and Ubuntu for doing this project. It will be great if you have dual operating systems on your computer.

Let's see how to install all this software first.

Installing dependent ROS packages

We have already installed and configured Ubuntu 16.04 and ROS Kinetic. Let's look at the dependent packages we need to install for this project.

Installing the usb_cam ROS package

Let's look at the use of the usb_cam package in ROS first. The usb_cam package is the ROS driver for **Video4Linux** (**V4L**) USB cameras. V4L is a collection of device drivers in Linux for real-time video capture from webcams. The usb_cam ROS package works using V4L devices and publishes the video stream from devices as ROS image messages. We can subscribe to it and perform our own processing using it. The official ROS page of this package is given in the previous table. You can check out this page for different settings and configurations this package offers.

Creating a ROS workspace for dependencies

Before starting to install the usb_cam package, let's create a ROS workspace for storing the dependencies of all the projects mentioned in the book. We can create another workspace for keeping the project code.

Create a ROS workspace called ros_project_dependencies_ws in the home folder. Clone the usb_cam package into the src folder:

```
$ git clone https://github.com/bosch-ros-pkg/usb_cam.git
```

Build the workspace using catkin_make.

After building the package, install the v4l-util Ubuntu package. It is a collection of command-line V4L utilities used by the usb_cam package:

```
$ sudo apt-get install v4l-utils
```

Configuring a webcam on Ubuntu 16.04

After installing these two, we can connect the webcam to the PC to check whether it is properly detected by our PC.

Open a Terminal and execute the `dmesg` command to check the kernel logs. If your camera is detected in Linux, it may give you logs like this:

```
$ dmesg
```

```
[   86.483102] usb 1-1.5: new high-speed USB device number 6 using ehci-pci
[   86.620403] usb 1-1.5: New USB device found, idVendor=0c45, idProduct=6340
[   86.620409] usb 1-1.5: New USB device strings: Mfr=2, Product=1, SerialNumber=3
[   86.620412] usb 1-1.5: Product: iBall Face2Face Webcam C12.0
[   86.620414] usb 1-1.5: Manufacturer: iBall Face2Face Webcam C12.0
[   86.620416] usb 1-1.5: SerialNumber: iBall Face2Face Webcam C12.0
[   86.657389] media: Linux media interface: v0.10
[   86.677503] Linux video capture interface: v2.00
[   86.703833] usb 1-1.5: 3:1: cannot get freq at ep 0x84
[   86.722072] usbcore: registered new interface driver snd-usb-audio
[   86.722096] uvcvideo: Found UVC 1.00 device iBall Face2Face Webcam C12.0 (0c45:6340)
[   86.735670] input: iBall Face2Face Webcam C12.0 as /devices/pci0000:00/0000:00:1a.0/
t/input16
[   86.735747] usbcore: registered new interface driver uvcvideo
[   86.735749] USB Video Class driver (1.1.1)
```

Figure 1: Kernels logs of the webcam device

You can use any webcam that has driver support in Linux. In this project, an iBall Face2Face (http://www.iball.co.in/Product/Face2Face-C8-0-Rev-3-0-/90) webcam is used for tracking. You can also go for the popular Logitech C310 webcam mentioned as a hardware prerequisite. You can opt for that for better performance and tracking.

If our webcam has support in Ubuntu, we can open the video device using a tool called **Cheese**. Cheese is simply a webcam viewer.

Enter the command `cheese` in the Terminal. If it is not installed, you can install it using the following command:

```
$ sudo apt-get install cheese
```

If the driver and device are proper, you will get a video stream from the webcam, like this:

Figure 2: Webcam video streaming using Cheese

Congratulations! Your webcam is working well in Ubuntu, but are we done with everything? No. The next thing is to test the ROS usb_cam package. We have to make sure that it's working well in ROS!

The complete source code of this project can be cloned from the following Git repository. The following command will clone the project repo:
```
$ git clone
https://github.com/qboticslabs/ros_robotics_projects
```

Interfacing the webcam with ROS

Let's test the webcam using the `usb_cam` package. The following command is used to launch the `usb_cam` nodes to display images from a webcam and publish ROS image topics at the same time:

```
$ roslaunch usb_cam usb_cam-test.launch
```

If everything works fine, you will get the image stream and logs in the Terminal, as shown here:

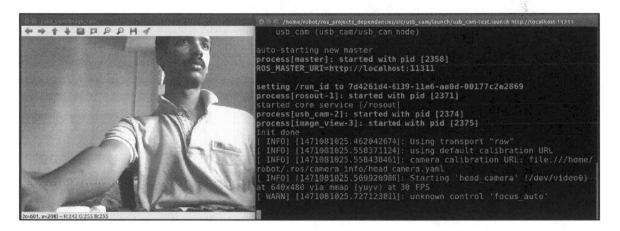

Figure 3: Working of the usb_cam package in ROS

The image is displayed using the `image_view` package in ROS, which is subscribed to the topic called `/usb_cam/image_raw`.

Here are the topics that `usb_cam` node is publishing:

```
robot@robot-pc: ~
/home/robot/ros_projects_dependencies/src/usb_c...    ×        robot@robot-pc: ~
robot@robot-pc:~$ rostopic list
/image_view/parameter_descriptions
/image_view/parameter_updates
/rosout
/rosout_agg
/usb_cam/camera_info
/usb_cam/image_raw
/usb_cam/image_raw/compressed
/usb_cam/image_raw/compressed/parameter_descriptions
/usb_cam/image_raw/compressed/parameter_updates
/usb_cam/image_raw/compressedDepth
/usb_cam/image_raw/compressedDepth/parameter_descriptions
/usb_cam/image_raw/compressedDepth/parameter_updates
/usb_cam/image_raw/theora
/usb_cam/image_raw/theora/parameter_descriptions
/usb_cam/image_raw/theora/parameter_updates
robot@robot-pc:~$
```

Figure 4: The topics being published by the usb_cam node

We've finished interfacing a webcam with ROS. So what's next? We have to interface an AX-12 Dynamixel servo with ROS. Before proceeding to interfacing, we have to do something to configure this servo.

Next, we are going to see how to configure a Dynamixel AX-12A servo.

Configuring a Dynamixel servo using RoboPlus

The Dynamixel servo can be configured using a program called **RoboPlus**, provided by *ROBOTIS INC* (http://en.robotis.com/index/), the manufacturer of Dynamixel servos.

To configure Dynamixel, you have to switch your operating system to Windows. The RoboPlus tool works on Windows. In this project, we are going to configure the servo in Windows 7.

Here is the link to download RoboPlus:

```
http://www.robotis.com/download/software/RoboPlusWeb%28v1.1.3.0%29.exe
```

If the link is not working, you can just search in Google for RoboPlus 1.1.3. After installing the software, you will get the following window. Navigate to the **Expert** tab in the software to get the application for configuring Dynamixel:

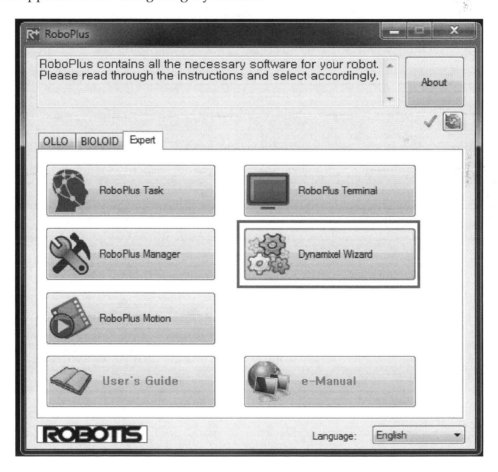

Figure 5: Dynamixel manager in RoboPlus

Before starting Dynamixel Wizard and configuring, we have to connect the Dynamixel and properly power it up. The following are images of the AX-12A servo we are using for this project and a diagram of its pin connection:

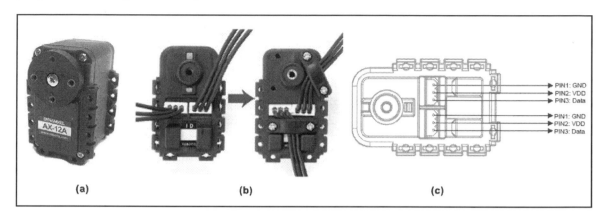

Figure 6: The AX-12A Dynamixel and its connection diagram

Unlike other RC servos, AX-12 is an intelligent actuator having a microcontroller that can monitor every parameter of a servo and customize all of them. It has a geared drive, and the output of the servo is connected to a servo horn. We can connect any link to this servo horn. There are two connection ports behind each servo. Each port has pins such as VCC, GND, and Data. The ports of the Dynamixel are daisy-chained, so we can connect one servo to another servo. Here is the connection diagram of the Dynamixel with a computer:

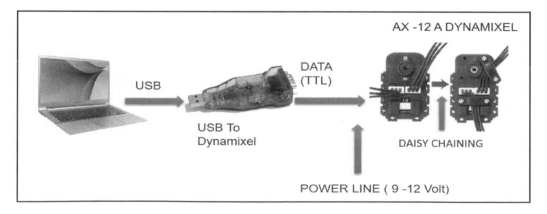

Figure 7: The AX-12A Dynamixel and its connection diagram

The main hardware component interfacing Dynamixel with the PC is called a USB-to-Dynamixel adapter. This is a USB-to-serial adapter that can convert USB to RS232, RS 484, and TTL. In AX-12 motors, data communication is done using TTL. From the previous figure, we can see that there are three pins in each port. The data pin is used to send to and receive from AX-12, and power pins are used to power the servo. The input voltage range of the AX-12A Dynamixel is from 9V to 12V. The second port in each Dynamixel can be used for daisy chaining. We can connect up to 254 servos using such chaining.

Official links of the AX-12A servo and USB-to-Dynamixel adapter:
AX-12A:
`http://www.trossenrobotics.com/dynamixel-ax-12-robot-actuator.aspx`
USB-to-Dynamixel:
`http://www.trossenrobotics.com/robotis-bioloid-usb2dynamixel.aspx`

To work with Dynamixel, we should know some more things. Let's have a look at some of the important specifications of the AX-12A servo. The specifications are taken from the servo manual.

- Weight :   54.6g (AX-12A)
- Dimension :   32mm * 50mm * 40mm
- Resolution :   0.29°
- Gear Reduction Ratio :   254 : 1
- Stall Torque :   1.5N.m (at 12.0V, 1.5A)
- No load speed :   59rpm (at 12V)
- Running Degree :   0° ~ 300°, Endless Turn
- Running Temperature : -5°C ~ +70°C
- Voltage :   9 ~ 12V (Recommended Voltage 11.1V)
- Command Signal :   Digital Packet
- Protocol Type :   Half duplex Asynchronous Serial Communication (8bit,1stop,No Parity)
- Link (Physical) : TTL Level Multi Drop (daisy chain type Connector)
- ID :   254 ID (0~253)
- Communication Speed : 7343bps ~ 1 Mbps
- Feedback :   Position, Temperature, Load, Input Voltage, etc.
- Material :   Engineering Plastic

Figure 8: AX-12A specifications

The Dynamixel servo can communicate with the PC at a maximum speed of 1 Mbps. It can also provide feedback about various parameters, such as its position, temperature, and current load. Unlike RC servos, this can rotate up to 300 degrees, and communication is mainly done using digital packets.

Powering and connecting the Dynamixel to a PC

Now, we are going to connect the Dynamixel to a PC. The following is a standard way of doing that:

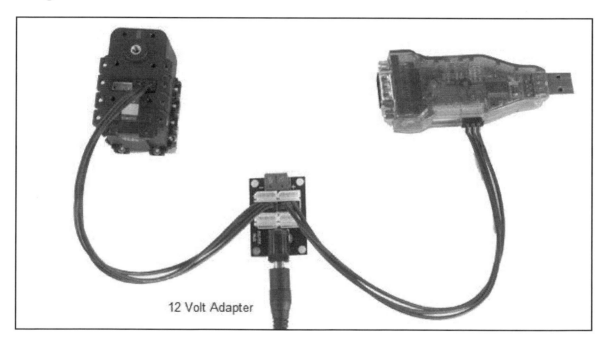

Figure 9: Connecting the Dynamixel to a PC

The three-pin cable is first connected to any of the ports of the AX-12, and the other side has to connect to the way to connect a six-port power hub. From the six-port power hub, connect another cable to the USB-to-Dynamixel. We have to set the switch of the USB-to-Dynamixel to TTL mode. The power can be either be connected through a 12V adapter or through a battery. The 12V adapter has a 2.1 x 5.5 female barrel jack, so you should check the specifications of the male adapter plug while purchasing.

Setting up the USB-to-Dynamixel driver on the PC

We have already discussed that the USB-to-Dynamixel adapter is a USB-to-serial converter with an FTDI chip (`http://www.ftdichip.com/`) on it. We have to install a proper FTDI driver on the PC in order to detect the device. The driver is required for Windows but not for Linux, because FTDI drivers are already present in the Linux kernel. If you install the RoboPlus software, the driver may already be installed along with it. If it is not, you can manually install from the RoboPlus installation folder.

Plug the USB-to-Dynamixel into the Windows PC, and check **Device Manager**. (Right-click on **My Computer** and go to **Properties** | **Device Manager**). If the device is properly detected, you'll see something like this:

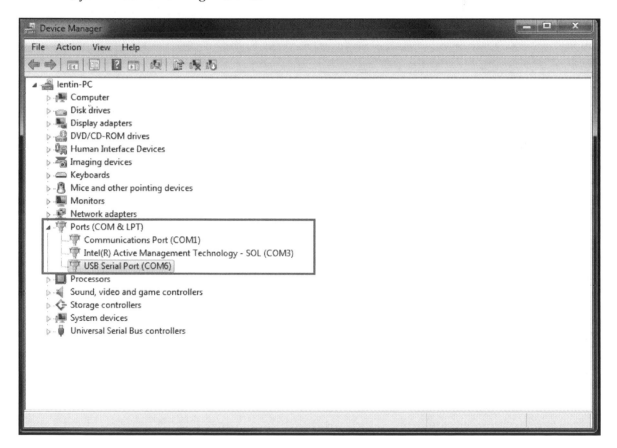

Figure 10: COM port of the USB-to-Dynamixel

If you are getting a COM port for the USB-to-Dynamixel, you can start Dynamixel manager from RoboPlus. You can connect to the serial port number from the list and click on the **Search** button to scan for Dynamixel, as shown in the next screenshot.

Select the COM port from the list, and connect to the port marked **1**. After connecting to the COM port, set the default baud rate to 1 Mbps, and click on the **Start searching** button:

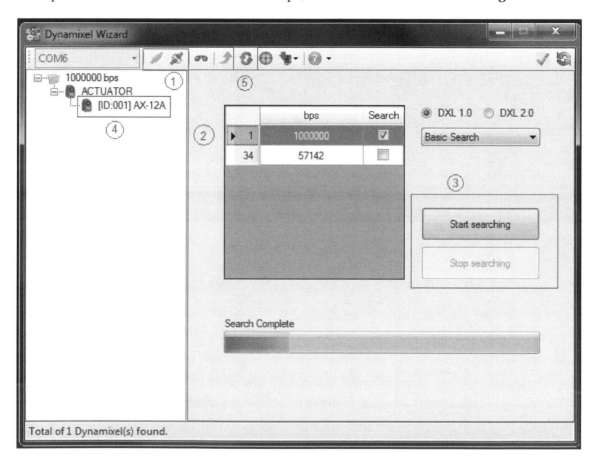

Figure 11: COM Port of the USB-to-Dynamixel

If you are getting a list of servos in the left-hand side panel, it means that your PC has detected a Dynamixel servo. If the servo is not being detected, you can perform the following steps to debug:

1. Make sure that the supply and connections are proper using a multimeter. Make sure that the servo LED on the back is blinking when power is on; if it is not coming on, it can indicate a problem with the servo or power supply.

2. Upgrade the firmware of the servo using Dynamixel manager from the option marked 6. The wizard is shown in the next set of screenshots. While using the wizard, you may need to power off the supply and turn it back on in order to detect the servo.

3. After detecting the servo, you have to select the servo model and install the new firmware. This may help you detect the servo in Dynamixel manager if the existing servo firmware is outdated.

Figure 12: The Dynamixel recovery wizard

If the servos are being listed in Dynamixel Manager, click on one, and you can see its complete configuration. We have to modify some values inside the configurations for our current face-tracker project. Here are the parameters:

- **ID**: Set the ID to 1
- **Baud rate**: 1
- **Moving Speed**: 100
- **Goal Position**: 512

The modified servo settings are shown in the following figure:

Addr	Description	Value		Addr	Description	Value
0	Model Number	12		14	Max Torque	1023
2	Version of Firmware	24		16	Status Return Level	2
3	ID	1		17	Alarm LED	0
4	Baud Rate	1		18	Alarm Shutdown	37
5	Return Delay Time	250		24	Torque Enable	1
6	CW Angle Limit (Joint / Wheel Mode)	0		25	LED	0
8	CCW Angle Limit (Joint / Wheel Mode)	1023		26	CW Compliance Margin	1
11	The Highest Limit Temperature	70		27	CCW Compliance Margin	1
12	The Lowest Limit Voltage	60		28	CW Compliance Slope	32
13	The Highest Limit Voltage	140		29	CCW Compliance Slope	32
14	Max Torque	1023		30	Goal Position	512
16	Status Return Level	2		32	Moving Speed	83
17	Alarm LED	0		34	Torque Limit	1023
18	Alarm Shutdown	37		36	Present Position	511
				38	Present Speed	1028

Figure 13: Modified Dynamixel firmware settings

After making these settings, you can check whether the servo is working well or not by changing its **Goal position**.

Nice! You are done configuring Dynamixel; congratulations! What next? We'll want to interface Dynamixel with ROS.

 The complete source code of this project can be cloned from the following Git repository. The following command will clone the project repo:
```
$ git clone
https://github.com/qboticslabs/ros_robotics_projects
```

Interfacing Dynamixel with ROS

If you successfully configured the Dynamixel servo, then it will be very easy to interface Dynamixel with ROS running on Ubuntu. As we've already discussed, there is no need of an FTDI driver in Ubuntu because it's already built into the kernel. The only thing we have to do is install the ROS Dynamixel driver packages.

The ROS Dynamixel packages are available at the following link:

`http://wiki.ros.org/dynamixel_motor`

You can install the Dynamixel ROS packages using commands we'll look at now.

Installing the ROS dynamixel_motor packages

The ROS `dynamixel_motor` package stack is a dependency for the face tracker project, so we can install it to the `ros_project_dependencies_ws` ROS workspace.

Open a Terminal and switch to the `src` folder of the workspace:

> **$ cd ~/ros_project_dependencies_ws/src**

Clone the latest Dynamixel driver packages from GitHub:

> **$ git clone https://github.com/arebgun/dynamixel_motor**

Remember to do a `catkin_make` to build the entire packages of the Dynamixel driver.

If you can build the workspace without any errors, you are done with meeting the dependencies of this project.

Congratulations! You are done with the installation of the Dynamixel driver packages in ROS. We have now met all the dependencies required for the face tracker project.

So let's start working on face tracking project packages.

Creating face tracker ROS packages

Let's start creating a new workspace for keeping the entire ROS project files for this book. You can name the workspace `ros_robotics_projects_ws`.

Download or clone the source code of the book from GitHub using the following link.

> **$ git clone https://github.com/qboticslabs/ros_robotics_projects**

Now, you can copy two packages named `face_tracker_pkg` and `face_tracker_control` from the `chapter_2_codes` folder into the `src` folder of `ros_robotics_projects_ws`.

Do a `catkin_make` to build the two project packages!

Yes, you have set up the face tracker packages on your system, but what if you want to create your own package for tracking? First, delete the current packages that you copied to the `src` folder, and use the following commands to create the packages.

 Note that you should be in the `src` folder of `ros_robotics_projects_ws` while creating the new packages, and there should not be any existing packages from the book's GitHub code.

Switch to the `src` folder:

```
$ cd ~/ros_robotics_projects_ws/src
```

The next command will create the `face_tracker_pkg` ROS package with the main dependencies, such as `cv_bridge`, `image_transport`, `sensor_msgs`, `message_generation`, and `message_runtime`.

We are including these packages because these packages are required for the proper working of the face tracker package. The face tracker package contain ROS nodes for detecting faces and determining the centroid of the face:

```
$ catkin_create_pkg face_tracker_pkg roscpp rospy cv_bridge
image_transport sensor_msgs std_msgs message_runtime    message_generation
```

Next, we need to create the `face_tracker_control` ROS package. The important dependency of this package is `dynamixel_controllers`. This package is used to subscribe to the centroid from the face tracker node and control the Dynamixel in a way that the face centroid will always be in the center portion of the image:

```
$ catkin_create_pkg face_tracker_pkg roscpp rospy std_msgs
dynamixel_controllers message_generation
```

Okay, you have created the ROS packages on your own. What's next? Before starting to code, you may have to understand some concepts of OpenCV and its interface with ROS. Also, you have to know how to publish ROS image messages. So let's master the concepts first.

The interface between ROS and OpenCV

Open Source Computer Vision (OpenCV) is a library that has APIs to perform computer vision applications. The project was started in Intel Russia, and later on, it was supported by Willow Garage and Itseez. In 2016, Itseez was acquired by Intel.

 OpenCV website: `http://opencv.org/`
Willow Garage: `http://www.willowgarage.com/`
Itseez: `http://itseez.com`

OpenCV is a cross-platform library that supports most operating systems. Now, it also has an open source BSD license, so we can use it for research and commercial applications. The OpenCV version interfaced with ROS Kinetic is 3.1. The 3.x versions of OpenCV have a few changes to the APIs from the 2.x versions.

The OpenCV library is integrated into ROS through a package called `vision_opencv`. This package was already installed when we installed `ros-kinetic-desktop-full` in *Chapter 1, Getting Started with ROS Robotics Application Development*.

The `vision_opencv` metapackage has two packages:

- `cv_bridge`: This package is responsible for converting the OpenCV image data type (`cv::Mat`) into ROS `Image` messages (`sensor_msgs/Image.msg`).
- `image_geometry`: This package helps us interpret images geometrically. This node will aid in processing such as camera calibration and image rectification.

Out of these two packages, we are mainly dealing with `cv_bridge`. Using `cv_bridge`, the face tracker node can convert ROS `Image` messages from `usb_cam` to the OpenCV equivalent, `cv::Mat`. After converting to `cv::Mat`, we can use OpenCV APIs to process the camera image.

Here is a block diagram that shows the role of `cv_bridge` in this project:

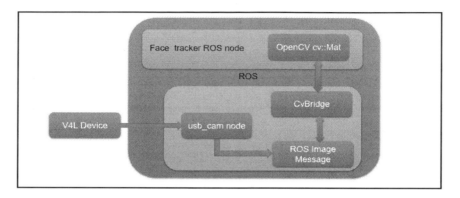

Figure 14: The role of cv_bridge

Here, `cv_bridge` is working between the `usb_cam` node and face-tracking node. We'll learn more about the face-tracking node in the next section. Before that, it will be good if you get an idea of its working.

Another package we are using to transport ROS `Image` messages between two ROS nodes is `image_transport` (http://wiki.ros.org/image_transport). This package is always used to subscribe to and publish image data in ROS. The package can help us transport images in low bandwidth by applying compression techniques. This package is also installed along with the full ROS desktop installation.

That's all about OpenCV and the ROS interface. In the next section, we are going to work with the first package of this project: `face_tracker_pkg`.

The complete source code of this project can be cloned from the following Git repository. The following command will clone the project repo:
```
$ git clone
https://github.com/qboticslabs/ros_robotics_projects
```

Working with the face-tracking ROS package

We have already created or copied the `face_tracker_pkg` package to the workspace and have discussed some of its important dependencies. Now, we are going to discuss what this package exactly does!

This package consists of a ROS node called `face_tracker_node` that can track faces using OpenCV APIs and publish the centroid of the face to a topic. Here is the block diagram of the working of `face_tracker_node`:

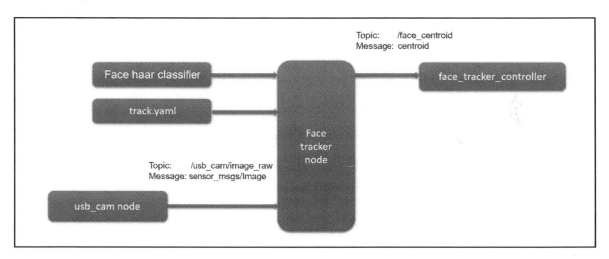

Figure 15: Block diagram of face_tracker_node

Let's discuss the things connected to `face_tracker_node`. One of the sections that may be unfamiliar to you is the face Haar classifier:

- **Face Haar classifier**: The Haar feature-based cascade classifier is a machine learning approach for detecting objects. This method was proposed by Paul Viola and Michael Jones in their paper *Rapid Object detection using a boosted cascade of simple features* in 2001. In this method, a cascade file is trained using a positive and negative sample image, and after training, that file is using for object detection.

  - In our case, we are using a trained Haar classifier file along with OpenCV source code. You will get these Haar classifier files from the OpenCV `data` folder (`https://github.com/opencv/opencv/tree/master/data`). You can replace the desired Haar file according to your application. Here, we are using the face classifier. The classifier will be an XML file that has tags containing features of a face. Once the features inside the XML match, we can retrieve the **region of interest (ROI)** of the face from the image using the OpenCV APIs. You can check the Haar classifier of this project from `face_tracker_pkg/data/face.xml`.

- `track.yaml`: This is a ROS parameter file having parameters such as the Haar file path, input image topic, output image topic, and flags to enable and disable face tracking. We are using ROS configuration files because we can change the node parameters without modifying the face tracker source code. You can get this file from `face_tracker_pkg/config/track.xml`.
- `usb_cam` node: The `usb_cam` package has a node publishing the image stream from the camera to ROS `Image` messages. The `usb_cam` node publishes camera images to the `/usb_cam/raw_image` topic, and this topic is subscribed to by the face tracker node for face detection. We can change the input topic in the `track.yaml` file if we require.
- `face_tracker_control`: This is the second package we are going to discuss. The `face_tracker_pkg` package can detect faces and find the centroid of the face in the image. The centroid message contains two values, *X* and *Y*. We are using a custom message definition to send the centroid values. These centroid values are subscribed by the controller node and move the Dynamixel to track the face. The Dynamixel is controlled by this node.

Here is the file structure of `face_tracker_pkg`:

```
── CMakeLists.txt
── config
│   └── track.yaml
── data
│   └── face.xml
── include
│   └── face_tracker_pkg
── launch
│   ├── start_dynamixel_tracking.launch
│   ├── start_tracking.launch
│   └── start_usb_cam.launch
── msg
│   └── centroid.msg
── package.xml
── src
    └── face_tracker_node.cpp

7 directories, 9 files
```

Figure 16: File structure of face_tracker_pkg

Let's see how the face-tracking code works. You can open the CPP file at `face_tracker_pkg/src/face_tracker_node.cpp`. This code performs the face detection and sends the centroid value to a topic.

We'll look at, and understand, some code snippets.

Understanding the face tracker code

Let's start with the header file. The ROS header files we are using in the code lie here. We have to include `ros/ros.h` in every ROS C++ node; otherwise, the source code will not compile. The remaining three headers are image-transport headers, which have functions to publish and subscribe to image messages in low bandwidth. The `cv_bridge` header has functions to convert between OpenCV ROS data types. The `image_encoding.h` header has the image-encoding format used during ROS-OpenCV conversions:

```
#include <ros/ros.h>
#include <image_transport/image_transport.h>
#include <cv_bridge/cv_bridge.h>
#include <sensor_msgs/image_encodings.h>
```

The next set of headers is for OpenCV. The `imgproc` header consists of image-processing functions, `highgui` has GUI-related functions, and `objdetect.hpp` has APIs for object detection, such as the Haar classifier:

```
#include <opencv2/imgproc/imgproc.hpp>
#include <opencv2/highgui/highgui.hpp>
#include "opencv2/objdetect.hpp"
```

The last header file is for accessing a custom message called **centroid**. The `centroid` message definition has two fields, `int32 x` and `int32 y`. This can hold the centroid of the file. You can check this message definition from the `face_tracker_pkg/msg/centroid.msg` folder:

```
#include <face_tracker_pkg/centroid.h>
```

The following lines of code give a name to the raw image window and face-detection window:

```
static const std::string OPENCV_WINDOW = "raw_image_window";
static const std::string OPENCV_WINDOW_1 = "face_detector";
```

The following lines of code create a C++ class for our face detector. The code snippet is creates handles of `NodeHandle`, which is a mandatory handle for a ROS node; `image_transport`, which helps send ROS `Image` messages across the ROS computing graph; and a publisher for the face centroid, which can publish the centroid values using the `centroid.msg` file defined by us. The remaining definitions are for handling parameter values from the parameter file `track.yaml`:

```
class Face_Detector
{
  ros::NodeHandle nh_;

  image_transport::ImageTransport it_;

  image_transport::Subscriber image_sub_;

  image_transport::Publisher image_pub_;

  ros::Publisher face_centroid_pub;

  face_tracker_pkg::centroid face_centroid;

  string input_image_topic, output_image_topic, haar_file_face;

int face_tracking, display_original_image,  display_tracking_image,
center_offset, screenmaxx;
```

The following is the code for retrieving ROS parameters inside the `track.yaml` file. The advantage of using ROS parameters is that we can avoid hard-coding these values inside the program and modify the values without recompiling the code:

```
try{
nh_.getParam("image_input_topic", input_image_topic);
nh_.getParam("face_detected_image_topic", output_image_topic);
nh_.getParam("haar_file_face", haar_file_face);
nh_.getParam("face_tracking", face_tracking);
nh_.getParam("display_original_image", display_original_image);
nh_.getParam("display_tracking_image", display_tracking_image);
nh_.getParam("center_offset", center_offset);
nh_.getParam("screenmaxx", screenmaxx);

ROS_INFO("Successfully Loaded tracking parameters");
}
```

The following code creates a subscriber for the input image topic and publisher for the face-detected image. Whenever an image arrives on the input image topic, it will call a function called `imageCb`. The names of the topics are retrieved from ROS parameters. We create another publisher for publishing the centroid value, which is the last line of the code snippet:

```
image_sub_ = it_.subscribe(input_image_topic, 1,
&Face_Detector::imageCb, this);
image_pub_ = it_.advertise(output_image_topic, 1);

face_centroid_pub = nh_.advertise<face_tracker_pkg::centroid>
("/face_centroid",10);
```

The next bit of code is the definition of `imageCb`, which is a callback for `input_image_topic`. What it basically does is it converts the `sensor_msgs/Image` data into the `cv::Mat` OpenCV data type. The `cv_bridge::CvImagePtr cv_ptr` buffer is allocated for storing the OpenCV image after performing the ROS-OpenCV conversion using the `cv_bridge::toCvCopy` function:

```
void imageCb(const sensor_msgs::ImageConstPtr& msg)
{

  cv_bridge::CvImagePtr cv_ptr;
  namespace enc = sensor_msgs::image_encodings;

  try
  {
    cv_ptr = cv_bridge::toCvCopy(msg,
sensor_msgs::image_encodings::BGR8);
  }
```

We have already discussed the Haar classifier; here is the code to load the Haar classifier file:

```
  string cascadeName = haar_file_face;
  CascadeClassifier cascade;
if( !cascade.load( cascadeName ) )
  {
    cerr << "ERROR: Could not load classifier cascade" << endl;
  }
```

We are now moving to the core part of the program, which is the detection of the face performed on the converted OpenCV image data type from the ROS `Image` message. The following is the function call of `detectAndDraw()`, which is performing the face detection, and in the last line, you can see the output image topic being published. Using `cv_ptr->image`, we can retrieve the `cv::Mat` data type, and in the next line, `cv_ptr->toImageMsg()` can convert this into a ROS `Image` message. The arguments of the `detectAndDraw()` function are the OpenCV image and cascade variables:

```
detectAndDraw( cv_ptr->image, cascade );
image_pub_.publish(cv_ptr->toImageMsg());
```

Let's understand the `detectAndDraw()` function, which is adopted from the OpenCV sample code for face detection: The function arguments are the input image and cascade object. The next bit of code will convert the image into grayscale first and equalize the histogram using OpenCV APIs. This is a kind of preprocessing before detecting the face from the image. The `cascade.detectMultiScale()` function is used for this purpose (`http://docs.opencv.org/2.4/modules/objdetect/doc/cascade_classification.html`).

```
Mat gray, smallImg;
cvtColor( img, gray, COLOR_BGR2GRAY );
double fx = 1 / scale ;
resize( gray, smallImg, Size(), fx, fx, INTER_LINEAR );
equalizeHist( smallImg, smallImg );
t = (double)cvGetTickCount();
cascade.detectMultiScale( smallImg, faces,
    1.1, 15, 0
    |CASCADE_SCALE_IMAGE,
    Size(30, 30) );
```

The following loop will iterate on each face that is detected using the `detectMultiScale()` function. For each face, it finds the centroid and publishes to the `/face_centroid` topic:

```
for ( size_t i = 0; i < faces.size(); i++ )
{
    Rect r = faces[i];
    Mat smallImgROI;
    vector<Rect> nestedObjects;
    Point center;
    Scalar color = colors[i%8];
    int radius;

    double aspect_ratio = (double)r.width/r.height;
    if( 0.75 < aspect_ratio && aspect_ratio < 1.3 )
    {
        center.x = cvRound((r.x + r.width*0.5)*scale);
```

```
        center.y = cvRound((r.y + r.height*0.5)*scale);
        radius = cvRound((r.width + r.height)*0.25*scale);
        circle( img, center, radius, color, 3, 8, 0 );

    face_centroid.x = center.x;
    face_centroid.y = center.y;

        //Publishing centroid of detected face
          face_centroid_pub.publish(face_centroid);

    }
```

To make the output image window more interactive, there are text and lines to alert about the user's face on the left or right or at the center. This last section of code is mainly for that purpose. It uses OpenCV APIs to do this job. Here is the code to display text such as **Left**, **Right**, and **Center** on the screen:

```
        putText(img, "Left", cvPoint(50,240),
    FONT_HERSHEY_SIMPLEX, 1,
        cvScalar(255,0,0), 2, CV_AA);
        putText(img, "Center", cvPoint(280,240),
    FONT_HERSHEY_SIMPLEX,
        1, cvScalar(0,0,255), 2, CV_AA);
        putText(img, "Right", cvPoint(480,240),
    FONT_HERSHEY_SIMPLEX,
        1, cvScalar(255,0,0), 2, CV_AA);
```

Excellent! We're done with the tracker code; let's see how to build it and make it executable.

Understanding CMakeLists.txt

The default CMakeLists.txt file made during the creation of the package has to be edited in order to compile the previous source code. Here is the CMakeLists.txt file used to build the face_tracker_node.cpp class.

The first two lines state the minimum version of cmake required to build this package, and next line is the package name:

```
    cmake_minimum_required(VERSION 2.8.3)
    project(face_tracker_pkg)
```

The following line searches for the dependent packages of `face_tracker_pkg` and raises an error if it is not found:

```
find_package(catkin REQUIRED COMPONENTS
  cv_bridge
  image_transport
  roscpp
  rospy
  sensor_msgs
  std_msgs
  message_generation


)
```

This line of code contains the system-level dependencies for building the package:

```
find_package(Boost REQUIRED COMPONENTS system)
```

As we've already seen, we are using a custom message definition called `centroid.msg`, which contains two fields, `int32 x` and `int32 y`. To build and generate C++ equivalent headers, we should use the following lines:

```
add_message_files(
   FILES
   centroid.msg
 )

## Generate added messages and services with any dependencies
listed here
 generate_messages(
   DEPENDENCIES
   std_msgs
 )
```

The `catkin_package()` function is a catkin-provided CMake macro that is required to generate `pkg-config` and CMake files.

```
catkin_package(
   CATKIN_DEPENDS roscpp rospy std_msgs message_runtime
 )
include_directories(
   ${catkin_INCLUDE_DIRS}
 )
```

Here, we are creating the executable called `face_tracker_node` and linking it to catkin and OpenCV libraries:

```
add_executable(face_tracker_node src/face_tracker_node.cpp)
target_link_libraries(face_tracker_node
   ${catkin_LIBRARIES}
   ${OpenCV_LIBRARIES}
 )
```

The track.yaml file

As we discussed, the `track.yaml` file contains ROS parameters, which are required by the `face_tracker_node`. Here are the contents of `track.yaml`:

```
image_input_topic: "/usb_cam/image_raw"
face_detected_image_topic: "/face_detector/raw_image"
haar_file_face:
"/home/robot/ros_robotics_projects_ws/
src/face_tracker_pkg/data/face.xml"
face_tracking: 1
display_original_image: 1
display_tracking_image: 1
```

You can change all the parameters according to your needs. Especially, you may need to change `haar_file_face`, which is the path of the Haar face file. If we set `face_tracking:1`, it will enable face tracking, otherwise not. Also, if you want to display the original and face-tracking image, you can set the flag here.

The launch files

The launch files in ROS can do multiple tasks in a single file. The launch files have an extension of `.launch`. The following code shows the definition of `start_usb_cam.launch`, which starts the `usb_cam` node for publishing the camera image as a ROS topic:

```
<launch>
  <node name="usb_cam" pkg="usb_cam" type="usb_cam_node"
output="screen" >
    <param name="video_device" value="/dev/video0" />
    <param name="image_width" value="640" />
    <param name="image_height" value="480" />
    <param name="pixel_format" value="yuyv" />
    <param name="camera_frame_id" value="usb_cam" />
```

```
            <param name="auto_focus" value="false" />
            <param name="io_method" value="mmap"/>
        </node>
    </launch>
```

Within the `<node>...</node>` tags, there are camera parameters that can be change by the user. For example, if you have multiple cameras, you can change the `video_device` value from `/dev/video0` to `/dev/video1` to get the second camera's frames.

The next important launch file is `start_tracking.launch`, which will launch the face-tracker node. Here is the definition of this launch file:

```
<launch>
<!-- Launching USB CAM launch files and Dynamixel controllers -->
    <include file="$(find
face_tracker_pkg)/launch/start_usb_cam.launch"/>

<!-- Starting face tracker node -->
    <rosparam file="$(find face_tracker_pkg)/config/track.yaml"
command="load"/>

    <node name="face_tracker" pkg="face_tracker_pkg"
type="face_tracker_node" output="screen" />
</launch>
```

It will first start the `start_usb_cam.launch` file in order to get ROS image topics, then load `track.yaml` to get necessary ROS parameters, and then load `face_tracker_node` to start tracking.

The final launch file is `start_dynamixel_tracking.launch`; this is the launch file we have to execute for tracking and Dynamixel control. We will discuss this launch file at the end of the chapter after discussing the `face_tracker_control` package.

Running the face tracker node

Let's launch the `start_tracking.launch` file from `face_tracker_pkg` using the following command. Note that you should connect your webcam to your PC:

```
$ roslaunch face_tracker_pkg start_tracking.launch
```

If everything works fine, you will get output like the following; the first one is the original image, and the second one is the face-detected image:

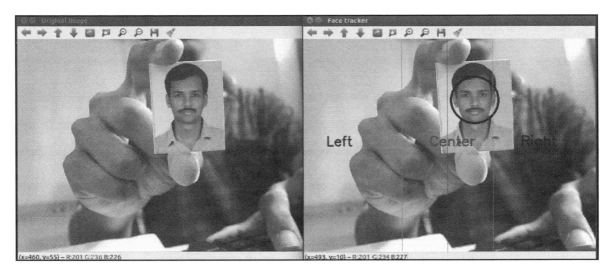

Figure 17: Face-detected image

We have not enabled Dynamixel now; this node will just find the face and publish the centroid values to a topic called /face_centroid.

So the first part of the project is done-what is next? It's the control part, right? Yes, so next, we are going to discuss the second package, face_tracker_control.

The face_tracker_control package

The face_tracker_control package is the control package used to track the face using the AX-12A Dynamixel servo.

Given here is the file structure of the `face_tracker_control` package:

```
├── CMakeLists.txt
├── config
│   ├── pan.yaml
│   └── servo_param.yaml
├── include
│   └── face_tracker_control
├── launch
│   ├── start_dynamixel.launch
│   └── start_pan_controller.launch
├── msg
│   └── centroid.msg
├── package.xml
└── src
    └── face_tracker_controller.cpp

6 directories, 8 files
```

Figure 18: File organization in the face_tracker_control package

We'll look at the use of each of these files first.

The start_dynamixel launch file

The `start_dynamixel` launch file starts Dynamixel Control Manager, which can establish a connection to a USB-to-Dynamixel adapter and Dynamixel servos. Here is the definition of this launch file:

```
<!-- This will open USB To Dynamixel controller and search for
servos -->
<launch>
    <node name="dynamixel_manager" pkg="dynamixel_controllers"
    type="controller_manager.py" required="true"
  output="screen">
        <rosparam>
            namespace: dxl_manager
            serial_ports:
                pan_port:
                    port_name: "/dev/ttyUSB0"
                    baud_rate: 1000000
                    min_motor_id: 1
                    max_motor_id: 25
                    update_rate: 20
        </rosparam>
```

```
    </node>
<!-- This will launch the Dynamixel pan controller -->
  <include file="$(find
face_tracker_control)/launch/start_pan_controller.launch"/>
</launch>
```

We have to mention the `port_name` (you can get the port number from kernel logs using the `dmesg` command). The `baud_rate` we configured was 1 Mbps, and the motor ID was 1. The `controller_manager.py` file will scan from servo ID 1 to 25 and report any servos being detected.

After detecting the servo, it will start the `start_pan_controller.launch` file, which will attach a ROS joint position controller for each servo.

The pan controller launch file

As we can see from the previous subsection, the pan controller launch file is the trigger for attaching the ROS controller to the detected servos. Here is the definition for the `start_pan_controller.launch` file:

This will start the pan joint controller:

```
<launch>
    <!-- Start tilt joint controller -->
    <rosparam file="$(find face_tracker_control)/config/pan.yaml"
 command="load"/>
    <rosparam file="$(find
face_tracker_control)/config/servo_param.yaml" command="load"/>

    <node name="tilt_controller_spawner"
pkg="dynamixel_controllers" type="controller_spawner.py"
        args="--manager=dxl_manager
            --port pan_port
            pan_controller"
        output="screen"/>
</launch>
```

The `controller_spawner.py` node can spawn a controller for each detected servo. The parameters of the controllers and servos are included in `pan.yaml` and `servo_param.yaml`.

The pan controller configuration file

The pan controller configuration file contains the configuration of the controller that the controller spawner node is going to create. Here is the `pan.yaml` file definition for our controller:

```
pan_controller:
    controller:
        package: dynamixel_controllers
        module: joint_position_controller
        type: JointPositionController
    joint_name: pan_joint
    joint_speed: 1.17
    motor:
        id: 1
        init: 512
        min: 316
        max: 708
```

In this configuration file, we have to mention the servo details, such as ID, initial position, minimum and maximum servo limits, servo moving speed, and joint name. The name of the controller is `pan_controller`, and it's a joint position controller. We are writing one controller configuration for ID 1 because we are only using one servo.

The servo parameters configuration file

The `servo_param.yaml` file contains the configuration of the `pan_controller`, such as the limits of the controller and step distance of each movement; also, it has screen parameters such as the maximum resolution of the camera image and offset from the center of the image. The offset is used to define an area around the actual center of the image:

```
servomaxx: 0.5    #max degree servo horizontal (x) can turn
servomin: -0.5    # Min degree servo horizontal (x) can turn
screenmaxx: 640   #max screen horizontal (x)resolution
center_offset: 50 #offset pixels from actual center to right and
left
step_distancex: 0.01 #x servo rotation steps
```

The face tracker controller node

As we've already seen, the face tracker controller node is responsible for controlling the Dynamixel servo according to the face centroid position. Let's understand the code of this node, which is placed at
`face_tracker_control/src/face_tracker_controller.cpp`.

The main ROS headers included in this code are as follows. Here, the `Float64` header is used to hold the position value message to the controller:

```
#include "ros/ros.h"
#include "std_msgs/Float64.h"
#include <iostream>
```

The following variables hold the parameter values from `servo_param.yaml`:

```
int servomaxx, servomin,screenmaxx, center_offset, center_left,
center_right;
float servo_step_distancex, current_pos_x;
```

The following message headers of `std_msgs::Float64` are for holding the initial and current positions of the controller, respectively. The controller only accepts this message type:

```
std_msgs::Float64 initial_pose;
std_msgs::Float64 current_pose;
```

This is the publisher handler for publishing the position commands to the controller:

```
ros::Publisher dynamixel_control;
```

Switching to the `main()` function of the code, you can see following lines of code. The first line is the subscriber of `/face_centroid`, which has the centroid value, and when a value comes to the topic, it will call the `face_callback()` function:

```
ros::Subscriber number_subscriber =
node_obj.subscribe("/face_centroid",10,face_callback);
```

The following line will initialize the publisher handle in which the values are going to be published through the `/pan_controller/command` topic:

```
dynamixel_control = node_obj.advertise<std_msgs::Float64>
("/pan_controller/command",10);
```

The following code creates new limits around the actual center of image. This will be helpful for getting an approximated center point of the image:

```
center_left = (screenmaxx / 2) - center_offset;
center_right = (screenmaxx / 2) + center_offset;
```

Here is the callback function executed while receiving the centroid value coming through the /face_centroid topic. This callback also has the logic for moving the Dynamixel for each centroid value.

In the first section, the x value in the centroid is checking against center_left, and if it is in the left, it just increments the servo controller position. It will publish the current value only if the current position is inside the limit. If it is in the limit, then it will publish the current position to the controller. The logic is the same for the right side: if the face is in the right side of the image, it will decrement the controller position.

When the camera reaches the center of image, it will pause there and do nothing, and that is the thing we want too. This loop is repeated, and we will get a continuous tracking:

```
void track_face(int x, int y)
{
    if (x < (center_left)){
      current_pos_x += servo_step_distancex;
      current_pose.data = current_pos_x;
    if (current_pos_x < servomaxx and current_pos_x > servomin ){
      dynamixel_control.publish(current_pose);
    }

    }

    else if(x > center_right){
current_pos_x -= servo_step_distancex;
current_pose.data = current_pos_x;
  if (current_pos_x < servomaxx and current_pos_x > servomin ){
       dynamixel_control.publish(current_pose);
}

    }

    else if(x > center_left and x < center_right){

;
}

}
```

Creating CMakeLists.txt

Like the first tracker package, there is no special difference in the control package; the difference is in the dependencies. Here, the main dependency is dynamixel_controllers. We are not using OpenCV in this package, so there's no need to include it:

```
cmake_minimum_required(VERSION 2.8.3)
project(face_tracker_control)
find_package(catkin REQUIRED COMPONENTS
  dynamixel_controllers
  roscpp
  rospy
  std_msgs
  message_generation
)
find_package(Boost REQUIRED COMPONENTS system)
add_message_files(
   FILES
   centroid.msg
 )
## Generate added messages and services with any dependencies
listed here
 generate_messages(
   DEPENDENCIES
  std_msgs
 )
catkin_package(
  CATKIN_DEPENDS dynamixel_controllers roscpp rospy std_msgs
)
include_directories(
  ${catkin_INCLUDE_DIRS}
)
add_executable(face_tracker_controller
src/face_tracker_controller.cpp)
target_link_libraries(face_tracker_controller ${catkin_LIBRARIES})
```

The complete source code of this project can be cloned from the following Git repository. The following command will clone the project repo:
```
$ git clone
https://github.com/qboticslabs/ros_robotics_projects
```

Testing the face tracker control package

We have seen most of the files and their functionalities. So let's test this package first. We have to ensure that it is detecting the Dynamixel servo and creating the proper topic.

Before running the launch file, we may have to change the permission of the USB device, or it will throw an exception. The following command can be used to get permissions on the serial device:

> $ **sudo chmod 777 /dev/ttyUSB0**

Note that you must replace ttyUSB0 with your device name; you can retrieve it by looking at kernel logs. The dmesg command can help you find it.

Start the start_dynamixel.launch file using the following command:

> $ **roslaunch face_tracker_control start_dynamixel.launch**

```
 * /servomin: -0.5
 * /step_distancex: 0.01

NODES
 /
    dynamixel_manager (dynamixel_controllers/controller_manager.py)
    tilt_controller_spawner (dynamixel_controllers/controller_spawner.py)

auto-starting new master
process[master]: started with pid [6997]
ROS_MASTER_URI=http://localhost:11311

setting /run_id to 6b4d648e-62c8-11e6-ac5f-00177c2e2869
process[rosout-1]: started with pid [7010]
started core service [/rosout]
process[dynamixel_manager-2]: started with pid [7027]
process[tilt_controller_spawner-3]: started with pid [7028]
[INFO] [WallTime: 1471252362.231754] pan_port controller_spawner: waiting for controller_manager dxl_manager
to startup in global namespace...
[INFO] [WallTime: 1471252362.661902] pan_port: Pinging motor IDs 1 through 25...
[INFO] [WallTime: 1471252364.696276] pan_port: Found 1 motors - 1 AX-12 [1], initialization complete.
[INFO] [WallTime: 1471252364.951534] pan_port controller_spawner: All services are up, spawning controllers..

[INFO] [WallTime: 1471252364.979589] Controller pan_controller successfully started.
[tilt_controller_spawner-3] process has finished cleanly
log file: /home/robot/.ros/log/6b4d648e-62c8-11e6-ac5f-00177c2e2869/tilt_controller_spawner-3*.log
```

Figure 19: Finding Dynamixel servos and creating controllers

If everything is successful, you will get a message as shown in the previous figure.

 If any errors occur during the launch, check the servo connection, power, and device permissions.

The following topics are generated when we run this launch file:

```
robot@robot-pc:~$ rostopic list
/diagnostics
/motor_states/pan_port
/pan_controller/command
/pan_controller/state
/rosout
/rosout_agg
robot@robot-pc:~$
```

Figure 20: Face tracker control topics

Bringing all the nodes together

Next, we'll look at the final launch file, which we skipped while covering the face_tracker_pkg package, and that is start_dynamixel_tracking.launch. This launch file starts both face detection and tracking using Dynamixel motors:

```
<launch>
<!-- Launching USB CAM launch files and Dynamixel controllers -->
  <include file="$(find
face_tracker_pkg)/launch/start_tracking.launch"/><include
file="$(find
face_tracker_control)/launch/start_dynamixel.launch"/>
<!-- Starting face tracker node -->

<node name="face_controller" pkg="face_tracker_control"
type="face_tracker_controller" output="screen" />

</launch>
```

Fixing the bracket and setting up the circuit

Before doing the final run of the project, we have to do something on the hardware side. We have to fix the bracket to the servo horn and fix the camera to the bracket. The bracket should be connected in such a way that it is always perpendicular to the center of the servo. The camera is mounted on the bracket, and it should be pointed toward the center position.

The following image shows the setup I did for this project. I simply used tape to fix the camera to the bracket. You can use any additional material to fix the camera, but it should always be aligned to the center first:

Figure 21: Fixing camera and bracket to the AX-12A

If you are done with this, then you are ready to go for the final run of this project.

The final run

I hope that you have followed all instructions properly; here is the command to launch all the nodes for this project and start tracking using Dynamixel:

```
$ roslaunch face_tracker_pkg start_dynamixel_tracking.launch
```

You will get the following windows, and it would be good if you could use a photo to test the tracking, because you will get continuous tracking of the face:

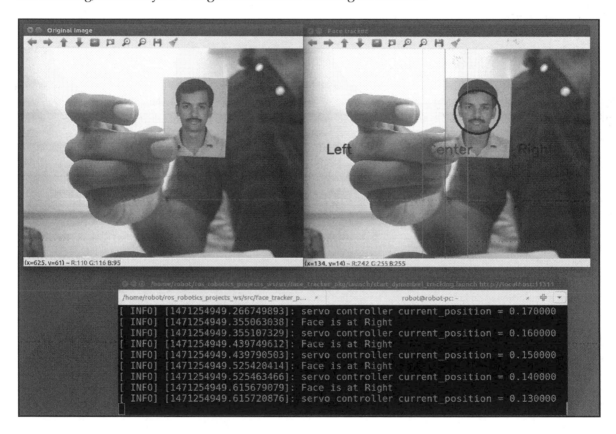

Figure 22: Final face tracking

Here, you can see the Terminal message that says the image is in the right and the controller is reducing the position value to achieve the center position.

Questions

- What is the main function of the `usb_cam` ROS package?
- What is the use of the `dynamixel_motor` package in ROS?
- What is the package for interfacing ROS and OpenCV?
- What is the difference between `face_tracker_pkg` and `face_tracker_control`?

Summary

This chapter was about building a face tracker using a webcam and Dynamixel motor. The software we used was ROS and OpenCV. Initially, we saw how to configure the webcam and Dynamixel motor, and after configuration, we were trying to build two packages for tracking. One package was for face detection, and the second package was a controller that can send a position command to Dynamixel to track the face. We have discussed the use of all the files inside the packages and did a final run to demonstrate the complete working of the system.

3
Building a Siri-Like Chatbot in ROS

Artificial intelligence, machine learning, and deep learning are getting very popular nowadays. All these technologies are linked, and the common goal is to mimic human intelligence. There are numerous applications for these fields; some of the relevant ones are as follows:

- **Logical reasoning**: This will generate logical conclusions from existing data. Reasoning using AI techniques is widely used in areas such as robotics, computer vision, and analytics.
- **Knowledge representation**: This is the study of how a computer could store knowledge fragments like our brains do. This is possible using AI techniques.
- **Planning**: This concept is heavily used in robotics; there are AI algorithms such as A* (star) and Dijkstra for planning a robot's path from its current position to a goal position. It is also heavily used in swarm robotics for robot planning.
- **Learning**: Humans can learn, right? What about machines? Using machine learning techniques, we can train artificial neural networks to learn data.
- **Natural language processing**: This is the ability to understand human language, mainly from text data.
- **Perception**: A robot can have various kinds of sensors, such as camera and mic. Using AI, we can analyze this sensor data and understand the meaning of it.
- **Social intelligence**: This is one of the trending fields of AI. Using AI, we can build social intelligence in a machine or robot. Robots such as Kismet and Jibo have social intelligence.

In this chapter, we will discuss knowledge representation and social intelligence. If you are going to build a robot that has skills to interact with people, you may need to store the knowledge and create some social skills. This chapter will teach you how to build a base system for such robots. Before discussing the implementation of this system, let's take a look at some social and service robots and its characteristics.

MIT Kismet:
http://www.ai.mit.edu/projects/humanoid-robotics-group/kismet/kismet.html
Jibo: https://www.jibo.com/

Social robots

In simple words, social robots are personal companions or assistive robots that can interact with human beings using speech, vision, and gestures. These robots behave like pets that can express emotions like us and can communicate their emotions using speech or gestures.

Nowadays, most social robots have an LCD display on their heads, actuators for movement, speakers and microphone for communication, and cameras for perception.

Here are some images of popular social robots:

Figure 1: Famous social robots

Let's learn about them:

- **Kismet(a)**: This is a social robot from MIT by Dr. Cynthia Breazeal and team, made in the 1990s. Kismet can identify people and objects and simulate different emotions. Kismet was just a research robot, not a commercial product.
- **Jibo(b)**: Jibo was conceived by Dr. Cynthia and team in 2014. Jibo has a rotating head with a screen, and it can communicate with people using speech recognition and can recognize them using perception techniques.
- **Pepper(c)**: Pepper is a humanoid social robot from Softbank. Unlike other social robots, this robot has two arms and a mobile base similar to a humanoid robot. Like other social robots, it can communicate with people and has tactile sensors on its body.
- **Buddy(d)**: This robot buddy has similar characteristics to the previous robots. It has a mobile base for movement and a screen on the head to express emotions.

Pepper: `https://www.ald.softbankrobotics.com/en/cool-robots/pepper`
Buddy: `http://www.bluefrogrobotics.com/en/home/`

These may have high intelligence and social skills. But most of the robots' source code is not open source, so we can't explore much about the software platforms and algorithms they use to implement them. But in this chapter, we are going to look at some of the open source solutions to build intelligence and social skills in robots.

Building social robots

A service or social robot may have capabilities to perceive the world using inbuilt cameras, interact with humans using speech and make decisions using artificial intelligence algorithms. These kinds of robots are a bit complicated in design, we can see a typical building block diagram of a social robot in the following figure.

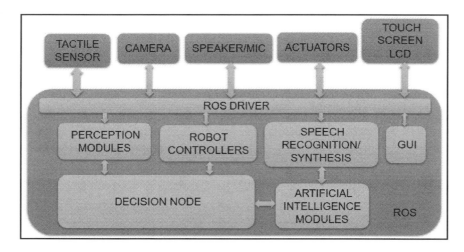

Figure 2: Block diagram of a typical social robot

The robot has sensors such as tactile sensor, camera, microphone, and touch screen and will have some actuators for its movement. The actuators will help the robot to move its head or body. There may be mobile service robots which has extra motors for navigation.

Inside the software block, you may can find modules for perception which handle camera data and finding necessary objects from the scene, speech recognition/synthesis, artificial intelligence modules, robot controller modules for controlling the actuators, decision-making node which combine all data from sensors and makes the final decision on what to do next. The ROS driver layer help to interface all sensors, actuators to ROS and the GUI can be an interactive visualization in the LCD panel.

In this chapter, we are going to implement the speech recognition or synthesis block with artificial intelligence which can communicate with people using text and speech. The reply from the bot should be like a human's.

We are going to implement a simple AI Chatbot using **AIML** (**Artificial Intelligence Markup Language**) which can be integrated to a social robot.

Let's see how to make software for such an interactive robot, starting with the prerequisites to build the software.

Prerequisites

Here are the prerequisites for doing this project:

- Ubuntu 16.04 LTS
- Python 2.7
- PyAIML: AIML interpreter in Python
- ROS Kinetic
- The `sound_play` ROS package: text-to-speech package in ROS

Let's get start with AIML.

Getting started with AIML

AIML (**Artificial Intelligence Markup Language**) is an XML-based language to store segments of knowledge inside XML tags. AIML files help us store knowledge in a structured way so that we can easily access it whenever required.

AIML was developed by *Richard Wallace* and the free software community worldwide between 1995 and 2002. You may have heard about chatter bots such as **Artificial Linguistic Internet Computer Entity** (**A.L.I.C.E.**) and **ELIZA**. AIML is the base of these chatter bots. The dataset of the A.L.I.C.E. chatter bot is available under the GNU GPL license, and there are open source AIML interpreters available in C++, Python, Java, and Ruby. We can use these interpreters to feed our input to the knowledge base and retrieve the best possible reply from it.

AIML tags

There is a set of AIML tags to represent knowledge inside files. The following are some of the important tags and their uses:

- `<aiml>`: Each AIML file starts with this tag and ends with the `</aiml>` tag. Basically, it holds the version of AIML and character encoding of the file. The `<aiml>` tag is not mandatory, but it will be useful when handling a huge AIML dataset. Here is the basic usage of the `<aiml>` tag:

```
<aiml version="1.0.1" encoding="UTF-8"?>
</aiml>
```

- `<category>`: Each knowledge segment is kept under this tag. This tag holds the input pattern from the user and outputs a response for it. The possible input from the user is kept under the `<pattern>` tag, and the corresponding response is under the `<template>` tag. Here is an example of the category, pattern, and template tags:

```
<aiml version="1.0.1" encoding="UTF-8">
  <category>
    <pattern> WHAT IS YOUR NAME </pattern>
    <template> MY NAME IS ROBOT </template>
  </category>
</aiml>
```

When a user asks the robot, "What is your name?", the robot replies, "My name is Robot." This is how we store knowledge for the robot.

- `<pattern>`: This tag consists of user input. From the preceding code, we can see that WHAT IS YOUR NAME is the user input. There will only be one pattern inside a category, placed after the category tag. Inside a pattern, we can include wild cards such as * or –, which can replace a string in the corresponding position.

- `<template>`: The template tag consists of responses to user input. In the previous code, MY NAME IS ROBOT is the response.

- `<star index = "n" />`: This tag helps extract a word from a sentence. The n indicates which word of the sentence is to be extracted:

    `<star index= "1" />`: This indicates the first fragment of the template sentence.

`<star index= "2" />`: This indicates the second fragment of the template sentence.

Using the star index, we can extract the word from user input and insert the word into the response if needed.

Here is an example of using wildcards and a start index:

```
<aiml version="1.0.1" encoding="UTF-8">
  <category>
    <pattern> MY NAME IS * </pattern>
      <template>
        NICE TO SEE YOU <star index="1"/>
      </template>
  </category>

  <category>
    <pattern> MEET OUR ROBOTS * AND * </pattern>
      <template>
        NICE TO SEE <star index="1"/> AND <star
    index="2"/>.
      </template>
  </category>
</aiml>
```

Here, we can reuse the word that comes in the * position in the `<template>` tag. Consider this input:

```
You: MY NAME IS LENTIN
Robot: NICE TO SEE YOU LENTIN
```

In the second category, you will get the following reply from the robot for the given input:

```
You: MEET OUR ROBOTS ROBIN AND TURTLEBOT
Robot: NICE TO SEE ROBIN AND TURTLEBOT
```

These are the basic tags used inside AIML files. Next, we'll see how to load these files and retrieve an intelligent reply from the AIML knowledge base for a random input from the user.

The following link will give you the list of AIML tags:
http://www.alicebot.org/documentation/aiml-reference.html

The PyAIML interpreter

There are AIML interpreters in many languages used to load the AIML knowledge base and interact with it. One of the easiest ways of loading and interacting with AIML files is using an AIML interpreter in Python called PyAIML. The PyAIML module can read all the categories, patterns, and templates and can build a tree. Using a backtracking depth-first search algorithm, it can search for the appropriate response from the user in order to give the proper reply.

PyAIML can be installed on Windows, Linux, and Mac OS X. In Ubuntu, there are prebuilt DEB binaries that we can install from Software Center. We can also install PyAIML from source code. The current PyAIML will work well in Python 2.7. Let's look at how we can install it.

Installing PyAIML on Ubuntu 16.04 LTS

Installing PyAIML on Ubuntu is pretty easy and straightforward. We can install the package using the following command:

```
$ sudo apt-get install python-aiml
```

The version of PyAIML will be 0.86.

We can also install PyAIML from source code. Clone the source code from Git using the following command:

```
$ git clone https://github.com/qboticslabs/pyaiml
```

After cloning the package, switch to the PyAIML folder and install using the following command:

```
$ sudo python setup.py install
```

Great! You are done with the installation. Let's check whether your installation is correct.

Playing with PyAIML

Take a Python interpreter Terminal and just try to import the AIML module using the following command:

```
>>> import aiml
```

If the module is loaded properly, the pointer you will come to the next line without getting an error. Congratulations! Your installation is correct.

Let's see how to load an AIML file using this module.

To play with this module, first we need an AIML file. Save the following content in an AIML file called `sample.aiml` in the `home` folder. You can save the file anywhere, but it should be in the same path where the Python Terminal was started.

```xml
<aiml version="1.0.1" encoding="UTF-8">
  <category>
    <pattern> MY NAME IS * </pattern>
      <template>
        NICE TO SEE YOU <star/>
      </template>
  </category>

  <category>
    <pattern> MEET OUR ROBOTS * AND * </pattern>
      <template>
        NICE TO SEE <star index="1"/> AND <star index="2"/>.
      </template>
  </category>
</aiml>
```

After saving the AIML file, let's try to load it. The first step is to build an object of the PyAIML module called `Kernel()`. The object name here is `bot`:

```
>>> bot = aiml.Kernel()
```

`Kernel()` is the main class doing the searching from the AIML knowledge base.

We can set the robot name using the following command:

```
>>> bot.setBotPredicate("name", ROBIN)
```

The next step is to load the AIML files; we can load one or more AIML files to memory.

To learn a single AIML file, use the following command:

```
>>> bot.learn('sample.aiml")
```

If the AIML file is correct, then you will get a message like this:

```
Loading sample.aiml... done (0.02 seconds)
```

This means that the sample AIML file is loaded properly in memory.

We can retrieve the response from the AIML file using the following command:

```
>>> print bot.respond("MY NAME IS LENTIN")
'NICE TO SEE YOU LENTIN'
```

If the user input is not in the file, you will get the following message:

```
'WARNING: No match found for input:'
```

Loading multiple AIML files

We have seen how to load a single AIML file to memory and retrieve response for a user input. In this section, we are going to see how to load multiple AIML files to memory; we are going to use these files for our AIML-based bots. Various AIML datasets are available on the Web, and some are also included in the code bundle. Given here is a file called startup.xml that helps us load all AIML files in a single run. It's a simple AIML file with a pattern called LOAD AIML B. When it gets this input from the user, it will learn all AIML files in that path using <learn>*.aiml</learn> tags:

```
<aiml version="1.0">
  <category>
    <pattern>LOAD AIML B</pattern>
      <template>
        <!-- Load standard AIML set -->
        <learn>*.aiml</learn>
      </template>
  </category>
</aiml>
```

We can use the following code to load this XML file and "learn" all the XML files to memory. After loading the AIML files, we can save the memory contents as a brain file. The advantage is that we can avoid the reloading of AIML files. Saving into a brain file will be helpful when we have thousands of AIML files:

```python
#!/usr/bin/env python
import aiml
import sys
import os
#Changing current directory to the path of aiml files
#This path will change according to your location of aiml files
os.chdir('/home/robot/Desktop/aiml/aiml_data_files') bot =
aiml.Kernel()
#If there is a brain file named standard.brn, Kernel() will
  initialize using bootstrap() method
if os.path.isfile("standard.brn"): bot.bootstrap(brainFile =
"standard.brn") else:
#If there is no brain file, load all AIML files and save a new
brain bot.bootstrap(learnFiles = "startup.xml", commands = "load
aiml b") bot.saveBrain("standard.brn")
#This loop ask for response from user and print the output from
Kernel() object
while True: print bot.respond(raw_input("Enter input >"))
```

You can see that the AIML files are stored at
/home/robot/Desktop/aiml/aiml_data_files/. All AIML files including
startup.xml and AIML brain files are stored in the same folder. You can choose any folder you want. In the previous code, we are using a new API called bootstrap() for loading, saving, and learning AIML files. The program tries to load a brain file called standard.brn first, and if there is no brain file, it will learn from startup.xml and save the brain file as standard.brn. After saving the brain file, it will start a while loop to start interacting with the AIML file.

If you run the code and there is no brain file, you may get output like this:

```
robot@robot-pc: ~/Desktop/aiml
Loading reduction.names.aiml... done (0.85 seconds)
Loading geography.aiml... done (0.16 seconds)
Loading wallace.aiml... done (0.11 seconds)
Loading emotion.aiml... done (0.02 seconds)
Loading science.aiml... done (0.01 seconds)
Loading biography.aiml... done (0.08 seconds)
Loading computers.aiml... done (0.02 seconds)
Loading pyschology.aiml... done (0.11 seconds)
Loading date.aiml... done (0.00 seconds)
Loading psychology.aiml... done (0.10 seconds)
Loading politics.aiml... done (0.01 seconds)
Loading mp1.aiml... done (0.62 seconds)
Loading mp0.aiml... done (1.08 seconds)
Loading mp6.aiml... done (0.37 seconds)
PARSE ERROR: Unexpected <category> tag (line 40, column 0)
PARSE ERROR: Unexpected </category> tag (line 43, column 0)
Loading ai.aiml... done (0.04 seconds)
PARSE ERROR: Unexpected </category> tag (line 104, column 0)
PARSE ERROR: Unexpected </category> tag (line 144, column 0)
Loading update_mccormick.aiml... done (0.01 seconds)

Kernel bootstrap completed in 12.90 seconds
Saving brain to standard.brn... done (0.65 seconds)
Enter input >
```

Figure 3: Loading multiple AIML files

Creating an AIML bot in ROS

The previous subsections were about understanding AIML tags and how to work with them using the PyAIML module. Let's see how to create an interactive AIML bot using ROS. The following figure shows the complete block diagram of the interactive bot:

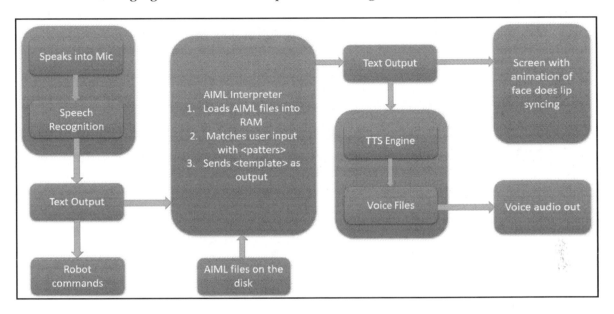

Figure 4: Interactive AIML bot

Here is how the entire system works: The speech of the user is converted into text using the speech recognition system in ROS. Then, it will input either to the AIML engine or send as a robot command. The robot commands are specific commands meant for robot control. If the text is not a robot command, it will send it to the AIML engine, which will give an intelligent reply from its database. The output of the AIML interpreter will be converted to speech using the text-to-speech module. The speech will be heard through speaker at the same time a virtual face of the robot will be animated on the screen, syncing with the speech.

In this chapter, we are mainly dealing with the AIML part and TTS using ROS; you can refer to other sources to perform speech recognition in ROS as well.

The AIML ROS package

In this section, we are going to create a simple package to load the AIML files to memory using ROS nodes. The following is the block diagram of the working AIML ROS package:

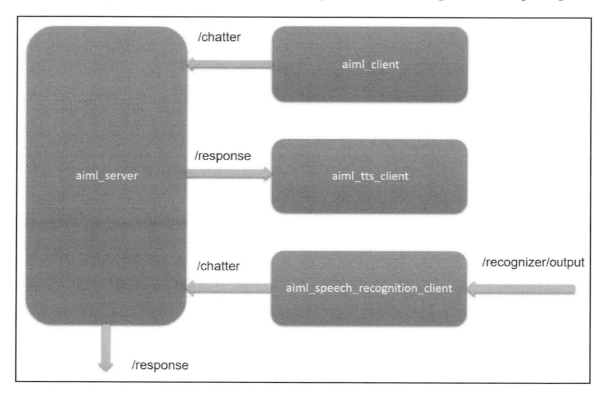

Figure 5: Working of the AIML ROS package

Here's the explanation for the nodes shown in the diagram:

- **aiml_server**: This ROS node loads AIML files from the database and saves them into brain files. It subscribes to a topic called **/chatter** (std_msgs/String). The string data from the **/chatter** topic is the input of the AIML interpreter. The response from the AIML interpreter is published through the **/response** (std_msgs/String) topic.
- **aiml_client**: This ROS node waits for user input, and once it gets the input, it will publish it to the **/chatter** topic.

- **aiml_tts_client**: The AIML server publishes the response to the **/response** topic. The `tts` client node will subscribe to this topic and convert it to speech.
- **aiml_speech_recognition_client**: This node will subscribe to the output from the speech recognition system and publish it to the **/chatter** topic.

The user can interact with AIML either by text chatting or speech. The speech recognition node will not do speech recognition; instead, it will receive the converted text from a speech recognition system and input it to the AIML server.

To create or install the `ros-aiml` package, you may need to install some dependency packages.

Installing the ROS sound_play package

The `sound_play` package is a **TTS** convertor package in ROS. You can obtain more information about the package from `http://wiki.ros.org/sound_play`. To install this package, you will need install some Ubuntu package dependencies. Let's go through the commands to install them.

Installing the dependencies of sound_play

Update your Ubuntu repositories using the following command:

```
$ sudo apt-get update
```

These are the dependencies required for the `sound_play` package:

```
$ sudo apt-get install libgstreamer1.0-dev libgstreamer-plugins-
base1.0-dev gstreamer1.0 gstreamer1.0-plugins-base gstreamer1.0-plugins-
good gstreamer1.0-plugins-ugly python-gi festival
```

After installing these Ubuntu packages, you can install the `sound_play` package using the following steps.

Installing the sound_play ROS package

Clone the `audio-common` packages into `ros_project_dependencies_ws`:

```
ros_project_dependencies_ws/src$ git clone
https://github.com/ros-drivers/audio_common
```

Install the packages using `catkin_make`.

After installing these packages, you can make sure it is properly installed using the following command:

```
$ roscd sound_play
```

If it switches to the `sound_play` package, you have installed it successfully.

Congratulations! You are done with all dependencies! Next, we will create the `ros-aiml` package.

 You can clone the source code discussed in the book from the following Git repository:
`https://github.com/qboticslabs/ros_robotics_projects`

Creating the ros_aiml package

Using the following command, we can create the `ros_aiml` package:

```
$ catkin_create_pkg ros_aiml rospy std_msgs sound_play
```

Inside the `ros_aiml` package, create folders called `data`, `scripts`, and `launch` to store the AIML files, Python scripts, and ROS launch files. This is the structure of the `ros_aiml` package:

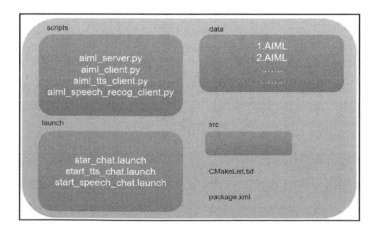

Figure 6: Structure of ros_aiml

You can keep the AIML files inside the `data` folder, and all launch files can be kept inside the `launch` folder. The scripts are saved inside the `scripts` folder. Let's look at each script.

The aiml_server node

As we've already discussed, `aiml_server` is responsible for loading and saving the AIML and AIM brain files. It is subscribed to the `/chatter` topic, which is the input of the AIML interpreter and publishes the `/response` topic, which is the response from the AIML interpreter. This is the main code snippet of `aiml_server.py`:

```python
def load_aiml(xml_file):

  data_path = rospy.get_param("aiml_path")
  print data_path
  os.chdir(data_path)

  if os.path.isfile("standard.brn"):
    mybot.bootstrap(brainFile = "standard.brn")

  else:
    mybot.bootstrap(learnFiles = xml_file, commands = "load aiml
b")
    mybot.saveBrain("standard.brn")

def callback(data):

  input = data.data
  response = mybot.respond(input)
  rospy.loginfo("I heard:: %s",data.data)
  rospy.loginfo("I spoke:: %s",response)
  response_publisher.publish(response)

def listener():

  rospy.loginfo("Starting ROS AIML Server")
  rospy.Subscriber("chatter", String, callback)

  # spin() simply keeps python from exiting until this node is
stopped
  rospy.spin()

if __name__ == '__main__':

  load_aiml('startup.xml')
  listener()
```

This ROS node is doing the same thing as the code that we used to load and save the AIML files. That code is converted into a ROS node that can accept input and send the response through a topic.

 You can clone the source code discussed in the book from the following Git repository:
`https://github.com/qboticslabs/ros_robotics_projects`

The AIML client node

The client code will wait for user input and publish the user input to the /chatter topic:

```python
#!/usr/bin/env python
import rospy
from std_msgs.msg import String
pub = rospy.Publisher('chatter', String,queue_size=10)
rospy.init_node('aiml_client')
r = rospy.Rate(1) # 10hz

while not rospy.is_shutdown():
    input = raw_input("\nEnter your text :> ")
    pub.publish(input)
    r.sleep()
```

The aiml_tts client node

The TTS client subscribes to the /response topic and converts the response to speech using the sound_play APIs:

```python
#!/usr/bin/env python
import rospy, os, sys
from sound_play.msg import SoundRequest
from sound_play.libsoundplay import SoundClient
from std_msgs.msg import String
rospy.init_node('aiml_soundplay_client', anonymous = True)

soundhandle = SoundClient()
rospy.sleep(1)
soundhandle.stopAll()
print 'Starting TTS'

def get_response(data):
  response = data.data
  rospy.loginfo("Response ::%s",response)
  soundhandle.say(response)
```

```
def listener():
  rospy.loginfo("Starting listening to response")
  rospy.Subscriber("response",String, get_response,queue_size=10)
  rospy.spin()
if __name__ == '__main__':
  listener()
```

The AIML speech recognition node

The speech recognition node subscribes to `/recognizer/output` and publishes to the `/chatter` topic:

```python
#!/usr/bin/env python
import rospy
from std_msgs.msg import String
rospy.init_node('aiml_speech_recog_client')
pub = rospy.Publisher('chatter', String,queue_size=10)
r = rospy.Rate(1) # 10hz

def get_speech(data):
  speech_text=data.data
  rospy.loginfo("I said:: %s",speech_text)
  pub.publish(speech_text)

def listener():
  rospy.loginfo("Starting Speech Recognition")
  rospy.Subscriber("/recognizer/output", String, get_speech)
  rospy.spin()

while not rospy.is_shutdown():
  listener()
```

The `/recognizer/output` topic is published by ROS speech recognition packages such as Pocket Sphinx (`http://wiki.ros.org/pocketsphinx`).

Next, we'll look at the launch files used for starting each node.

start_chat.launch

The `start_chat.launch` launch file launches the `aiml_server` and `aiml_client` nodes.
Before running this launch file, you have to set the data folder path that is set as the ROS
parameter. You can set it as your AIML data folder path:

```
<launch>
  <param name="aiml_path"
value="/home/robot/ros_robotics_projects_ws/src/ros_aiml/data" />
  <node name="aiml_server" pkg="ros_aiml" type="aiml_server.py"
output="screen">
  </node>
  <node name="aiml_client" pkg="ros_aiml" type="aiml_client.py"
output="screen">
  </node>
</launch>
```

start_tts_chat.launch

The launch file launches the `aiml_server`, `aiml_client`, and `aiml_tts` nodes. The
difference between the previous launch file and this one is that this will convert the AIML
server response into speech:

```
<launch>


  <param name="aiml_path"
 value="/home/robot/ros_robotics_projects_ws/src/ros_aiml/data" />
  <node name="aiml_server" pkg="ros_aiml" type="aiml_server.py"
output="screen">
  </node>
  <include file="$(find sound_play)/soundplay_node.launch">
</include>
  <node name="aiml_tts" pkg="ros_aiml" type="aiml_tts_client.py"
output="screen">
  </node>
  <node name="aiml_client" pkg="ros_aiml" type="aiml_client.py"
output="screen">
  </node>
</launch>
```

start_speech_chat.launch

The `start_speech_chat.launch` launch file will start the AIML server, AIML TTS node, and speech recognition node:

```
<launch>
  <param name="aiml_path"
value="/home/robot/ros_robotics_projects_ws/src/ros_aiml/data" />
  <node name="aiml_server" pkg="ros_aiml" type="aiml_server.py"
output="screen">
  </node>
  <include file="$(find sound_play)/soundplay_node.launch">
  </include>
  <node name="aiml_tts" pkg="ros_aiml" type="aiml_tts_client.py"
output="screen">
  </node>
  <node name="aiml_speech_recog" pkg="ros_aiml"
type="aiml_speech_recog_client.py" output="screen">
  </node>
</launch>
```

After creating the launch file, change its permission using the following command:

```
$ sudo chmod +x *.launch
```

Use the following command to start interacting with the AIML interpreter:

```
$ roslaunch ros_aiml start_chat.launch
```

We can use the following command to start interacting with the AIML interpreter. The response will be converted to speech as well:

```
$ roslaunch ros_aiml start_tts_chat.launch
```

The following command will enable speech recognition and TTS:

```
$ roslaunch ros_aiml start_speech_chat.launch
```

If you set up the `pocketsphinx` package for speech recognition, you can run it using the following command:

```
$ roslaunch pocketsphinx robotcup.launch
```

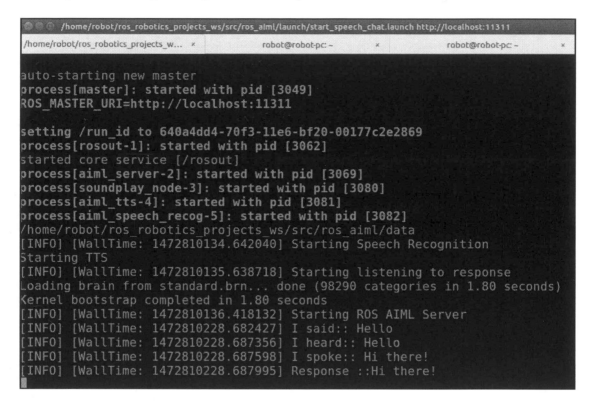

Figure 7: Output of the start_speech_chat launch file

Here are the topics generated when we run this launch file:

Figure 8: List of ROS topics

We can test the entire system without the speech recognition system too. You can manually publish the string to the `/recognizer/output` topic, as shown here:

Figure 9: Manually publishing input to speech topic

Questions

- What are the various applications of AI in robotics?
- What is AIML and why is it used?
- What is a pattern and template in AIML?
- What is PyAIML and what are its functions?

Summary

In this chapter, we discussed building a ROS package to make a robot interactive using artificial intelligence. Using this package, we can talk to a robot and the robot can answer your queries, like human-to-human interaction. The entire chapter was about building this communication system using AIML, which is the main component of this project. We discussed AIML tags, how to work with AIML files using Python, and ultimately, how to build a ROS package based on AIML for an interactive robot. In the next chapter, we will discuss interfacing boards with the ROS.

4
Controlling Embedded Boards Using ROS

Do you know how a robot makes decisions according to its sensor data? It has a processing unit, right? The processing unit can be either a computer or a microcontroller. We are using high-end computers to process data if the robot has sensors such as camera, laser scanners, and LIDARs. On the other hand, microcontrollers are commonly used in all kind of robots for interfacing low-bandwidth sensors and for performing real-time tasks. Both these units are commonly found in a standard robotic system.

In small robots such as line follower, we may do everything using a single controller. The sensors such as ultrasonic distance sensors, Imus can easily interface with a microcontroller. So in a robotic system, these two units can work independently, and there will be some kind of communication happening between them.

In this chapter, we will discuss how we can communicate with an embedded controller board from a computer running on ROS. It is very useful to acquire sensor data from a controller using a computer, and you can do the remaining processing on the computer. In most of the high-end robots, both controller and computer are used for low-level and high-level control and processing.

We'll also look at some popular embedded boards and their interfacing techniques with ROS.

Here are the topics we will look in this chapter:

- Getting started with popular embedded boards
- Interfacing Arduino with ROS
- Interfacing STM32 with ROS
- Working with Raspberry Pi 2 and ROS
- Odroid and ROS

Getting started with popular embedded boards

In this section, we will look at some of the popular microcontroller boards and microcomputers that can be used in robots.

An introduction to Arduino boards

Arduino is one of the most popular embedded controller boards that can be used in robots. It is mainly used for prototyping electronics projects and robots. The boards mainly contain an AVR series controller, in which its pins are mapped as Arduino board pins. The main reason for the Arduino board's popularity is in its programming and easiness in prototyping. The Arduino APIs and packages are very easy to use. So we can prototype our application without much difficulty. The Arduino programming IDE is based on a software framework called **Wiring** (http://wiring.org.co/); we are coding using C/ C++ in a simplified way. The code is compiled using C/C++ compilers. Here is an image of a popular Arduino board, the Arduino Uno:

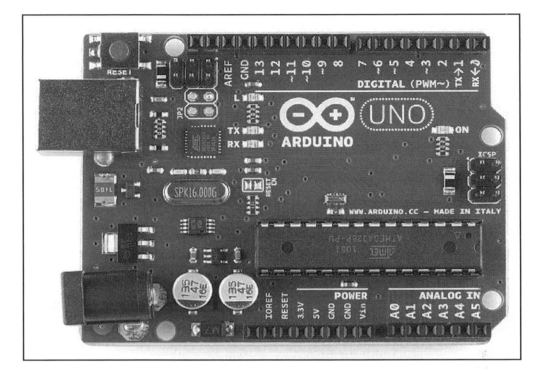

Figure 1: Arduino Uno board

How to choose an Arduino board for your robot

The following are some of the important specifications of this board that may be useful while selecting an Arduino board for your robot:

- **Speed**: Almost all Arduino boards work under 100 MHz. Most of the controllers on boards are 8 MHz and 16 MHz. If you want to do some serious processing such as implementing a PID on a single chip, then the Arduino may not be the best choice, especially if we want to run it at a higher rate. The Arduino is best suited for simple robot control. It is best for tasks such as controlling a motor driver and servo, reading from analog sensors, and interfacing serial devices using protocols such as **Universal Asynchronous Receiver/Transmitter** (**UART**), **Inter-Integrated Circuit** (**I2C**), and **Serial Peripheral Interface** (**SPI**).

- **GPIO pins**: Arduino boards provide different kinds of I/O pins to developers, such as **general purpose input/output (GPIO)**, **analog-to-digital converter (ADC)**, and **pulse width modulation (PWM)**, I2C, UART, and SPI pins. We can choose Arduino boards according to our pin requirements. There are boards having a pin count from 9 to 54. The more pins the board has, the larger will be the size of the board.

- **Working voltage levels**: There are Arduino boards working on TTL (5V) and CMOS (3.3V) voltage levels. For example, if the robot sensors are working only in 3.3V mode and our board is 5V, then we have to either convert 3.3V to the 5V equivalent using a level shifter or use an Arduino working at 3.3V. Most Arduino boards can be powered from USB itself.

- **Flash memory**: Flash memory is an important aspect when selecting an Arduino board. The output hex file generated by the Arduino IDE may not be optimized when compared with the hex of embedded C and assembly code. If your code is too big, it is better to go for higher flash memory, such as 256 KB. Most basic Arduino boards have only 32 KB of flash memory, so you should be aware of this issue before selecting the board.

- **Cost**: One of the final criteria is of course the cost of the board. If your requirement is just for a prototype, you can be flexible; you can take any board. But if you are making a product using this, cost will be a constraint.

Getting started with STM32 and TI Launchpads

What do we do if the Arduino is not enough for our robotic applications? No worries; there are advanced ARM-based controller boards available, such as STM32 microcontroller based development boards like NUCLEO and **Texas Instrument (TI)** microcontrollers based boards like Launchpads. The STM32 is a family of 32-bit microcontrollers from a company called **STMicroelectronics** (http://www.st.com/content/st_com/en.html). They manufacture microcontrollers based on different ARM architectures, such as the Cortex-M series. The STM32 controllers offer a lot more clock speed than Arduino boards. The range of STM32 controllers are from 24 MHz to 216 MHz, and the flash memory sizes are from 16 KB to 2 MB. In short, STM32 controllers offer a stunning configuration with a wider range of features than the Arduino. Most boards work at 3.3V and have a wide range of functionalities on the GPIO pins. You may be thinking about the cost now, right? But the cost is also not high: the price range is from 2 to 20 USD.

There are evaluation boards available in the market to test these controllers. Some famous families of evaluation boards are as follows:

- **STM32 Nucleo boards**: The Nucleo boards are ideal for prototyping. They are compatible with Arduino connectors and can be programmed using an Arduino-like environment called **mbed** (`https://www.mbed.com/en/`).
- **STM32 Discovery kits**: These boards are very cheap and come built in with components such as an accelerometer, mic, and LCD. The mbed environment is not supported on these boards, but we can program the board using IAR, Keil, and **Code Composer Studio (CCS)**.
- **Full evaluation boards**: These kinds of boards are comparatively expensive and are used to evaluate all features of the controller.
- **Arduino-compatible boards**: These are Arduino header-compatible boards having STM32 controllers. Examples of these boards are Maple, OLIMEXINO-STM32, and Netduino. Some of these boards can be programmed using the Wiring language, which is used to program Arduino.

The STM32 boards are not more popular in the hobby/DIY community than the Arduino, but they are mainly used in high-end robot controllers. Here is an STM 32 Nucleo board:

Figure 2: STM 32 NUCLEO board

The Tiva C Launchpad

One of the other alternatives to the Arduino is Launchpad from Texas Instruments. The TI controllers have specifications similar to STM32 controllers, and both are based on ARM's Cortex-M architecture. The clock speed of the controllers ranges from 48 MHz-330 MHz. The flash memory capacity is also high: up to 1 MB. The GPIO pins and cost are almost similar to STM32 boards. Some of the commonly used Launchpad boards are TM4C123G Launchpad and EK-TM4C1294XL, which is based on an ARM Cortex-M4F-based MCU. The 123G works at 80MHZ and 1294XL at 120 MHz.

The good thing about these boards is that we can program them using a modified Arduino IDE called **Energia** (http://energia.nu/).

This is how the EK-TM4C1294XL looks:

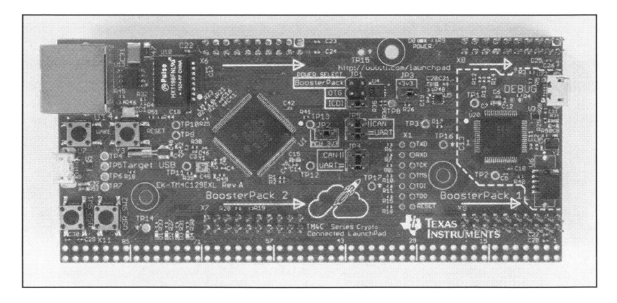

Figure 3: The EK-TM4C1294XL board

List of Arduino boards: https://www.arduino.cc/en/Main/Products
STM32 boards: https://goo.gl/w7qFuE
Tiva C Series Launchpad: http://processors.wiki.ti.com/index.php
/Tiva_C_Series_LaunchPads
Launchpad boards:
http://www.ti.com/lsds/ti/tools-software/launchpads/launchpads.p
age

We have seen some popular controllers; now let's look at some of the high-level embedded processing units that can be used in robots.

Introducing the Raspberry Pi

Raspberry Pi is another popular embedded board, and it's a single-board computer on which we can load an operating system and use it like a full-fledged PC. It has a **system on chip** (**SoC**) comprising of components such as an ARM processor, RAM, and GPU. There is an Ethernet port, USB ports, HDMI, GPIO pins, sound jack, camera connector, and LCD connector:

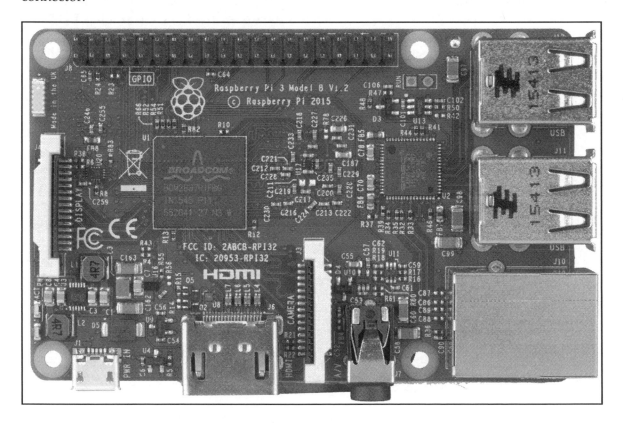

Figure 4: Raspberry Pi 3 board

List of Raspberry Pi boards:
`https://www.raspberrypi.org/products/`

How to choose a Raspberry Pi board for your robot

The following are some important specifications that may be useful while selecting this board for your robots:

- **Speed of the board**: The speed of the ARM processor in Raspberry Pi boards ranges from 700 MHz to 1.2 GHz. These boards are suitable for running an OS and building robotics applications on top of it. We can perform processor-intensive tasks such as image processing on the board. Don't pick this board if you have multiple image-processing applications and other tasks for the robot. They won't properly run on the board. It can freeze the entire system too. This board is perfectly suited for a single robotics application. The latest board, the Raspberry Pi 3, can offer you better performance for robotics applications.
- **Memory**: The RAM of the board ranges from 256 MB to 1 GB. If the robot application involves a lot of data processing, it may need a good amount of RAM. So for an image processing application, we should select a board with a large RAM size.
- **GPIO**: The main feature of Raspberry Pi boards is they have dedicated GPIO pins. The GPIO pins have multiple functions, such as I2C, UART, SPI, and PWM. We can't interface an analog sensor with the Pi because there are no inbuilt ADC pins. The GPIO pins are 3.3V compatible, so to interface with TTL logic, we may need a level shifter or voltage divider circuit. For interfacing analog sensors, we may need to interface an external ADC to the Raspberry Pi. The board has a maximum of 40 GPIO pins.
- **Power rating**: The Raspberry Pi works on 5V, which can take up to 2A current during operation. It will be good if you can provide this rating for the RPi. The RPi can even work from a computer USB port, but the power rating can vary according to the processing. So to be safe, it will be good if we can provide a 5V/2A rating.
- **Cost**: This is one of the most important criteria while choosing an RPi board. The price range of RPi boards is from 19 USD to 40 USD. You can choose the latest and most expensive board, the Raspberry Pi 3, to get maximum performance. The selection of board will depend on your robotics application.

The Odroid board

If you want more processing power than a Raspberry Pi board and with the same form factor, then Odroid is for you. The Odroid-C2 and Odroid-XU4 are the latest Odroid models, with 1.5 GHz and 2 GHz quad-core processors and 2 GB RAM, and almost the same power consumption as the RPi.

Odroid can be loaded with the latest version of Ubuntu, Android, and many flavors of Linux. It is a good choice if you are planning for an embedded powerhouse in a very small form factor. Let's discuss some of the models of Odroid.

The Odroid-XU4 is the most powerful and expensive board in the series. This board is ideal for running ROS and image-processing application. It has eight cores running at 2 GHz and with 2 GB of RAM.

The ODROID-C2 runs at 1.5 GHz, on a quad-core processor with 2 GB of RAM. The Odroid-C1+ and C1 have almost the same configuration as the C2, with the main difference being that the C1/C1+ only have 1 GB RAM, as opposed to the C2's 2 GB. These two boards are priced almost the same as Raspberry Pi's high-end boards. They are clear competitors to the Raspberry Pi.

ODROID XU4   ODROID C2   ODROID C1+

Figure 5: The Odroid board series

This subsection should be enough for you to get an idea of popular embedded boards that can be used for robots. Next, we can start discussing interfacing ROS with some of these boards. We are not going to discuss too deeply about the interfacing concept; rather than that, we will mainly focus on the procedures to get the board ready to work with ROS. We will also learn about some of the sensor interfacing, using which we can read sensor values using a controller board and read into ROS.

List of Odroid boards:
`http://www.hardkernel.com/main/products/prdt_info.php`

Interfacing Arduino with ROS

Interfacing an Arduino board with ROS simply means running a ROS node on Arduino that can publish/subscribe like a normal ROS node. An Arduino ROS node can be used to acquire and publish sensor values to a ROS environment, and other nodes can process it. Also, we can control devices, for example, actuators such as DC motors, by publishing values to an Arduino node. The main communication between PC and Arduino happens over UART. There is a dedicated protocol called ROS Serial (`http://wiki.ros.org/rosserial/Overview`), implemented as a ROS metapackage called `rosserial`, which can encode and decode ROS Serial messages. Using the ROS Serial protocol, we can publish and subscribe to Arduino like a ROS node over UART.

To start with ROS interfacing of Arduino, follow these steps:

1. First, we have to install some ROS packages on Ubuntu. The following commands can be used to install them.
2. Installing the `rosserial` metapackage:

    ```
    $ sudo apt-get install ros-kinetic-rosserial
    ```

3. The following command will install the `rosserial-arduino` client package on ROS. This client package helps create a client library of the Arduino IDE for ROS. Using this library, we can create Arduino ROS nodes that work like a normal ROS node.

    ```
    $ sudo apt-get install ros-kinetic-rosserial-arduino
    ```

4. After installing these packages, you need to download and set up the Arduino IDE. We need to download this IDE to program Arduino boards. You can download the latest Arduino IDE from (`https://www.arduino.cc/en/Main/Software`).

5. You can download the Arduino IDE for Linux 64/32-bit according to your OS configuration and run the `arduino` executable after extracting the package.

6. To add the ROS library for the Arduino IDE, first you have to go to **File | Preference** and set the **Sketchbook location,** as shown in this screenshot:

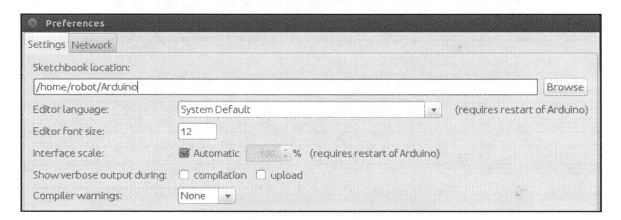

Figure 6: Arduino board preference

7. Go to the sketchbook location and create a folder called `libraries` if it is not present, and open a Terminal inside the `libraries` folder. We are keeping all Arduino libraries on this folder. Enter the following command to generate the `ros_lib` library for Arduino:

```
$ rosrun rosserial_arduino make_libraries.py .
```

8. You will see the following messages printing during the execution of the command. You may get an error after some time, but that's perfectly fine.

```
Exporting rosserial_msgs

  Messages:
    Log,TopicInfo,

  Services:
    RequestServiceInfo,RequestMessageInfo,RequestParam,

Exporting std_srvs

  Services:
    Trigger,Empty,SetBool,

Exporting std_msgs

  Messages:
    Time,Int32MultiArray,Byte,ColorRGBA,Int8MultiArray,Int32,Float32,String,Char
,UInt8MultiArray,UInt64MultiArray,Bool,Header,Float64MultiArray,MultiArrayDimens
ion,Float32MultiArray,UInt32,UInt64,Int16,Int64MultiArray,UInt8,UInt16MultiArray
,Int16MultiArray,Empty,MultiArrayLayout,Int8,UInt32MultiArray,Int64,Float64,Dura
tion,UInt16,ByteMultiArray,

Exporting geometry_msgs
```

Figure 7: Building the Arduino ROS library

9. After the execution of this command, a folder called `ros_lib` will be generated, which is the Arduino ROS serial client library.

10. Now, you can open the Arduino IDE and check that the option highlighted in the following figure is available. You can take any of the ROS examples and compile and check whether it is building without any errors:

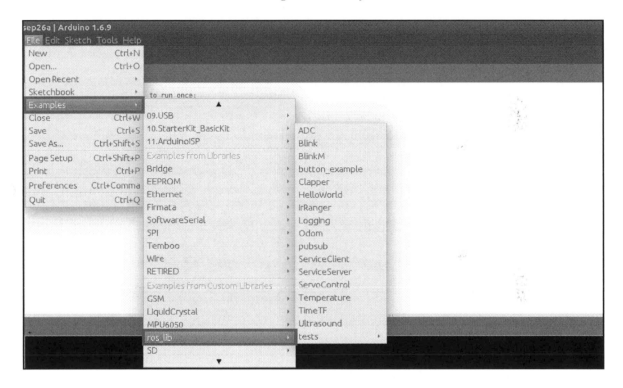

Figure 8: ros_lib on Arduino IDE

Congratulations! You have successfully set up `ros_lib` on Arduino. Now we can perform a few experiments using the ROS-Arduino interface.

Monitoring light using Arduino and ROS

We can start coding a basic Arduino-ROS node that can sense the amount of light using a **light-dependent resistor** (**LDR**). You can use any Arduino for this demo; here, we are going to use the Arduino Mega 2560. Given in the following figure is the circuit of an LDR with the Arduino. The characteristic of an LDR is that it is basically a resistor in which the resistance across it changes when light falls on it. The maximum resistance is when there is no light and minimum when light falls on it.

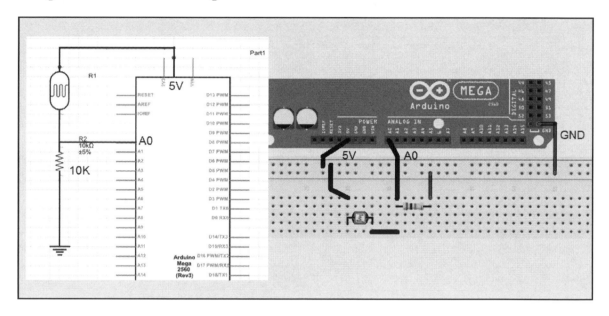

Figure 9: Arduino-LDR interfacing circuit

We have to connect one pin to 5V from the Arduino board and the next terminal to the Arduino's A0 pin. That terminal is connected to the GND pin through a 10 KΩ resistor. It is basically a voltage divider circuit. The equation for finding the voltage at A0 is as follows:

$V\_a0 = 5 * (R2 / (R1 + R2))$

From the equation, it is clear that when there is no light, we will get the minimum voltage, and when there is light, we'll get the maximum. This value can be read out using an Arduino program.

Here is the ROS code to read from an LDR:

```
#include <Arduino.h>
#include <ros.h>
#include <rosserial_arduino/Adc.h>

ros::NodeHandle nh;

rosserial_arduino::Adc adc_msg;
ros::Publisher p("adc", &adc_msg);

void setup()
{
 nh.initNode();
 nh.advertise(p);
}

//We average the analog reading to elminate some of the noise
int averageAnalog(int pin){
   int v=0;
   for(int i=0; i<4; i++) v+= analogRead(pin);
   return v/4;
}

long adc_timer;

void loop()
{
   adc_msg.adc0 = averageAnalog(0);
   p.publish(&adc_msg);
   nh.spinOnce();
   delay(50);
}
```

Here is the explanation of the code:

```
#include <Arduino.h>
#include <ros.h>
#include <rosserial_arduino/Adc.h>
```

The `<Arduino.h>` library contains definitions of Arduino-specific functions. The `<ros.h>` library contains Arduino-to-ROS client functionalities. The `<rosserial_arduino/Adc.h>` header contains message definitions for carrying several ADC values in a single message.

```
ros::NodeHandle nh;
```

This create a ROS node handle. Like other ROS nodes, we are using this handle to publish and subscribe to Arduino.

```
rosserial_arduino::Adc adc_msg;
ros::Publisher p("adc", &adc_msg);
```

This code will create an `adc_msg` instance and create a publisher object.

```
void setup()
{
 nh.initNode();
 nh.advertise(p);
}
```

This will initialize the node and bind the publisher object to start publishing the topic called `/adc`.

```
void loop()
{
  adc_msg.adc0 = averageAnalog(0);
  p.publish(&adc_msg);
  nh.spinOnce();
  delay(50);
}
```

In the loop, the Analog value from pin `A0` is read and the average is computed. The average value will be published to the `/adc` topic.

After compiling the code, you can select the board from **Tools | Board** and **Serial Port** from the list. You can now burn the code into the Arduino board.

Running ROS serial server on PC

After burning the code, to start subscribing or publishing to the Arduino board, we should start the ROS serial server on the PC side. Let's see how to do so:

1. Initialize `roscore`:

   $ roscore

2. Run the ROS serial server on the PC. The argument of the server is the serial device name of the Arduino device:

   $ rosrun rosserial_python serial_node.py /dev/ttyACM0

3. Now, you can see the /adc topic using the following command:

```
$ rostopic list
```

4. You can echo the /adc topic using the following command:

```
$ rostopic echo /adc/adc0
```

5. You may get following values:

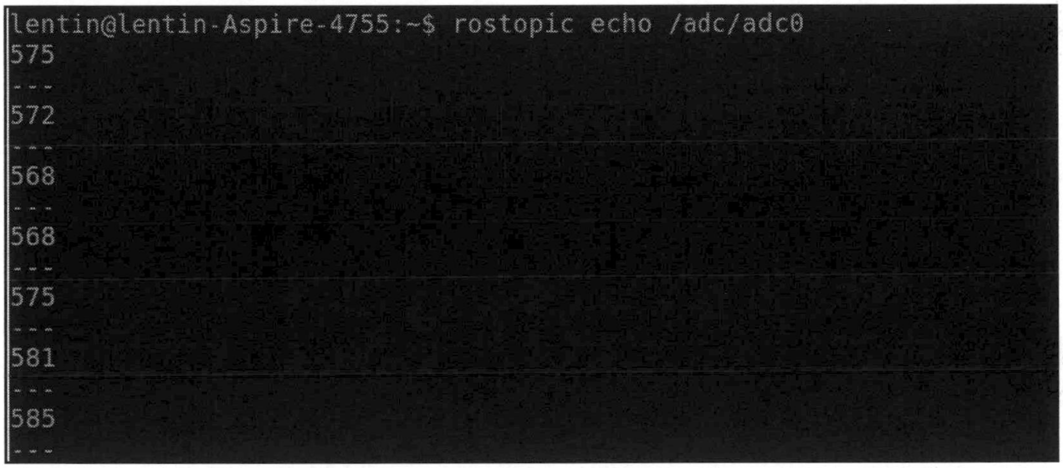

```
lentin@lentin-Aspire-4755:~$ rostopic echo /adc/adc0
575
- - -
572
- - -
568
- - -
568
- - -
575
- - -
581
- - -
585
- - -
```

Figure 10: Displaying LDR values from the ROS topic

We can also visualize the sensor value using `rqt_plot` using the following command. Now you can vary the light around the sensor and can check the variation of the values. The readings of the LDR are mapped from 1 to 1023. If there is no light, that means there's a high resistance in the LDR, so there'll be a low voltage across it and low reading on the Arduino, and vice versa.

```
$ rqt_plot adc/adc0
```

You can see this in the following graph:

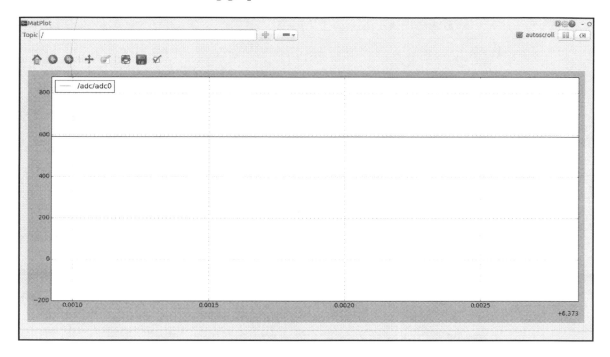

Figure 11: Visualizing LDR values in rqt_plot

Interfacing STM32 boards to ROS using mbed

If Arduino is not enough for your application, the STM 32 boards are ready to serve you. To demonstrate ROS interfacing, we are going to use an STM 32 NUCLEO L476RG (https://developer.mbed.org/platforms/ST-Nucleo-L476RG/). Before we begin programming, let's understand the mbed platform. The mbed platform is a software platform for programming 32-bit ARM Cortex-M microcontrollers. The mbed platform developed as a collaborative project by ARM its technology partners. We can use the online mbed IDE or offline compilers for programming the boards. The advantage of using the online IDE is it will be updated and will have more hardware support.

Let's start programming the STM 32 board:

1. The first step is to create an account on the mbed website, which is `https://developer.mbed.org`.

2. After creating an account, go to the following link to check our board has support in the mbed platform: `https://developer.mbed.org/platforms/`.

3. You can select your board from this website; for this demo, you should choose the NUCLEO L476RG board, which is available at `https://developer.mbed.org/platforms/ST-Nucleo-L476RG/`.

4. You can see an option called **Add to your mbed compiler** on the right-hand side of this page. You have to click on this button to add this board to the mbed compiler. We can add any number of boards to the mbed compiler; also, we can choose the board before compiling.

5. After adding the board to the compiler, we can compile a ROS node for this board. As we've already discussed, we can program the board using the online IDE or an offline compiler such as gcc4embed (`https://github.com/adamgreen/gcc4mbed`). Using offline compilers, we can only program a limited number of boards, but the online IDE can handle the latest boards.

6. The programming APIs of the ROS node in STM 32 are the same as those for Arduino, only the environment and tools are different.

7. The online `ros_lib` files for mbed are available at `https://developer.mbed.org/users/garyservin/code/`. You can find `ros_lib` for the Kinetic, Jade, and Indigo versions. You can try with the ROS version you are working on.

8. You can look at Hello World code for each ROS distribution from the preceding link.

You can check out examples for ROS Kinetic at `https://developer.mbed.org/users/garyservin/code/ros_lib_kinetic`.

For ROS Jade, the link is `https://developer.mbed.org/users/garyservin/code/ros_lib_jade/`.
For ROS Indigo:
`https://developer.mbed.org/users/garyservin/code/ros_lib_indigo/`

9. You can import the code into the compiler using the following option:

Figure 12: Importing code to mbed in the online compiler

10. This will open the source code in the mbed online IDE, as shown in the next screenshot. Here, we are testing with Hello World code for ROS Indigo.

11. The area marked **1** is the board we have added to the compiler. Area **2** is imported source code and `ros_lib` for mbed, and area **3** is the button to compile the source code. You can see the debugging details at the bottom of the compiler:

Figure 13: The mbed online compiler

12. The APIs are the same as those of Arduino we saw in the previous section. In this code, we are publishing a string message, `Hello from STM32 NUCLEO`, to a topic called `/chatter`. You can display this string on a PC by running the ROS serial server.

13. Click on the **Compile** button to download the binary file, which can be copied to the board. Plug the board to your PC, and you will see a flash drive of the board. You can copy the downloaded binary file to the flash storage, as shown here:

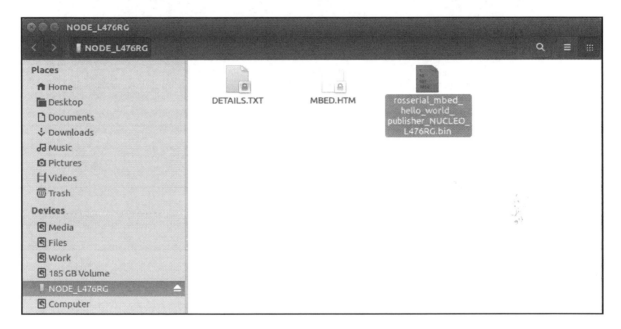

Figure 14: Binary file on flash drive

14. When we copy the binary file, the board will automatically start running it. Now, the procedures have been completed. Just start the ROS server on the PC side to display topics from the board.

15. Start `roscore`:

        $ roscore

16. Start the ROS server:

        $ rosrun rosserial_python serial_node.py /dev/ttyACM0

17. Now you can echo the topic using the following command:

        $ rostopic echo /chatter

18. You will get following messages on the Terminal:

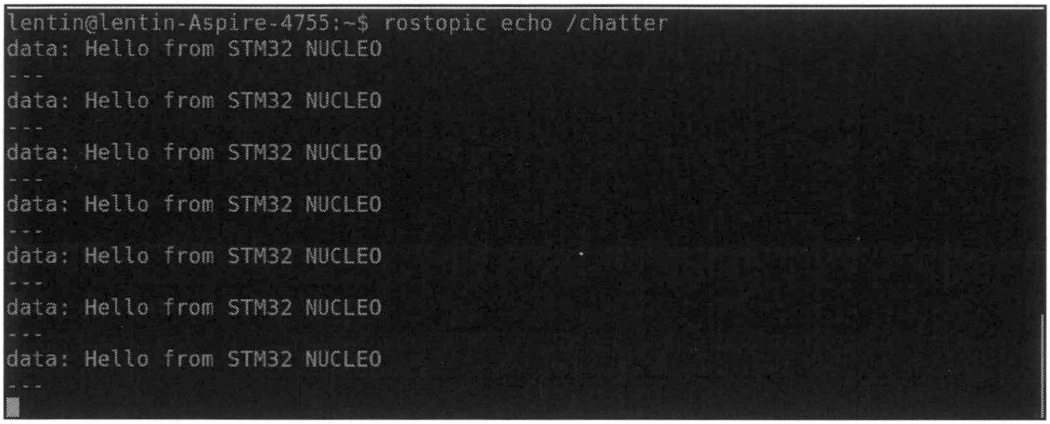

```
lentin@lentin-Aspire-4755:~$ rostopic echo /chatter
data: Hello from STM32 NUCLEO
---
data: Hello from STM32 NUCLEO
---
data: Hello from STM32 NUCLEO
---
data: Hello from STM32 NUCLEO
---
data: Hello from STM32 NUCLEO
---
data: Hello from STM32 NUCLEO
---
data: Hello from STM32 NUCLEO
---
```

Figure 15: String message from an STM 32 board

Interfacing Tiva C Launchpad boards with ROS using Energia

Interfacing Tiva C Launchpads in ROS is very much similar to Arduino. The IDE we are using to program Tiva C boards such as the EK-TM4C123GXL and EK-TM4C1294XL is called Energia (http://energia.nu/). The Energia IDE is a modified version of the Arduino IDE. The procedure to generate the ROS serial client library is the same as Arduino. We have to install a few packages on Ubuntu before we start working with the Energia ROS serial client for Energia.

The following command will install the ROS serial client library for the Energia IDE:

        $ sudo apt-get install ros-kinetic-rosserial-tivac

The following command will install the C libraries for the i386 platform. This library is required if you run Energia on 64-bit Ubuntu.

        $ sudo dpkg --add-architecture i386
        $ sudo apt-get update
        $ sudo apt-get install libc6:i386

After installing these packages, you can download and extract the Energia IDE. You can download the latest Energia version from `http://energia.nu/download/`. We are using Energia-018 here, and you can launch Energia by running `energia` from the extracted folder. You will get an IDE like this, which is very much like the Arduino IDE except the color:

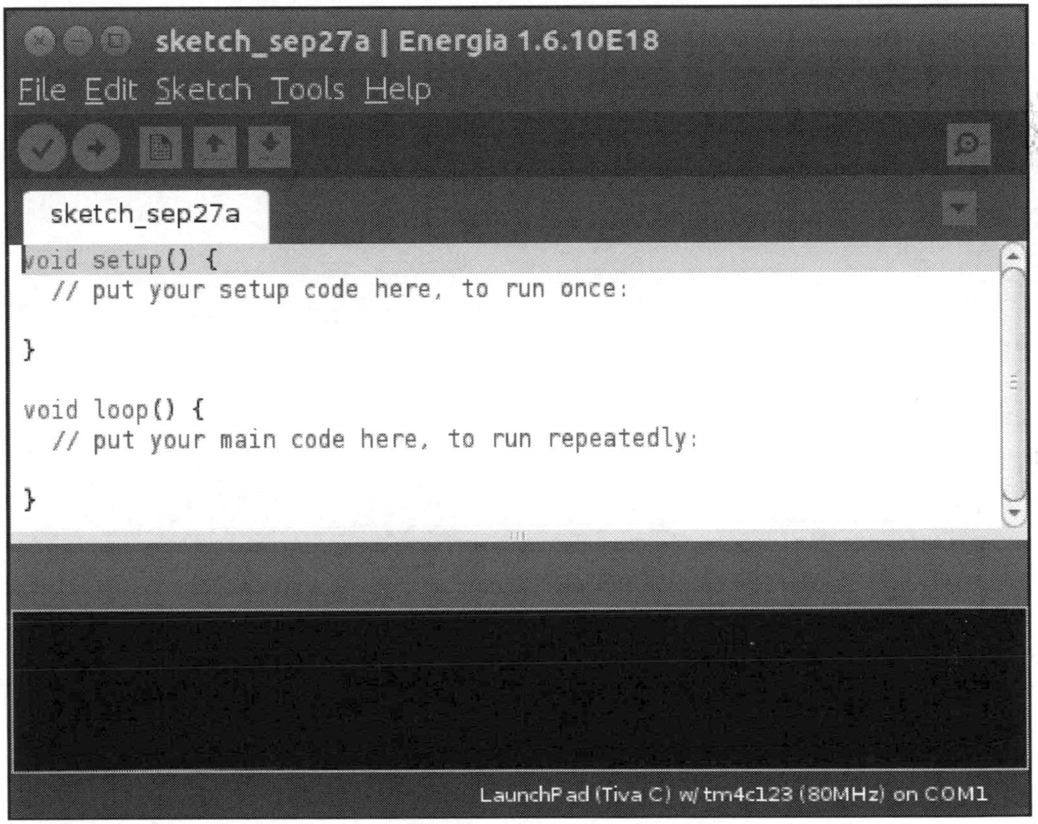

Figure 16: Energia IDE

Creating the ROS library for Energia is the same as for Arduino:

1. Go to **File** | **Preference** and set the sketchbook location.
2. Create a folder called `libraries` if one doesn't exist inside this location, and run the following command to create `ros_lib`:

```
$ rosrun rosserial_tivac make_libraries_energia
```

3. If everything works fine, you can access the ROS examples like this:

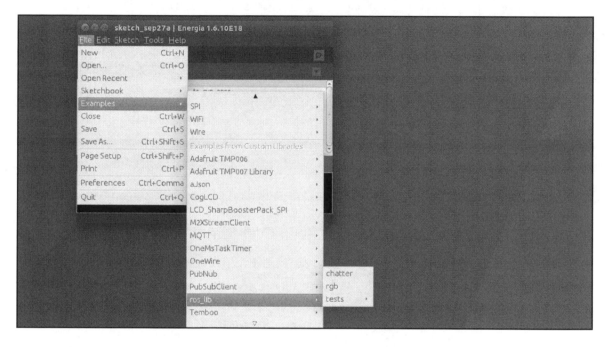

Figure 17: ros_lib in the Energia IDE

We can try with the `rgb` example first. The Tiva C board has a tricolor LED integrated with some port pins. Using this code, we can publish RGB values to a topic, and the board will turn on and off the LED according to the topic values. We can input values 0 or 1 for each LED. If the value is 0, that LED will be off, and if it is 1, it will have maximum brightness.

We can compile the code and upload it to the desired board and start the ROS serial server using the following set of commands.

Starting `roscore`:

```
$ roscore
```

Starting the ROS serial server:

```
$ rosrun rosserial_python serial_node.py /dev/ttyACM0
```

We will get a topic called `/led` when we start the ROS serial server, and we can publish the values to the topic using the following command:

```
$ rostopic pub led std_msgs/ColorRGBA "r: 0.0 g: 0.0 b: 1.0 a: 1.0"
```

Here, the type of `/led` topic is `std_msgs/ColorRGBA`, and r, g, and b correspond to red, green, and blue, and A is for alpha or transparency. We are not using the alpha value.

We have seen how to make a controller board as an ROS node, and now we will see how to run ROS on a single-board computer.

Running ROS on Raspberry Pi and Odroid boards

As we discussed earlier, Raspberry Pi and Odroid boards work like a PC. We can install customized Linux on each board and install ROS on it. There are two methods to run ROS on these boards. We can either install a fresh version of a Linux OS on it and install ROS from scratch or download a prebuilt image of the OS with ROS. The first option is a long procedure, and it will take a while to build ROS on Linux. You can follow the procedure at `https://goo.gl/LvW2ZN` to install ROS from scratch. In this section, we are dealing with ROS installation from a prebuilt binary.

Here is the link to download Raspberry Pi 2 images with ROS preinstalled:

`http://www.mauriliodicicco.com/raspberry-pi2-ros-images/`

Also, you can download Odroid-ROS images from the following links:

`http://forum.odroid.com/viewtopic.php?f=112&t=11994`

You can burn the OS to an SD card using the following tools:

On Windows, you can use Win32DiskImager, which can be downloaded from the following link:

`https://sourceforge.net/projects/win32diskimager/`

For Odroid, we need a customized version of Win32DiskImager, and it can be downloaded from the following link:

```
http://dn.odroid.com/DiskImager_ODROID/Win32DiskImager-odroid-v1.3.zip
```

This is what Win32DiskImage looks like in Odroid:

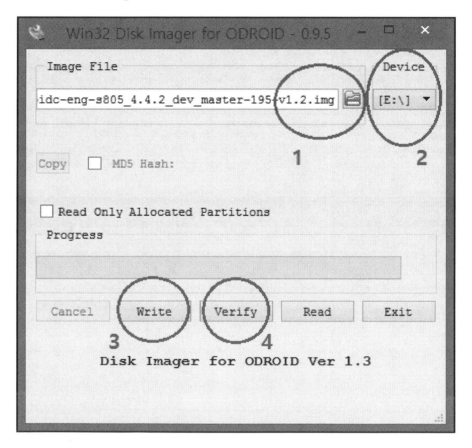

Figure 18: Win32DiskImager for Odroid

In Linux, you can use a tool called **dd** (Disk Dump); the following command helps you install OS images to an SD card:

```
$ sudo apt-get install pv
```

The `pv` tool can help you monitor the progress of this operation:

```
$ dd bs=4M if=image_name.img | pv | sudo dd of=/dev/mmcblk0
```

Here, `image_name.img` is the OS image name, and `/dev/mmcblk0` is the SD card reader device.

Boot the board from the SD card and check whether the board is booting properly. If it is, we can communicate with the board using Wi-Fi or wired LAN with the PC.

Now let's look at the methods to connect a single board computer to your PC.

Connecting Raspberry Pi and Odroid to PC

We can connect the RPi and Odroid boards in two ways to a PC. One is through a router in which both devices are on same network, or we can directly connect to a PC without a router. The connection through a router is simple and straightforward. Each device will get an IP address, and we can communicate with each device using it. But using direct communication, there is no IP assigned; we can do it using a Wi-Fi hotspot or wired LAN hotspot from a PC.

The following is the procedure to create a wired hotspot on Ubuntu for interfacing these boards:

1. Click on **Edit Connection...** from the network option in Ubuntu, as shown in the following figure. Click **Add** button to create a new connection.

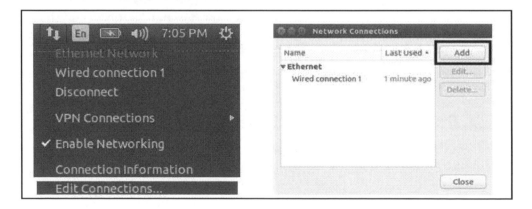

Figure 19: Creating a new network connection in Ubuntu

2. Create a new **Ethernet** connection, name the connection Share, and in the connection settings, change the IPV4 setting to **Shared to other Computers**, as shown here:

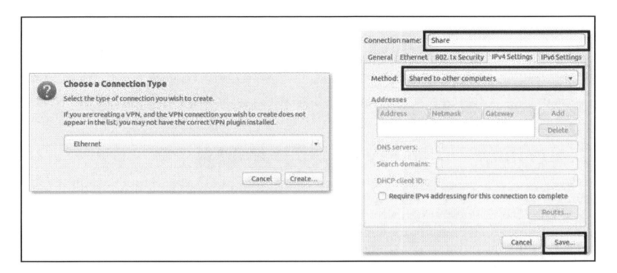

Figure 20: Creating a new Ethernet connection in Ubuntu

3. After creating the connection, you can plug the micro SD card to the board and boot the device; also, connect the wired LAN cable from the board to the PC.

4. When the board boots up, it will automatically connect to the **Share** network. If it is not connecting, you can manually click on the **Share** network name to connect to it. When it is connected, it means the board has an IP address and the PC can communicate with the board using this IP; also, the important thing is that the PC is sharing its Internet connection if it has one.

5. But how do we find the IP of a board that is connected to a PC? There is a way to find out. The following command will unveil the IP:

```
$ cat /var/lib/misc/dnsmasq.leases
```

6. The dnsmasq utility is a lightweight DNS and DHCP server. We can get an active client connected to the server by looking at the file called dnsmasq.leases. The output of this command is as follows:

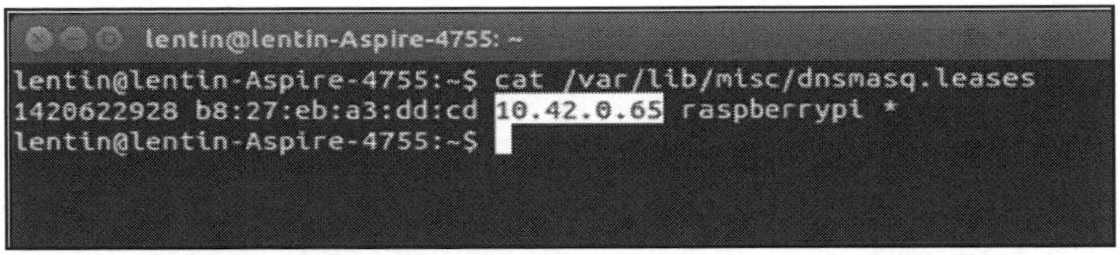

```
lentin@lentin-Aspire-4755: ~
lentin@lentin-Aspire-4755:~$ cat /var/lib/misc/dnsmasq.leases
1420622928 b8:27:eb:a3:dd:cd 10.42.0.65 raspberrypi *
lentin@lentin-Aspire-4755:~$
```

Figure 21: The IP of active clients connected to dnsmasq

7. Great going! If you get the IP, you can communicate with the board using **Secure Shell (SSH)**. Here are the commands to start an SSH shell from a PC to each board:

  - From PC to Raspberry Pi:

    $ **ssh pi@ip_address_of_board**

  - The password is raspberry

  - From PC to Odroid:

    $ **ssh odroid@ip_adress_of_board**

  - The password is odroid

If everything works fine, you will get the board's shell, and you can access the ROS commands from the shell.

Controlling GPIO pins from ROS

In Arduino and other controller boards, what we have created a did was make a hardware ROS node. But RPi and Odroid are single-board computers, so we can run ROS on the board itself. We can run ROS on these two boards in three ways. We can run ROS on the same board, or we can run the ROS master on the board and connect other ROS nodes from the PC or make the PC the ROS master and make the board the client.

In this section, we are going to create a simple demo to blink an LED using ROS topics from the same board. To work with Raspberry Pi and Odroid, we have to use a library called `wiringpi`.

Here are the commands to install `wiringpi` on Raspberry Pi:

```
$ git clone git clone git://git.drogon.net/wiringPi
$ cd wiringPi
$ sudo ./build
```

And these are the commands to install `wiringpi` on Odroid:

```
$ git clone https://github.com/hardkernel/wiringPi.git
$ cd wiringPi
$ sudo ./build
```

After installing `wiringpi`, we should know the GPIO pin layout of each board in order to program it. The GPIO pin layout of the boards is as follows:

WiringPi Pin	BCM GPIO	Name	Header		Name	BCM GPIO	WiringPi Pin
		P1: The Main GPIO connector					
WiringPi Pin	BCM GPIO	Name	Header		Name	BCM GPIO	WiringPi Pin
		3.3v	1	2	5v		
8	Rv1:0 - Rv2:2	SDA	3	4	5v		
9	Rv1:1 - Rv2:3	SCL	5	6	0v		
7	4	GPIO7	7	8	TxD	14	15
		0v	9	10	RxD	15	16
0	17	GPIO0	11	12	GPIO1	18	1
2	Rv1:21 - Rv2:27	GPIO2	13	14	0v		
3	22	GPIO3	15	16	GPIO4	23	4
		3.3v	17	18	GPIO5	24	5
12	10	MOSI	19	20	0v		
13	9	MISO	21	22	GPIO6	25	6
14	11	SCLK	23	24	CE0	8	10
		0v	25	26	CE1	7	11
WiringPi Pin	BCM GPIO	Name	Header		Name	BCM GPIO	WiringPi Pin
		P5: Secondary GPIO connector (Rev. 2 Pi only)					
WiringPi Pin	BCM GPIO	Name	Header		Name	BCM GPIO	WiringPi Pin
		5v	1	2	3.3v		
17	28	GPIO8	3	4	GPIO9	29	18
19	30	GPIO10	5	6	GPIO11	31	20
		0v	7	8	0v		
WiringPi Pin	BCM GPIO	Name	Header		Name	BCM GPIO	WiringPi Pin

Figure 22: GPIO pin layout of Raspberry Pi

The pin layout of Odroid is similar to RPi. Here is the GPIO pin layout of Odroid C1/C2:

		Power Pin
		Special Function
		GPIO/Special Function

ODROID-C1 40pin Layout

WiringPi GPIO#	Export GPIO#	ODROID-C PIN		Label	HEADER		Label	ODROID-C PIN		Export GPIO#	WiringPi GPIO#
				3V3	1	2	5V0				
			I2CA_SDA	SDA1	3	4	5V0				
			I2CA_SCL	SCL1	5	6	GND				
7	83		GPIOY.BIT3	#83	7	8	TXD1	TXD_B		113	
				GND	9	10	RXD1	RXD_B		114	
0	88		GPIOY.BIT8	#88	11	12	#87	GPIOY.BIT7		87	1
2	116		GPIOX.BIT19	#116	13	14	GND				
3	115		GPIOX.BIT18	#115	15	16	#104	GPIOX.BIT7		104	4
				3V3	17	18	#102	GPIOX.BIT5		102	5
12	107	MOSI	GPIOX.BIT10	MOSI	19	20	GND				
13	106	MISO	GPIOX.BIT9	MISO	21	22	#103	GPIOX.BIT6		103	6
14	105	SCLK	GPIOX.BIT8	SCLK	23	24	CE0	GPIOX.BIT20	CE0	117	10
				GND	25	26	#118	GPIOX.BIT21		118	11
			I2CB_SDA	SDA2	27	28	SCL2	I2CB_SCL			
21	101		GPIOX.BIT4	#101	29	30	GND				
22	100		GPIOX.BIT3	#100	31	32	#99	GPIOX.BIT2		99	26
23	108		GPIOX.BIT11	#108	33	34	GND				
24	97		GPIOX.BIT0	#97	35	36	#98	GPIOX.BIT1		98	27
			ADC.AIN1	AIN1	37	38	1V8	1V8			
				GND	39	40	AIN0	ADC.AIN0			

Figure 23: GPIO pin layout of Odroid

Creating a ROS package for the blink demo

We are done with installing `wiringpi`; let's create a ROS package for the LED blink demo. I hope you have already created a ROS workspace on the board. For this demo, we are connecting the LED anode to the twelfth pin of the board (first pin in `wiringpi`). The LED cathode is connected to GND.

The following figure shows the circuit of the demo. It is applicable to RPi and Odroid.

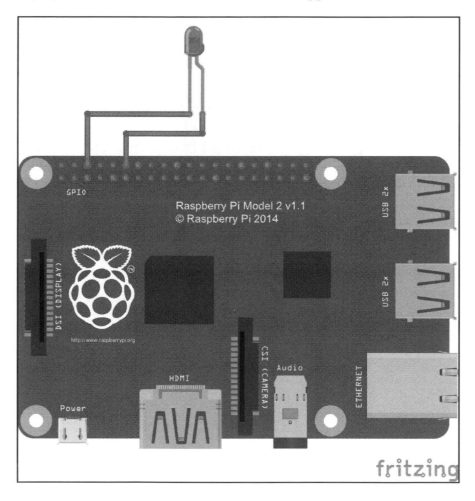

Figure 24: Board connected to an LED

Okay! Let's make a ROS package for creating a blinking ROS node. Here is the command to create a ROS package for this demo:

```
$ catkin_create_pkg ros_wiring_example roscpp std_msgs
```

You will also get the complete package from chapter_4_codes/ros_wiring_example.

Create an `src` folder inside the new package, and copy the `blink.cpp` file from the existing code. The blink code is and is as follows:

```cpp
#include "ros/ros.h"
#include "std_msgs/Bool.h"

#include <iostream>
#include "wiringPi.h"

//Wiring PI 1
#define LED 1

void blink_callback(const std_msgs::Bool::ConstPtr& msg)
{

  if(msg->data == 1){

    digitalWrite (LED, HIGH) ;
    ROS_INFO("LED ON");


    }
  if(msg->data == 0){

    digitalWrite (LED, LOW) ;
    ROS_INFO("LED OFF");

    }
}

int main(int argc, char** argv)
{

    ros::init(argc, argv,"blink_led");
    ROS_INFO("Started Odroid-C1 Blink Node");
    wiringPiSetup ();
    pinMode(LED, OUTPUT);


    ros::NodeHandle n;
    ros::Subscriber sub =
     n.subscribe("led_blink",10,blink_callback);
    ros::spin();

    }
```

The preceding code will subscribe to a topic called /led_blink, which is a Boolean type. If the value is true, the LED will turn on, otherwise it'll be off.

The following is the CMakeLists.txt file for compiling the code:

```
cmake_minimum_required(VERSION 2.8.3)
project(ros_wiring_examples)

find_package(catkin REQUIRED COMPONENTS
  roscpp
  std_msgs
)

find_package(Boost REQUIRED COMPONENTS system)


set(wiringPi_include "/usr/local/include")


include_directories(
  ${catkin_INCLUDE_DIRS}
  ${wiringPi_include}
)

LINK_DIRECTORIES("/usr/local/lib")


add_executable(blink_led src/blink.cpp)

target_link_libraries(blink_led
    ${catkin_LIBRARIES} wiringPi
  )
```

After changing CMakeLists.txt, we can perform a catkin_make to build the ROS node.

If everything builds successfully, we can run the demo using the following procedure.

Running the LED blink demo on Raspberry Pi and Odroid

To run the demo, launch multiple SSH Terminals and execute each command in each Terminal.

Start roscore:

```
$ roscore
```

Run the executable as root in another Terminal. We are running the node with root privilege, because GPIO handling needs root. If you are working with RPi, the username will be `pi` instead of `odroid`:

```
$ sudo -s
# cd /home/odroid/catkin_ws/build/ros_wiring_examples
#./blink_led
```

You can publish 1 and 0 to `/led_blink` to test the node working from another Terminal:

```
$ rostopic pub /led_blink std_msgs/Bool 1
$ rostopic pub /led_blink std_msgs/Bool 0
```

To run on the Raspberry Pi, we have to perform few more steps. We have to add the following lines to the `.bashrc` folder of the root user. You can do so using the following command:

```
$ sudo -i
$ nano .bashrc
```

Add the following lines to the `.bashrc` file:

```
source /opt/ros/<ros_version>/setup.sh
source /home/pi/catkin_ws/devel/setup.bash
export ROS_MASTER_URI=http://localhost:11311
```

Questions

- What are ROS serial client libraries?
- What are the functions of a ROS serial server?
- What are mbed and Energia?
- What are the functions of `wiringpi`?

Summary

In this chapter, we dealt with ROS interfacing of embedded controller boards and single-board PCs. We started by discussing popular controller boards, such as Arduino, STM 32-based boards and Tiva C boards. In the single-board computer category, we went through Raspberry Pi and Odroid. After discussing each board, we learned about interfacing ROS with controllers and single computers. We covered LDR interfacing with the Arduino, Hello World example on the STM 32, and RGB demo on the Tiva C Launchpad. For single-board computers, we created a basic LED blink demo using ROS.

In the next chapter, we will discuss teleoperating a robot using hand gestures.

5

Teleoperate a Robot Using Hand Gestures

As you all know, robots can be controlled mainly in the following modes:

- **Manual**: In manual control, the robot is controlling manually by a human. The controlling is done using a remote controller or teach pendant.
- **Semiautonomous**: The semiautonomous robot will have both manual and autonomous control. For simple task, it can work autonomously but in complex task it may change its mode to manual.
- **Fully autonomous**: An autonomous robot has complete control over its action and can think for itself. It can learn and adapt, and very much everything is controlled by the robot itself.

We can choose the model of robot control based on our application. In this chapter, we are mainly discussing implementing a manual robot control; we can call it distance control or teleoperation. In teleoperation, the robot and human can be far apart, and the operator may not able to see the real robot moving but may get some visual feedback. Rather than manual control, some teleoperated robots have different levels of autonomy integrated. The robots can take action entirely by following the commands sent by the operator or only receiving high-level commands and taking care of other stuff autonomously.

We are going to be discussing a project to teleoperate a robot using hand gestures. The major component that we are using to detect the gestures is an **inertial measurement unit (IMU)**. The IMU is fitted into a hand glove, and with specific hand gestures, we can move or rotate the robot. The project uses the Arduino-ROS combination to compute IMU orientation and send it to PC. A ROS node runs on the PC, which maps the orientation data into twist messages (`geometry_msgs/Twist`), which is the command velocity of the robot. We will look at more analysis of the project design in the upcoming sections.

We are going to discuss following topics in this chapter:

- Teleoperating a TurtleBot using a keyboard
- Gesture teleop: teleoperating using hand gestures
- Setting up the project
- Interfacing the IMU MPU-9250 with the Arduino and ROS
- Visualizing the IMU TF on Rviz
- Converting IMU data into twist messages
- Integration and final run
- Teleoperating using an Android phone

Teleoperating ROS Turtle using a keyboard

This section is for beginners who haven't worked with teleoperation in ROS yet. In this section, we will see how to teleoperate a robot manually using a keyboard. Using a keyboard, we can translate and rotate the robot. One of the basic example to demonstrate keyboard teleoperation is ROS `turtlesim`.

The following commands launch `turtlesim` with keyboard teleoperation. You can run each command on separate Terminals.

Run `roscore`:

```
$ roscore
```

Run a `turtlesim` node using the following command. This command will launch the `turtlesim` window:

```
$ rosrun turtlesim turtlesim_node
```

Run the keyboard teleoperation node. We can change the turtle's position by pressing arrow keys on the keyboard:

```
$ rosrun turtlesim turtle_teleop_key
```

The screenshot of the moving turtle using arrow keys is shown here:

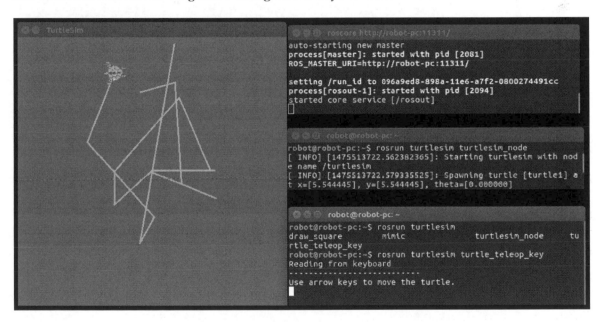

Figure 1: Turtlesim keyboard teleoperation

In ROS, most of the robot packages are bundled with a teleop node for manual control of the robot. This control can either be through keyboard, joystick, or some other input device.

Teleoperating using hand gestures

The idea of this project is converting IMU orientation into the linear and angular velocity of the robot. Here is the overall structure of this project.

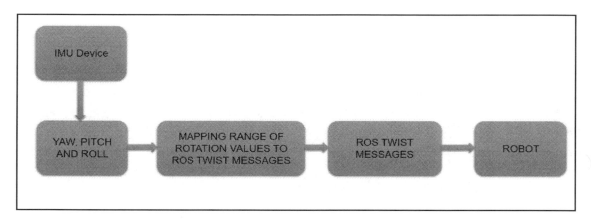

Figure 2: Basic structure of the gesture teleop project

For the IMU device, we are using an IMU called MPU-9250 (`https://www.invensense.com /products/motion-tracking/9-axis/mpu-9250/`). The IMU will interface with an Arduino board using the I2C protocol. The orientation values from the IMU are computed by the Arduino and send to PC through the `rosserial` protocol. The orientation values are received on the PC side as ROS topics and converted into twist messages using a ROS node.

Here is the project block diagram with the **MPU 9250** and Arduino board:

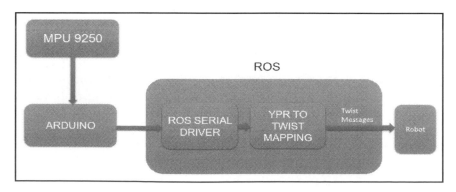

Figure 3: Functional block diagram of the robot teleop project

We are using a hand glove in which an Arduino board is fixed in the palm area and an MPU-9250 is fixed on the finger area, as shown in the following image:

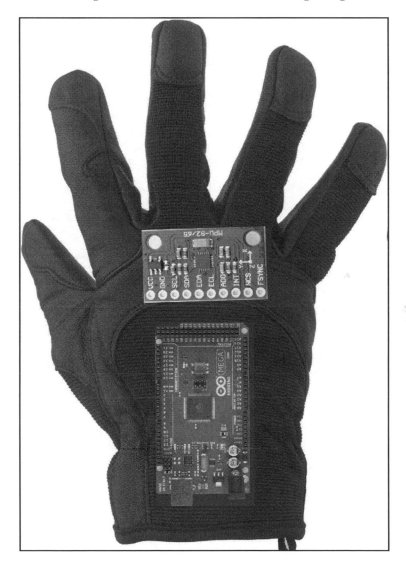

Figure 4: Hand glove with Arduino and MPU-9250

There are four kinds of arm gestures used in this project:

- Vertical elbow rotation:
    - Clockwise
    - Anticlockwise
- Up pitch movement of hand
- Down pitch movement of hand

Vertical elbow rotation is mapped to the rotation of the robot in the z direction, and up and down pitch movement of the hand is mapped into forward and reverse movement of the robot. Here's a depiction of how the movements of our arm and motion of the robot are mapped:

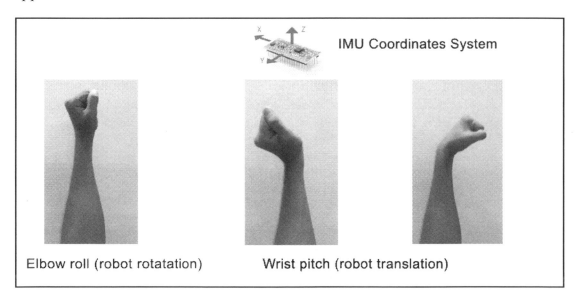

Figure 5: Hand gestures and corresponding motion mapping

The mapping goes like this: the robot will stop the movement when the IMU in the hand is horizontal to the ground. We can call this the home position. In the home position, the robot will not move. When the elbow starts rotating about the vertical axis, the robot's velocity will be such that it will rotate along the z axis. The robot's rotation will depend on how many degrees the elbow is rotated. The robot will keep on rotating until the IMU reaches the home position. For moving the robot forward and backward, we can pitch the hand as shown in the preceding figure. If the hand pitching is upward, the resultant robot velocity can move the robot backward, and vice versa.

Here is the coordinate-system representation of the IMU and movement happening along each axis and the motion assigned to each hand movement:

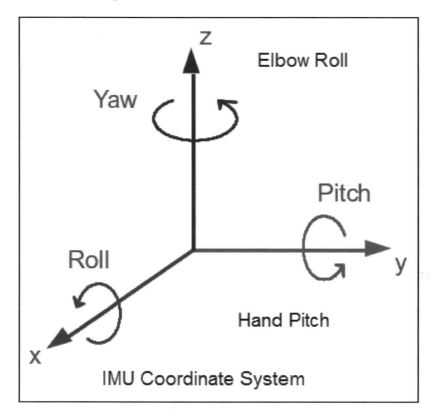

Figure 6: Hand gestures and its motion mapping

The following table will give you a quick idea about the mapping of hand gestures and robot motion:

Hand movement	Robot motion
Elbow rotation clockwise (IMU yaw)	Robot rotates clockwise
Elbow rotation anticlockwise (IMU yaw)	Robot rotates anticlockwise
Hand pitch upward (IMU pitch)	Robot moves backward
Hand pitch downward (IMU pitch)	Robot moves forward

Note that we are using two components of rotation from the IMU, which are yaw and pitch. The yaw rotation of the IMU is facing upward, and pitch rotation is facing toward you. When we rotate the elbow, the yaw value of the IMU changes, and when we pitch the hand, the pitch value of the IMU changes. These changes will converted to the linear and angular velocity of the robot.

Setting up the project

Let's set up the project. To finish this project, you may need the following electronic components. You can see the component name and the link to buy it from the following table:

No	Name	Link
1	Arduino Mega – 2560 with USB cable	https://www.sparkfun.com/products/11061
2	MPU – 9250 breakout	https://amzn.com/B00OPNUO9U
3	Male to Female jumper wires	https://amzn.com/B00PBZMN7C
4	Hand glove	https://amzn.com/B00WH4NXLA

You can use any Arduino having I2C communication. You can also use MPU – 6050 /9150, both of which are compatible with this project. A few words about the MPU – 9250 IMU: it is a 9-axis motion tracking device consisting of a gyro, accelerometer, and compass. MPU – 6050/9150/9250 models have an inbuilt **Digital Motion Processor (DMP)**, which can fuse the accelerometer, gyro, and magnetometer values to get accurate 6DOF/9DOF motion components. In this project, we are only taking the yaw and pitch rotation components.

 If you want to learn more about I2C, check out the following link:
https://learn.sparkfun.com/tutorials/i2c
Read more about the MPU series:
https://www.invensense.com/technology/motion/

Interfacing the MPU-9250 with the Arduino and ROS

So the first step in this project is to interface the IMU to the Arduino to get the rotation values and send those values to ROS. We're essentially making an Arduino-ROS node that is receiving IMU values and publishing the yaw, pitch, and roll as well as the **transformation (TF)** corresponding to the IMU movement as ROS topics.

The following figure shows the interfacing of IMU with the Arduino. The IMU is interfaced using the I2C protocol:

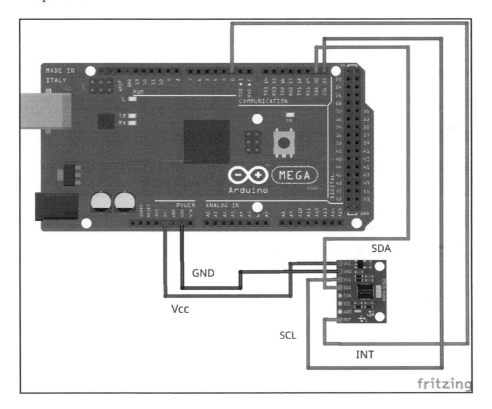

Figure 7: Interfacing MPU 9250/9150/6050 with Arduino

The connection from Arduino to MPU-9250 is shown in this table:

Arduino pins	MPU – 9250 pins
5V	VCC
GND	GND
SCL (21)	SCL
SDA (20)	SDA
Digital PIN2	INT

To start working on IMU values in ROS, we have to create a ROS-Arduino node that is receiving IMU values and send it as ROS topics. I hope you have set up the Arduino IDE in your system. For running this code, you will need the Arduino library for the MPU – 9250. Note that you can use the MPU – 9150 library for working with this IMU, and you can clone that library's files using the following command:

```
$ git clone
https://github.com/sparkfun/MPU-9150_Breakout/tree/master/firmware
```

Copy `firmware/I2Cdev` and `MPU6050` into the `arduino_sketch_location/libraries` folder. The sketchbook location can be obtained from the **File | Preferences** IDE option.

Once you've copied both of these folders, you can compile the ROS-Arduino node. You can open the code from `chapter_5_codes/MPU9250_ROS_DMP`. Just try to compile the code and check whether it's working or not. I hope that you have already set the Arduino ROS serial client library , which is `ros_lib`. The entire procedure was mentioned in `Chapter 4`, *Controlling Embedded Boards Using ROS*.

The following figure shows the flowchart of the complete code. We'll go through a detailed explanation of code after this.

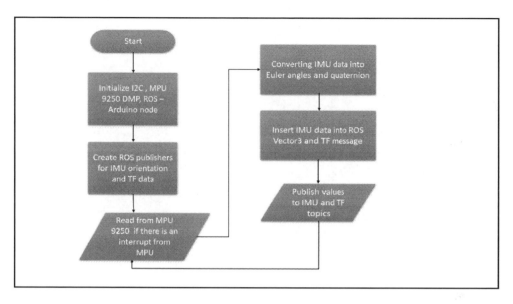

Figure 8: Flowchart of Arduino-ROS node

The Arduino-IMU interfacing code

Let's discuss the code from the beginning. The following Arduino headers help us read IMU values using the I2C protocol. The `MPU6050_6Axis_MotionApps20.h` header has functions to enable DMP and retrieve values from it.

```
#include "Wire.h"
#include "I2Cdev.h"
#include "MPU6050_6Axis_MotionApps20.h"
```

The following line of code will create an `MPU6050` handle, which can be used for the MPU-9250. We can use this object to initialize and retrieve values from the IMU.

```
MPU6050 mpu;
```

As you know, we have to include `ros.h` to access ROS serial client APIs. We are also including `Vector3.h`, which has the definition of the `Vector3` ROS message. This message can carry three values of orientation. The `tf/transform_broadcaster.h` header has TF broadcaster classes, which basically send transforms of IMU values with respect to a fixed frame:

```
#include <ros.h>
#include <geometry_msgs/Vector3.h>
#include <tf/transform_broadcaster.h>
```

After defining headers, we have to define handles of the TF message and broadcaster, as given here:

```
geometry_msgs::TransformStamped t;
tf::TransformBroadcaster broadcaster;
```

In the next line of code, we are creating a `NodeHandle`, which essentially helps us subscribe to and publish ROS topics like a normal ROS node:

```
ros::NodeHandle nh;
```

To hold the orientation values, which are yaw, pitch, and roll, we are creating a `Vector3` ROS message. This message is published by the Arduino node on a topic named `/imu_data`.

```
geometry_msgs::Vector3 orient;
```

The following line of code creates a publisher object for the `/imu_data` topic. We are publishing the orientation using this object.

```
ros::Publisher imu_pub("imu_data", &orient);
```

The `frameid` value is `/base_link`, which is static, and the `child` frame is `/imu_frame` which moves according to the IMU data.

```
char frameid[] = "/base_link";
char child[] = "/imu_frame";
```

These are variables to hold orientation values, such as `Quaternion`, `gravity` vector, and yaw, pitch, and roll:

```
Quaternion q;
VectorFloat gravity;
float ypr[3];
```

Here is the interrupt-detection routine, for whenever data is ready to be read from the IMU. The routine basically sets the `mpuInterrupt` variable as `true`.

```
volatile bool mpuInterrupt = false;
void dmpDataReady() {
    mpuInterrupt = true;
}
```

Next is the `setup()` function of Arduino, which does several I2C initializations for the Arduino, ROS node handler, TF broadcaster, ROS publisher, MPU object, and DMP inside MPU:

```
void setup() {
    Wire.begin();
    nh.initNode();
    broadcaster.init(nh);
    nh.advertise(imu_pub);
    mpu.initialize();
    devStatus = mpu.dmpInitialize();
```

If DMP is initialized, we can enable it and attach an interrupt on the Arduino's second digital pin, which is the first interrupt pin of the Arduino. Whenever data is ready to be read from buffer, the IMU will generate an interrupt. The code also checks the DMP status and sets a variable to check whether DMP is ready or not. This will be useful while executing the `loop()` function. We are also using a variable called `packetSize` to store the MPU buffer size.

```
    if (devStatus == 0) {
        mpu.setDMPEnabled(true);
        attachInterrupt(0, dmpDataReady, RISING);
        mpuIntStatus = mpu.getIntStatus();
        dmpReady = true;
        packetSize = mpu.dmpGetFIFOPacketSize();
    }
```

Inside the `loop()` function, the code checks whether `dmpReady` is true or not. If it is not true, that means DMP is not initialized, so it will not execute any code. If it is ready, it will wait for interrupts from the MPU.

```
    if (!dmpReady) return;
      while (!mpuInterrupt && fifoCount < packetSize) {
        ;
    }
```

If there is an interrupt, it will go to the dmpDataReady() interrupt-detection routine and set the mpuInterrupt flag as true. If it is true, then the previous while loop will exit and start running the following code. We are resetting the mpuInterrupt flag to false, reading the current status of the MPU, and retrieving the **first-in first-out (FIFO)** count. FIFO is basically a buffer, and the first entry to the buffer will be processed first.

```
mpuInterrupt = false;
mpuIntStatus = mpu.getIntStatus();
fifoCount = mpu.getFIFOCount();
```

After reading the status and FIFO count, we can reset the FIFO if an overflow is detected. Overflows can happen if your code is too inefficient.

```
if ((mpuIntStatus & 0x10) || fifoCount == 1024) {
    mpu.resetFIFO();
```

If the data is ready, we will again compare the FIFO buffer size and the DMP packet size; if equal, FIFO data will be dumped into the fifoBuffer variable.

```
else if (mpuIntStatus & 0x01) {
    while (fifoCount < packetSize) fifoCount =
    mpu.getFIFOCount();
    mpu.getFIFOBytes(fifoBuffer, packetSize);
    fifoCount -= packetSize;
```

After storing the DMP data in the buffer, we can extract the rotation components, such as quaternion, gravity vector, and Euler angle.

```
mpu.dmpGetQuaternion(&q, fifoBuffer);
mpu.dmpGetGravity(&gravity, &q);
mpu.dmpGetYawPitchRoll(ypr, &q, &gravity);
```

We need to get the Euler angle in degrees, and it is going to be published in the /imu_data topic. Here is the code for doing it. The ypr value we're getting from the MPU object will be in radians, which should be converted to degree using the following equations:

```
orient.x = ypr[0] * 180/M_PI;
orient.y = ypr[1] * 180/M_PI;
orient.z = ypr[2] * 180/M_PI;
imu_pub.publish(&orient);
```

Here is how we'll publish the TF data. We have to insert the frame, quaternion values, and time stamping to the TF message headers. Using the TF broadcaster, we can publish it.

```
t.header.frame_id = frameid;
t.child_frame_id = child;
t.transform.translation.x = 1.0;
t.transform.rotation.x = q.x;
t.transform.rotation.y = q.y;
t.transform.rotation.z = q.z;
t.transform.rotation.w = q.w;
t.header.stamp = nh.now();
broadcaster.sendTransform(t);
```

We have to call `nh.spinOnce()` to process each operation we have performed using ROS APIs, so the publishing and subscribing operations are performed only while calling the `spinOnce()` function. We are also blinking the onboard LED to indicate the program activity.

```
nh.spinOnce();
delay(200);
blinkState = !blinkState;
digitalWrite(LED_PIN, blinkState);
delay(200);
```

That is all about the ROS-Arduino node. Now what you can do is compile and upload this code to Arduino. Make sure that all other settings on the Arduino IDE are correct.

After uploading the code to the Arduino, the remaining work is on the PC side. We have to run the ROS serial server node to obtain the Arduino node topics. The first step to verify the IMU data from Arduino is by visualizing it. We can visualize the IMU data by observing the TF values in Rviz.

Visualizing IMU TF in Rviz

In this section, we are going to visualize the TF data from Arduino on Rviz. Here's the procedure to do that.

Plug the Arduino to the PC and find the Arduino's serial port. To get topics from the Arduino-ROS node, we should start a ROS serial server on the PC, listening on the Arduino serial port. We did this in `Chapter 4`, *Controlling Embedded Boards Using ROS*. Still, let's look at the commands again in this section too.

Starting `roscore` first:

```
$ roscore
```

Starting the ROS serial server:

```
$ rosrun rosserial_python serial_node.py /dev/ttyACM0
```

You can get the following topics when you run the previous node:

```
lentin@lentin-Aspire-4755:~$ rostopic list
/imu_data
/rosout
/rosout_agg
/tf
lentin@lentin-Aspire-4755:~$ 
```

Figure 9: Listing ROS topics from Arduino

You can simply echo these topics, or visualize the TF data on Rviz. You can run Rviz using the following command. The `base_link` option is the fixed frame, and we can mention that on the command line itself.

```
$ rosrun rviz rviz -f base_link
```

The Rviz window will pop up, and if there is no TF option on the left-hand side of Rviz, add it from the **Add** | **TF**.

You may get a visualization like shown here, where `imu_frame` will move according to the rotation of the IMU:

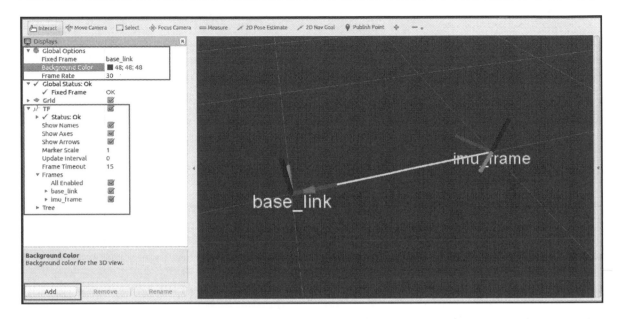

Figure 10: Visualizing IMU data in Rviz

Converting IMU data into twist messages

If you are able to the visualization in Rviz, you are done with the interfacing. The next step is to convert IMU orientation into command velocity as ROS twist messages. For this, we have to create a ROS package and a Python script. You can get this package from `chapter_5_codes/gesture_teleop`; look for a script called `gesture_teleop.py` from the `gesture_teleop/scripts` folder.

If you want to create the package from scratch, here is the command:

```
$ catkin_create_pkg gesture_teleop rospy roscpp std_msgs sensor_msgs
geometry_msgs
```

Now let's look at the explanation of `gesture_teleop.py`, which is performing the conversion from IMU orientation values to `twist` commands.

In this code, what we basically do is subscribe to the /imu_data topic and extract only the yaw and pitch values. When these values change in the positive or negative direction, a step value is added or subtracted from the linear and angular velocity variable. The resultant velocity is sent using ROS twist messages with a topic name defined by the user.

We need the following modules to perform this conversion. As you know, rospy is a mandatory header for a ROS Python node.

```
import rospy
from geometry_msgs.msg import Twist
from geometry_msgs.msg import Vector3
```

After importing the modules, you will see the initialization of some parameters; these parameters are keeping in a file called gesture_teleop/config/teleop_config.yaml. If the node can't retrieve parameters from the file, it will load the default values mentioned in the code.

Here is the subscriber for the /imu_data topic, in which the topic name is defined as a variable. The callback function is called Get_RPY and the message type is Vector3.

```
rospy.Subscriber(imu_topic,Vector3,Get_RPY)
```

The Get_RPY simply computes the delta value of the yaw and pitch values of the IMU data and sends those values along with the yaw value to another function called Send_Twist():

```
def Get_RPY(rpy_data):
    global prev_yaw
    global prev_pitch
    global dy,dp
    dy = rpy_data.x - prev_yaw
    dp = rpy_data.y - prev_pitch
    Send_Twist(dy,dp,rpy_data.y)
    prev_yaw = rpy_data.x
    prev_pitch = rpy_data.y
```

The following code is the definition of `Send_Twist()`. This is the function generating the twist message from the orientation values. Here, the linear velocity variable is `control_speed` and angular velocity variable is `control_turn`. When the pitch value is very less and change in yaw value is zero, the position is called home position. In home position, the IMU will be horizontal to the ground. In this position, the robot should stop its movement. We are assigning both the speeds as zero at this condition. In other cases, the control speed and control turn is computed up to the maximum or minimum speed limits. If the speed is beyond the limit, it will switch to the limiting speed itself. The computed velocities are assigned to a twist message header and published to the ROS environment.

```python
def Send_Twist(dy,dp,pitch):
    global pub
    global control_speed
    global control_turn
    dy = int(dy)
    dp = int(dp)
    check_pitch = int(pitch)
    if (check_pitch < 2 and check_pitch > -2 and dy == 0):
        control_speed = 0
        control_turn = 0
    else:
        control_speed = round(control_speed + (step_size * dp),2)
        control_turn = round(control_turn + ( step_size * dy),2)
        if (control_speed > high_speed):
            control_speed = high_speed
        elif (control_turn > high_turn):
            control_turn = high_turn
        if (control_speed < low_speed):
            control_speed = low_speed
        elif (control_turn < low_turn):
            control_turn = low_turn
        twist = Twist()
        twist.linear.x = control_speed; twist.linear.y = 0;
        twist.linear.z = 0
        twist.angular.x = 0; twist.angular.y = 0; twist.angular.z = control_turn
        pub.publish(twist)
```

That is all about the converter node, which converts orientation data to twist commands. Next is the configuration file of the `gesture_teleop.py` node. This node stores the essential parameters of the converter node. The file is named `teleop_config.yaml` and placed in the `gesture_teleop/config/` folder. The file consists of the IMU data topic, limits of linear and angular velocity, and step size.

```
imu_topic: "/imu_data"
low_speed: -4
high_speed: 4
low_turn: -2
high_turn: 2
step_size: 0.02
```

Integration and final run

We are almost done! But how to test this teleop tool? We can create some launch file that can start all these nodes and work with some robot simulation. The `gesture_teleop/launch` folder has three launch files. Let's take a look at them.

The `gesture_teleop.launch` file is a generic launch file that can be used for any robot. The only thing we need to edit is the command velocity topic. Here is the definition of this launch file:

```
<launch>
    <param name="teleop_topic" value="/cmd_vel"/>
    <rosparam command="load" file="$(find
      gesture_teleop)/config/teleop_config.yaml"/>
  <node name="rosserial_server_node" pkg="rosserial_python"
      type="serial_node.py" args="$(arg port)" output="screen"/>
  <node name="gesture_teleop_node" pkg="gesture_teleop"
      type="gesture_teleop.py" output="screen"/>
</launch>
```

This launch file defines `teleop_topic`. You can change the command velocity topic name according to each robot's configuration. It also loads the config file called `teleop_config.yaml`. Then, start the ROS serial server node and then the gesture teleop node.

The other two launch files are `gesture_teleop_turtlebot.launch` and
`gesture_teleop_turtlebot_2D.launch`. The first launch file starts the gesture teleop of
TurtleBot, which also launches the TurtleBot simulation in Gazebo, and the second launch
file launches the ROS turtlesim and its gesture teleop node.

Let's start turtlesim with its gesture teleop node:

```
$ roslaunch gesture_teleop gesture_teleop_turtlebot_2D.launch
```

You may get the turtlesim window and control the turtle using the gesture teleop:

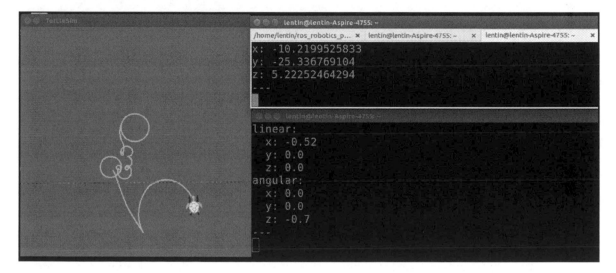

Figure 11: Gesture teleop on turtlesim

You can rotate the turtle by moving the IMU in the Z axis and can move forward and
backward by pitching in the Y-axis. You can stop the robot's movement by bringing the
IMU to the home position.

We can also teleop TurtleBot using the following launch file:

```
$ roslaunch gesture_teleop gesture_teleop_turtlebot.launch
```

You may get the following simulation in Gazebo if the TurtleBot packages are already installed on your system:

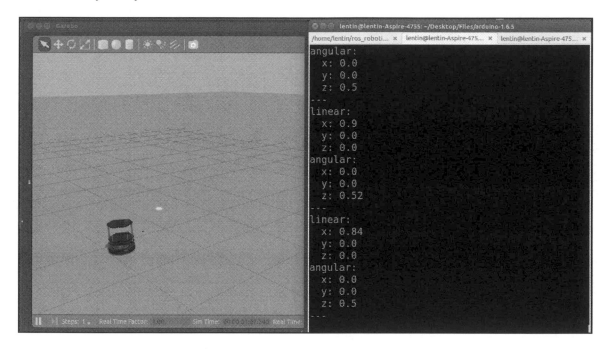

Figure 12: Gesture teleop on TurtleBot simulation.

Similar to turtlesim, we can rotate and translate TurtleBot using yaw and pitch movements.

Teleoperating using an Android phone

If it is difficult to build the previous circuit and set everything up, there is an easy way to do so with your Android phone. You can manually control either using a virtual joystick or the tilt of the phone.

Here is the Android application you can use for this:

```
https://play.google.com/store/apps/details?id=com.robotca.ControlApp.
```

The application's name is ROS Control. You can also search on Google Play Store for it.

Here is the procedure to connect your Android phone to a ROS environment:

Initially, you have to connect both your PC and Android device to a local Wi-Fi network in which each device can communicate with each other using IP addresses.

After connecting to the same network, you have to start `roscore` on the PC side. You can also note the IP address of the PC by entering the command `ifconfig`.

```
wlan0     Link encap:Ethernet  HWaddr 94:39:e5:4d:7d:da
          inet addr:192.168.1.102  Bcast:192.168.1.255  Mask:255.255.255.0
          inet6 addr: fe80::9639:e5ff:fe4d:7dda/64 Scope:Link
          UP BROADCAST RUNNING MULTICAST  MTU:1500  Metric:1
          RX packets:1963 errors:0 dropped:0 overruns:0 frame:0
          TX packets:2252 errors:0 dropped:0 overruns:0 carrier:0
          collisions:0 txqueuelen:1000
          RX bytes:345822 (345.8 KB)  TX bytes:248404 (248.4 KB)
```

Figure 13: Retrieving the IP address of a PC with ifconfig

1. After obtaining the IP address of the PC, you can start the app and create a robot configuration, as shown in this figure:

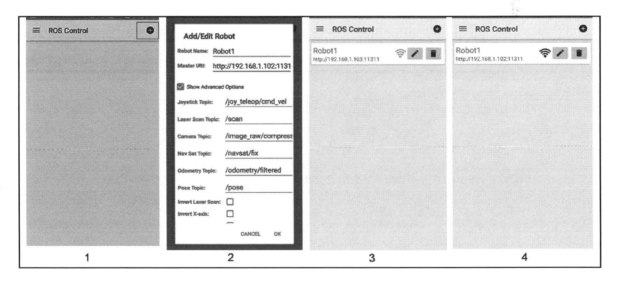

Figure 14: Configuring ROS Control app in Android

2. The + symbol in the top-right corner of the app is used to add a robot configuration in the app. Press it and you'll see a window to enter the various topic names, **Robot Name**, and **Master URI**.

3. You have to change the **Master URI** from localhost:11311 to IP_of_PC:11311; for example, it is 192.168.1.102.11311 in this case, which is shown in the preceding figure marked as **2**.

4. We can enter the topic name of the teleop here, so twist messages will be published to that topic. For TurtleBot, the topic name is /cmd_vel_mux/input/teleop. Press **OK** if you are done with the configuration, and you will see the third screen. In case your phone is not connected to the PC, press that configuration option and it will connect to the PC, which is shown as **4** in the figure.

5. When it connects to the PC, you will get another window, in which you can interact with the robot. Those windows are shown here:

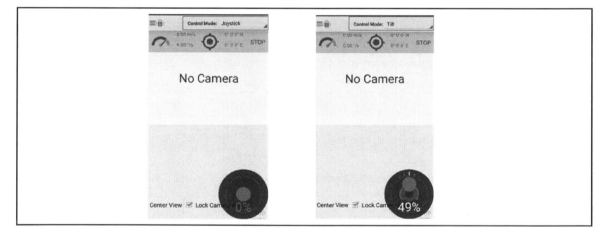

Figure 15: Controlling robot using virtual joystick and tilt of the phone.

6. The control mode can change from Joystick to Tilt, with which will work according to the tilting of phone. You can tilt the phone and change the robot's rotation and translation. Make sure you're running robot hardware or a simulation that accepts twist messages to move. You also need confirm that the topic name that you give the app is the same as the robot teleop topic.

7. After connecting your phone to the PC through the app, you will get the following topics on the PC side. You can confirm whether you're getting this before starting the robot simulation on the PC:

```
/clock
/cmd_vel_mux/input/teleop
/image_raw/compressed
/navsat/fix
/odometry/filtered
/pose
/rosout
/rosout_agg
/scan
```

Figure 16: Listing the ROS topics from the app

8. If you are getting these topics, you can start a robot simulation, such as TurtleBot, using the following command:

```
$ roslaunch turtlebot_gazebo turtlebot_empty_world.launch
```

9. Now you can see that the robot is moving with your commands from your phone. Here is a screenshot of this operation:

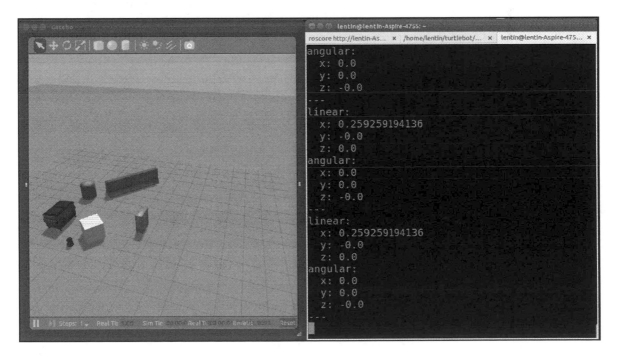

Figure 17: Controlling TurtleBot from Android app

Questions

- What are the main modes of controlling a differential drive robot?
- What is the twist message in ROS for?
- What is DMP and what is the use of DMP in this project?
- How can we teleoperate a robot from an Android phone?

Summary

This chapter was about making a gesture-based teleoperation project for a ROS-based robot. We used an IMU to detect gestures and interfaced with the Arduino to get the values from the IMU. The Arduino is interfaced with ROS using the ROS serial protocol. The PC is running a ROS node that can convert IMU orientation into linear and angular velocity and send it as a twist message. This twist message can be used in any robot just by changing the teleop topic name. We can also visualize the IMU orientation data in Rviz using TF data from Arduino. If it is too difficult to build this circuit, we can use an Android app called ROS Control that can move the robot using the inbuilt IMU on the phone.

In the next chapter, we'll be dealing with 3D object recognition using ROS.

6
Object Detection and Recognition

Object recognition has an important role in robotics. It is the process of identifying an object from camera images and finding its location. Using this, a robot can pick an object from the workspace and place it at another location.

This chapter will be useful for those who want to prototype a solution for a vision-related task. We are going to look at some popular ROS packages to perform object detection and recognition in 2D and 3D. We are not digging more into the theoretical aspects, but you may see short notes about the algorithm while we discuss their applications.

You will learn about the following topics:

- Getting started with object detection and recognition
- The `find_object_2d` package in ROS
- Installing `find_object_2d`
- Detecting and tracking an object using a webcam
- Detecting and tracking using 3D depth sensors
- Getting started with 3D object recognition
- Introducing the object-recognition package in ROS
- Installing object-recognition packages
- Detecting and recognizing objects using 3D meshes
- Training and detecting using real-time capture
- Final run

So let's begin with the importance of object detection and recognition in robotics.

Getting started with object detection and recognition

So what's the main difference between detection and recognition? Consider face detection and face recognition. In face detection, the algorithm tries to detect a face from an image, but in recognition, the algorithm can also state information about whose face is detected. It may be the person's name, gender, or something else.

Similarly, object detection involves the detection of a class of object and recognition performs the next level of classification, which tells which us the name of the object.

There is a vast number of applications that use object detection and recognition techniques. Here is a popular application that is going to be used in Amazon warehouses:

Figure 1: A photo from an Amazon Picking Challenge

Amazon is planning to automate the picking and placing of objects from the shelves inside their warehouses. To retrieve objects from the shelves, they are planning to deploy robotic arms such as the one shown in the previous image. Whenever the robot gets an order to retrieve a specific object and place it in a basket, it should identify the position of object first, right? So how does the robot understand the object position? It should need some kind of 3D sensor, right? And also, on the software side, it should have some object recognition algorithm for recognizing each object. The robot will get the object coordinates only after the recognition. The detected coordinates will be relative to the vision sensors, which have to transform into robot end-effector coordinates of the tip of the robot to reach the object position. After reaching the object position, what should be the robot do? It should grasp the object and place it in the basket, right? The task looks simple, doesn't it? But it's not as simple as we think. Here is the coordinate system of a robotic arm, end effector, Kinect, and the object:

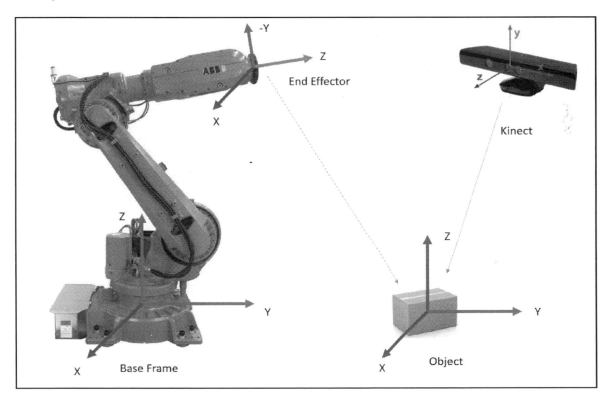

Figure 2: Coordinate system of each component

Amazon organizes a challenge called the Amazon Picking Challenge, which was first conducted as a part of ICRA 2015 (http://www.ieee-ras.org/conference/robot-challe nges), and in 2016, it was conducted along with Robocup (http://www.robocup2016.org/e n/events/amazon-picking-challenge/). The challenge was all about solving the pick-and-place problem we just discussed. In effect, the object recognition and detection tasks have immense scope in the industry, not only in Amazon but also in areas such as agriculture, defense, and space.

In the following section, we will see how to implement object detection and recognition in our applications. There are some good ROS packages to do this stuff. Let's discuss each package one by one.

The find_object_2d package in ROS

One of the advantages of ROS is that it has tons of packages that can be reused in our applications. In our case, what we want is to implement an object recognition and detection system. The find_object_2d package (http://wiki.ros.org/find_object_2d) implements SURF, SIFT, FAST, and BRIEF feature detectors (https://goo.gl/B8H9Zm) and descriptors for object detection. Using the GUI provided by this package, we can mark the objects we want to detect and save them for future detection. The detector node will detect the objects in camera images and publish the details of the object through a topic. Using a 3D sensor, it can estimate the depth and orientation of the object.

Installing find_object_2d

Installing this package is pretty easy. Here is the command to install it on Ubuntu 16.04 and ROS Kinetic:

```
$ sudo apt-get install ros-kinetic-find-object-2d
```

Installing from source code

Switch into the ROS workspace:

```
$ cd ~/catkin_ws/src
```

Clone the source code into the `src` folder:

```
$ git clone https://github.com/introlab/find-object.git
src/find_object_2d
```

Build the workspace:

```
$ catkin_make
```

Running find_object_2d nodes using webcams

Here is the procedure to run the detector nodes for a webcam. If we want to detect an object using a webcam, we first need to install the `usb_cam` package,which was discussed in `Chapter 2`, *Face Detection and Tracking Using ROS, OpenCV, and Dynamixel Servos*.

1. Start `roscore`:

```
$ roscore
```

2. Plug your USB camera into your PC, and launch the ROS `usb_cam` driver:

```
$ roslaunch usb_cam usb_cam-test.launch
```

   This will launch the ROS driver for USB web cameras, and you can list the topics in this driver using the `rostopic list` command. The list of topics in the driver is shown here:

```
robot@robot-pc:~$ rostopic list
/image_view/parameter_descriptions
/image_view/parameter_updates
/rosout
/rosout_agg
/usb_cam/camera_info
/usb_cam/image_raw
/usb_cam/image_raw/compressed
/usb_cam/image_raw/compressed/parameter_descriptions
/usb_cam/image_raw/compressed/parameter_updates
/usb_cam/image_raw/compressedDepth
/usb_cam/image_raw/compressedDepth/parameter_descriptions
/usb_cam/image_raw/compressedDepth/parameter_updates
/usb_cam/image_raw/theora
/usb_cam/image_raw/theora/parameter_descriptions
/usb_cam/image_raw/theora/parameter_updates
```

Figure 3: Topics being published from the camera driver

3. From the topic list, we are going to use the raw image topic from the cam, which is being published to the `/usb_cam/image_raw` topic. If you are getting this topic, then the next step is to run the object detector node. The following command will start the object detector node:

```
$ rosrun find_object_2d find_object_2d image:=/usb_cam/image_raw
```

This command will open the object detector window, shown in the previous screenshot, in which we can see the camera feed and the feature points on the objects.

4. So how can we use it for detecting an object? Here are the procedures to perform a basic detection using this tool:

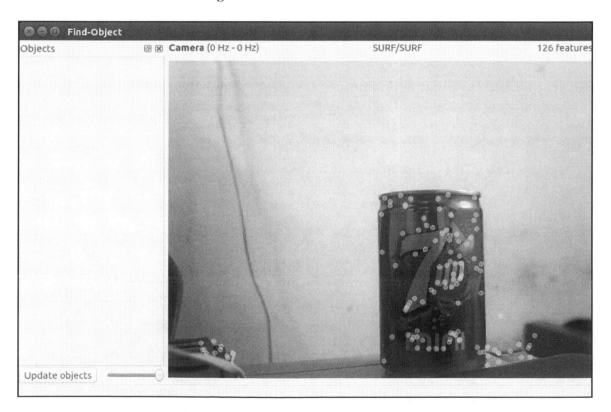

Figure 4: The Find-Object detector window

5. You can right-click on the left-hand side panel (**Objects**) of this window, and you will get an option to **Add objects from scene**. If you choose this option, you will be directed to mark the object from the current scene, and after completing the marking, the marked object will start to track from the scene. The previous screenshot shows the first step, which is taking a snap of the scene having the object.

6. After aligning the object toward the camera, press the **Take Picture** button to take a snap of the object:

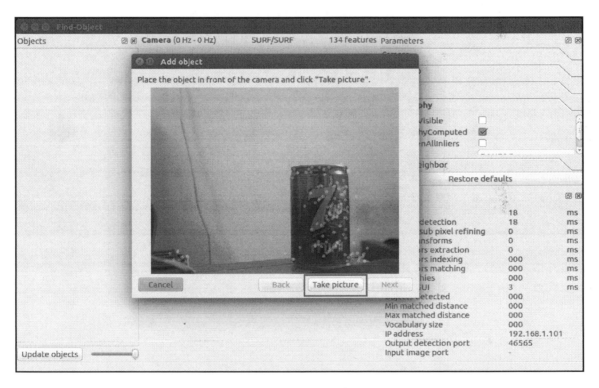

Figure 5: The Add object wizard for taking a snap of the object

7. The next window is for marking the object from the current snap. The following figure shows this. We can use the mouse pointer to mark the object. Click on the **Next** button to crop the object, and you can proceed to the next step:

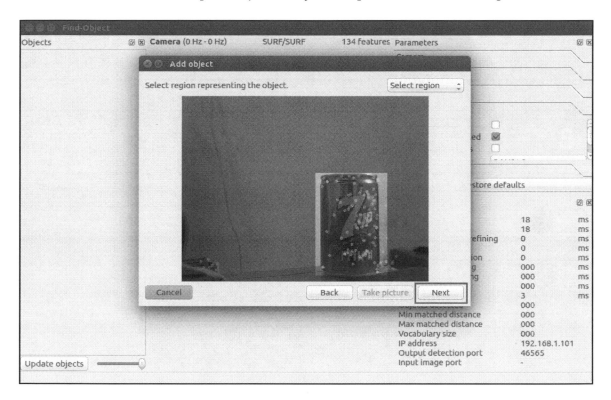

Figure 6: The Add object wizard for marking the object

8. After cropping the object, it will show you the total number of feature descriptors on the object, and you can press the **End** button to add the object template for detection. The following figure shows the last stage of adding an object template to this detector application:

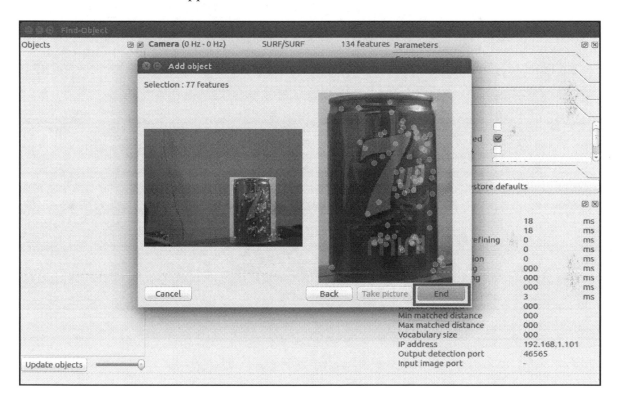

Figure 7: The last step of the Add object wizard

9. Congratulations! You have added an object for detection. Immediately after adding the object, you will be able to see the detection shown in the following figure. You can see a bounding box around the detected object:

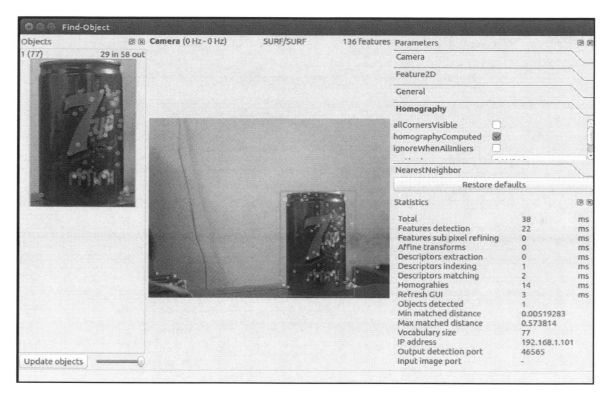

Figure 8: The Find-Object wizard starting the detection

10. Is that enough? What about the position of the object? We can retrieve the position of the object using the following command:

```
$ rosrun find_object_2d print_objects_detected
```

```
Object 1 detected, Qt corners at (349.005890,193.805511) (548.637444,194.173731) (347.
745106,476.882712) (546.294145,476.546963)
- - -
Object 1 detected, Qt corners at (348.654999,193.916397) (548.521667,194.306640) (347.
606602,477.062803) (546.462457,476.123968)
- - -
Object 1 detected, Qt corners at (349.047729,194.432526) (549.321203,192.786282) (348.
294037,476.387848) (546.751276,476.828125)
- - -
Object 1 detected, Qt corners at (348.831024,193.950211) (548.481769,194.160784) (347.
401401,477.281268) (546.429143,476.099446)
- - -
Object 1 detected, Qt corners at (348.817383,194.296692) (549.181819,193.494925) (347.
031157,477.201164) (546.595589,476.701254)
- - -
Object 1 detected, Qt corners at (348.775452,193.905640) (548.325150,194.470809) (347.
195352,477.604420) (546.620953,476.316763)
- - -
Object 1 detected, Qt corners at (349.173157,194.101913) (548.643213,193.599104) (348.
129605,476.705982) (546.500466,476.719158)
- - -
Object 1 detected, Qt corners at (349.087555,194.182556) (549.201040,193.357581) (348.
503663,475.883037) (546.713381,477.380333)
```

Figure 9: The object details

11. You can also get the complete information about the detected object from the /object topic. The topic publishes a multi-array that consist of the width and height of the object and the homography matrix to compute the position and orientation of the object and its scale and shear values. You can echo the /objects topic to get output like this:

```
objects:
  layout:
    dim: []
    data_offset: 0
  data: [3.0, 202.0, 393.0, 1.0872979164123535, 0.048006415367126465,
0.00016619441157672554, 0.008327833376824856, 1.057657241821289, 1.759
977385518141e-05, 280.7042236328125, 74.2943115234375, 1.0]
---
header:
  seq: 43
  stamp:
    secs: 1476380300
    nsecs: 630851717                        3x3 Homography matrix
  frame_id: usb_cam        Width & height
objects:
  layout:
    dim: []
    data_offset: 0
  data: [3.0, 202.0, 393.0  1.0946733951568604, 0.05213480815291405, 0
.00018432267825119197, 0.00999543722718954, 1.0606046915054321, 2.1411
471607279964e-05, 280.6572265625, 74.00088500976562, 1.0]
```

Figure 10: The /object topic values

12. We can compute the new position and orientation from the following equations:

$$
H = \begin{bmatrix} h_{00} & h_{01} & h_{02} \\ h_{10} & h_{11} & h_{12} \\ h_{20} & h_{21} & h_{22} \end{bmatrix} \quad \begin{bmatrix} x_1 \\ y_1 \\ 1 \end{bmatrix} = H \begin{bmatrix} x_2 \\ y_2 \\ 1 \end{bmatrix} = \begin{bmatrix} h_{00} & h_{01} & h_{02} \\ h_{10} & h_{11} & h_{12} \\ h_{20} & h_{21} & h_{22} \end{bmatrix} \begin{bmatrix} x_2 \\ y_2 \\ 1 \end{bmatrix}
$$

Figure 11: The equation to compute object position

Here, *H* is the homography 3×3 matrix, (*x1, y1*) is the object's position in the stored image, and (*x2, y2*) is the computed object position in the current frame.

You can check out the source code of the `print_objected_src` node to get the conversion using a homography matrix.
Here is the source code of this node:
`https://github.com/introlab/find-object/blob/master/src/ros/print_objects_detected_node.cpp`.

Running find_object_2d nodes using depth sensors

Using a webcam, we can only find the 2D position and orientation of an object, but what should we use if we need the 3D coordinates of the object? We could simply use a depth sensor like the Kinect and run these same nodes. For interfacing the Kinect with ROS, we need to install some driver packages. The Kinect can deliver both RGB and depth data. Using RGB data, the object detector detects the object, and using the depth value, it computes the distance from the sensor too.

Here are the dependent packages for working with the Kinect sensor:

- If you are using the Xbox Kinect 360, which is the first Kinect, you have to install the following package to get it working:

```
$ sudo apt-get install ros-kinetic-openni-launch
```

- If you have Kinect version 2, you may need a different driver package, which is available on GitHub. You may need to install it from the source code. The following is the ROS package link of the V2 driver. The installation instructions are also given:`https://github.com/code-iai/iai_kinect2`

If you are using the Asus Xtion Pro or other PrimeSense device, you may need to install the following driver to work with this detector:

```
$ sudo apt-get install ros-kinetic-openni2-launch
```

In this book, we will be working with the Xbox Kinect, which is the first version of Kinect.

Before starting the Kinect driver, you have to plug the USB to your PC and make sure that the Kinect is powered using its adapter. Once everything is done, you can launch the drivers using the following command:

```
$ roslaunch openni_launch openni.launch depth_registration:=true
```

1. If the driver is running without errors, you should get the following list of topics:

```
lentin@lentin-Aspire-4755:~$ rostopic list
/camera/depth/camera_info
/camera/depth/disparity
/camera/depth/image
/camera/depth/image/compressed
/camera/depth/image/compressed/parameter_descriptions
/camera/depth/image/compressed/parameter_updates
/camera/depth/image/compressedDepth
/camera/depth/image/compressedDepth/parameter_descriptions
/camera/depth/image/compressedDepth/parameter_updates
/camera/depth/image/theora
/camera/depth/image/theora/parameter_descriptions
/camera/depth/image/theora/parameter_updates
/camera/depth/image_raw
/camera/depth/image_raw/compressed
/camera/depth/image_raw/compressed/parameter_descriptions
/camera/depth/image_raw/compressed/parameter_updates
/camera/depth/image_raw/compressedDepth
```

Figure 12: List of topics from the Kinect openNI driver

2. If you are getting this, start the object detector and mark the object as you did for the 2D object detection. The procedure is the same, but in this case, you will get the 3D coordinates of the object. The following diagram shows the detection of the object and its TF data on Rviz. You can see the side view of the Kinect and the object position in Rviz.

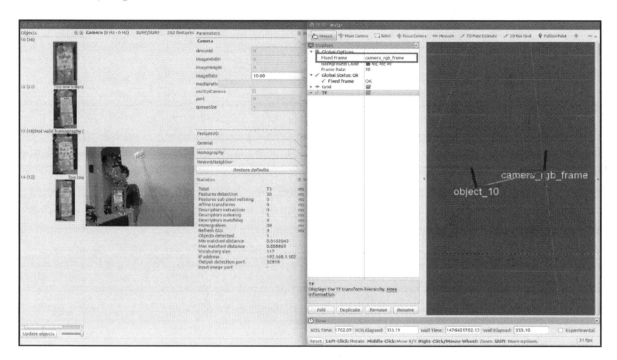

Figure 13: Object detection using Kinect

3. To start the object detection, you have to perform some tweaks in the existing launch file given by this package. The name of the launch file for object detection is find_object_3d.launch.

 You can directly view this file from the following link:
https://github.com/introlab/find-object/blob/master/launch/find_object_3d.launch.
This launch file is written for an autonomous robot that detects objects while navigating the surrounding.

4. We can modify this file a little bit because in our case, there is no robot, so we can modify it in such a way that the TF information should be published with respect to Kinect's `camera_rgb_frame`, which is shown in the previous diagram. Here is the launch file definition we want for the demo:

```
<launch>
    <node name="find_object_3d" pkg="find_object_2d"
    type="find_object_2d" output="screen">
    <param name="gui" value="true" type="bool"/>
    <param name="settings_path"
value="~/.ros/find_object_2d.ini" type="str"/>
   <param name="subscribe_depth" value="true"
      type="bool"/>
   <param name="objects_path" value="" type="str"/>
   <param name="object_prefix" value="object"
  type="str"/>
   <remap from="rgb/image_rect_color"
   to="camera/rgb/image_rect_color"/>
   <remap from="depth_registered/image_raw"
    to="camera/depth_registered/image_raw"/>
   <remap from="depth_registered/camera_info"
   to="camera/depth_registered/camera_info"/>
  </node>
</launch>
```

In this code, we just removed the static transform required for the mobile robot. You can also change the `object_prefix` parameter to name the detected object.

Using the following commands, you can modify this launch file, which is already installed on your system:

```
$ roscd find_object_2d/launch
$ sudo gedit find_object_3d.launch
```

Now, you can remove the unwanted lines of code and save your changes. After saving this launch file, launch it to start detection:

```
$ roslaunch find_object_2d find_object_3d.launch
```

You can mark the object and it will start detecting the marked object.

5. To visualize the TF data, you can launch Rviz, make the fixed frame `/camera_link` or `/camera_rgb_frame`, and add a TF display from the left panel of Rviz.

6. You can run Rviz using the following command:

```
$ rosrun rviz rviz
```

Other than publishing TF, we can also see the 3D position of the object in the detector Terminal. The detected position values are shown in the following screenshot:

```
[ INFO] [1476451737.207323202]: Object_10 [x,y,z] [x,y,z,w] in "/camera_rgb_fram
e" frame: [0.542000,0.131629,-0.077945] [0.077937,-0.007629,0.996919,-0.004438]
[ INFO] [1476451737.207384747]: Object_10 [x,y,z] [x,y,z,w] in "camera_rgb_optic
al_frame" frame: [-0.131629,0.077945,0.542000] [0.457895,0.461087,-0.531395,0.54
3462]
[ INFO] [1476451737.305781577]: Object_10 [x,y,z] [x,y,z,w] in "/camera_rgb_fram
e" frame: [0.542000,0.130596,-0.077945] [0.059449,0.011080,0.998159,-0.004555]
[ INFO] [1476451737.305822771]: Object_10 [x,y,z] [x,y,z,w] in "camera_rgb_optic
al_frame" frame: [-0.130596,0.077945,0.542000] [0.477172,0.461538,-0.532067,0.52
5542]
[ INFO] [1476451737.543368607]: Object_10 [x,y,z] [x,y,z,w] in "/camera_rgb_fram
e" frame: [0.542000,0.131629,-0.077945] [0.080979,-0.000803,0.996625,-0.013447]
[ INFO] [1476451737.543409748]: Object_10 [x,y,z] [x,y,z,w] in "camera_rgb_optic
al_frame" frame: [-0.131629,0.077945,0.542000] [0.464145,0.451501,-0.531677,0.54
5927]
```

Figure 14: Printing the 3D object's position

Getting started with 3D object recognition

In the previous section, we dealt with 2D object recognition using a 2D and 3D sensor. In this section, we will discuss 3D recognition. So what is 3D object recognition? In 3D object recognition, we take the 3D data or point cloud data of the surroundings and 3D model of the object. Then, we match the scene object with the trained model, and if there is a match found, the algorithm will mark the area of detection.

In real-world scenarios, 3D object recognition/detection is much better than 2D because in 3D detection, we use the complete information of the object, similar to human perception. But there are many challenges involved in this process too. Some of the main constrains are computational power and expensive sensors. We may need more expensive computers to process 3D information; also, the sensors for this purpose are costlier.

Some of the latest applications using 3D object detection and recognition are autonomous robots, especially self-driving cars. Self-driving cars have a LIDAR such as Velodyne (http://velodynelidar.com/) that can provide a complete 3D point cloud around the vehicle. The computer inside takes the 3D input and run various detectors to find pedestrians, cyclists, and other obstacles for a collision-free ride.

Like we discussed in the beginning, in the Amazon Picking Challenge and other such applications, the picking and placing needs 3D recognition capability. The following figure shows how an autonomous car perceives the world. The data shown around the car is the 3D point cloud, which helps it detect objects and predict a collision-free route.

Figure 15: Typical 3D data from an autonomous car

3D object recognition has many applications, and in this section, you are going to see how to perform a basic 3D object recognition using ROS and cheap depth sensors.

Introduction to 3D object recognition packages in ROS

ROS has packages for performing 3D object recognition. One of the popular packages we are dealing with in this section is the **Object Recognition Kitchen (ORK)**. This project was started at Willow Garage mainly for 3D object recognition. The ORK is a generic way to detect any kind of object, whether it be textured, nontextured, transparent, and so on. It is a complete kit in which we can run several object-recognition techniques simultaneously. It is not just a kit for object recognition, but it also provides non-vision aspects, such as database management to store 3D models, input/output handling, robot-ROS integration, and code reuse.

 ORK home page:
http://wg-perception.github.io/object_recognition_core/.
ORK ROS page:
http://wiki.ros.org/object_recognition

Installing ORK packages in ROS

Here are the installation instructions to set up the `object_recognition` package in ROS. We can install it using prebuilt binaries and source code. The easiest way to install is via binaries.

Here is the command to install ORK packages in ROS:

```
$ sudo apt-get install ros-kinetic-object-recognition-*
```

If you want to install these packages in ROS Indigo, replace `kinetic` with `indigo`.

This command will install the following ROS packages:

- `object-recognition-core`: This package contains tools to launch several recognition pipelines, train objects, and store models.
- `object-recognition-linemod`: This is an object recognition pipeline that uses linemod from OpenCV. The linemod pipeline is best for rigid body detection.

- `object-recognition-tabletop`: This is a pipeline use for pick-and-place operations from a flat surface
- `object-recognition-tod`: Textured Object Recognition is another pipeline for textured objects that uses features for detection.
- `object-recognition-reconstruction`: This is a basic 3D reconstruction of an object from aligned Kinect data.
- `object-recognition-renderer`: This is code that generates random views of an object.
- `object-recognition-msgs`: This package contains the ROS message and the `actionlib` definition used in `object_recognition_core`.
- `object-recognition-capture`: Capture is a set of tools to capture objects in 3D and perform odometry.
- `object-recognition-transparent-objects`: This is a technique to recognize and estimate poses of transparent objects.
- `object-recognition-ros-visualization`: This package contains Rviz plugins to visualize ORK detection results.

Here are the commands to install the packages from source. This command is basically based on the `rosinstall` tool, which helps set up a list of packages in a single command. You can run this commands from the `/home/<user>` folder.

```
$ mkdir ws && cd ws
$ wstool init src
https://raw.github.com/wg-perception/object_recognition_core/master/doc/sou
rce/ork.rosinstall.kinetic.plus
$ cd src && wstool update -j8
$ cd .. && rosdep install --from-paths src -i -y
$ catkin_make
$ source devel/setup.bash
```

You can find more about LINE-MODE from the following link:
http://far.in.tum.de/Main/StefanHinterstoisser
This is the GitHub repository of the object-recognition packages:
https://github.com/wg-perception
Here are the possible issues you may have while working with this package:
https://github.com/wg-perception/object_recognition_ros/issues

https://github.com/wg-perception/linemod/issues
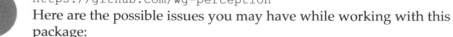
https://github.com/wg-perception/object_recognition_core/issues

Detecting and recognizing objects from 3D meshes

After installing these packages, let's start the detection. What are the procedures involved? Here are the main steps:

1. Building a CAD model of the object or capturing its 3D model
2. Training the model
3. Detecting the object using the trained model

The first step in the recognition process is building the 3D model of the desired object. We can do it using a CAD tool, or we can capture the real object using depth-sensing cameras. If the object is rigid, then the best procedure is CAD modelling, because it will have all the 3D information regarding the object. When we try to capture and build a 3D model, it may have errors and the mesh may not be look like the actual object because of the accumulation of errors in each stage. After building the object model, it will be uploaded to the object database. The next phase is the training of the uploaded object on the database. After training, we can start the detection process. The detection process will start capturing from the depth sensors and will match with the trained model in the database using different methods, such as **Random Sample Consensus (RANSAC)**. If there is a match, it will marked the area and print the result. We can see the final detection output in Rviz.

Let's see how to add a mesh of an object to the object database. There are ORK tutorial packages that provide meshes of some objects, such as soda bottles. We can use one of these object and add it to the object database.

Training using 3D models of an object

We can clone the ORK tutorial package using the following command:

```
$ git clone https://github.com/wg-perception/ork_tutorials
```

You can see that the `ork_tutorials/data` folder contains some mesh files that we can use for object detection. Navigate to that folder and execute the following commands from the same path. The following command will add an entry to the object database:

```
$ rosrun object_recognition_core object_add.py -n "coke" -d "A universal coke" --commit
```

The object name is mentioned after that −n argument and the object description after −d. The −commit argument is to commit these operations. When the operation is successful, you will get the ID of the object. This ID is used in the next command. The next command is to upload the mesh file of the object to the created entry:

```
$ rosrun object_recognition_core mesh_add.py <ID_OF_OBJECT> coke.stl --
commit
```

Here's an example:

```
$ rosrun object_recognition_core mesh_add.py
cfab1c4804c316ea23c698ecbf0026e4 coke.stl --commit
```

We are mentioning the name of object model–coke.stl–in this command, which is in the data folder. We are not mentioning the path here because we are already in that path. If not, we have to mention the absolute path of the model.

If it is successful, you will get output saying the model has been stored in the database.

Do you want to see the uploaded model? Here is the procedure:

1. Install couchapp. The object recognition package uses couchdb as the database. So we need the following application to view the model from the database:

```
$ sudo pip install git+https://github.com/couchapp/couchapp.git
```

2. After setting up the application, you can run the following command:

```
$rosrun object_recognition_core push.sh
```

3. If everything is successful, you will get a message like this:

   [INFO] Visit your CouchApp here:

   http://localhost:5984/or_web_ui/_design/viewer/index.html

4. Click on the link, and you will get the list of objects and their visualizations in your web browser. Here is a set of screenshots of this web interface:

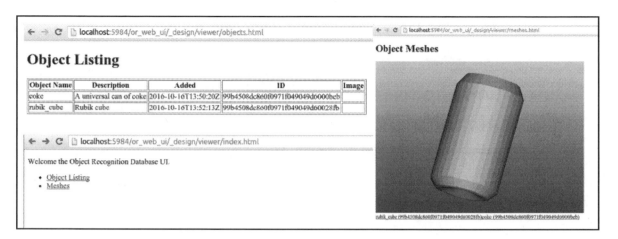

Figure 16: Web interface for viewing object models

All right! The object model has been properly uploaded to the database.

5. After uploading the model, we have to train it. You can use the following command:

```
$ rosrun object_recognition_core training -c `rospack find
object_recognition_linemod`/conf/training.ork
```

6. If the training is successful, you will see a message like this:

```
lentin@lentin-Aspire-4755:~/Desktop/Files/3d_obj_recog/ork_tutorials/data$ rosru
n object_recognition_core training -c `rospack find object_recognition_linemod`/
conf/training.ork
Training 1 objects.
computing object_id: cfab1c4804c316ea23c698ecbf0026e4
Info,  T0: Load /tmp/fileXdkkE5.stl
Info,  T0: Found a matching importer for this file format
Info,  T0: Import root directory is '/tmp/'
Info,  T0: Entering post processing pipeline
Info,  T0: Points: 0, Lines: 0, Triangles: 1, Polygons: 0 (Meshes, X = removed)
Error, T0: FindInvalidDataProcess fails on mesh normals: Found zero-length vecto
r
Info,  T0: FindInvalidDataProcess finished. Found issues ...
Info,  T0: GenVertexNormalsProcess finished. Vertex normals have been calculated
Error, T0: Failed to compute tangents; need UV data in channel0
Info,  T0: JoinVerticesProcess finished | Verts in: 1536 out: 258 | ~83.2%
Info,  T0: Cache relevant are 1 meshes (512 faces). Average output ACMR is 0.669
922
Info,  T0: Leaving post processing pipeline
Loading images 495/5737
```

Figure 17: Training 3D objects

Training from captured 3D models

If you don't have a 3D mesh of the object, you can also create one by capturing the 3D point cloud data and reconstructing the mesh. Here are the steps to capture and build the mesh of an object:

1. Before the capture, we have to print a pattern for better capturing and reconstruction. You can download the pattern from `http://wg-perception.github.io/capture/_downloads/capture_board_big_5x 3.svg.pdf`.

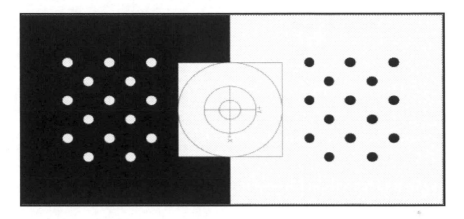

Figure 18: Capture pattern for 3D objects

2. Print the pattern, stick it to some hard board, and place it on a rotating mechanism that you can manually rotate the board along an axis. The object has to be placed at the center of the pattern. The size of the pattern doesn't matter, but the larger the size, the better the detection. We can place the object at the center and place the Kinect where it can detect all the markers. The capture program only capture the object once it detect the markers. Here is an example setup made for the object capture:

Figure 19: Capturing 3D model of object using patterns

3. If the setup is ready, we can start running the tools to capture the object mode. First, start `roscore`:

    ```
    $ roscore
    ```

4. Launch the Kinect driver node, ensuring that Kinect is properly powered on and plugged in to the PC:

    ```
    $ roslaunch openni_launch openni.launch
    ```

5. Set these parameters for the Kinect ROS driver:

    ```
    $ rosrun dynamic_reconfigure dynparam set /camera/driver
    depth_registration True
    $ rosrun dynamic_reconfigure dynparam set /camera/driver
    image_mode 2
    $ rosrun dynamic_reconfigure dynparam set /camera/driver
    depth_mode 2
    ```

6. The `topic_toolsrelay` parameter basically subscribes to the first topic and republished it in another name. You can run the following two commands on two Terminals:

    ```
    $ rosrun topic_tools relay /camera/depth_registered/image_raw
    /camera/depth/image_raw
    $ rosrun topic_tools relay /camera/rgb/image_rect_color
    /camera/rgb/image_raw
    ```

    This command will start the visualization and start capturing the object.

7. While running this command, you have to rotate the pattern board to acquire maximum features from the object. Here, `object.bag` is the bag file used to store the captured data.

    ```
    $ rosrun object_recognition_capture capture --seg_z_min 0.01 -o
    object.bag
    ```

Here is the screenshot of the capture operation:

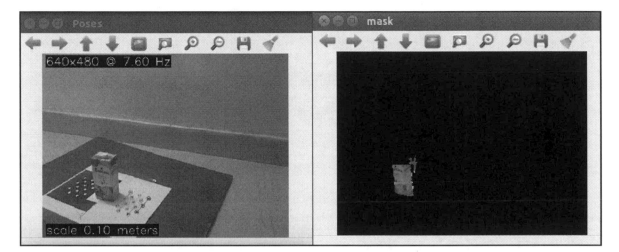

Figure 20: Capturing 3D model

8. If the detector gets enough 3D data of an object, it will print that it is satisfied with the data and quit.

9. After the capture, we need to upload the data to the database. We have to mention the bag file name, name of the object, and its description. Here is an example command to do that:

```
$ rosrun object_recognition_capture upload -i object.bag -n
'Tropicana'  It is a Tropicana --commit
```

10. The next phase is the reconstruction of the captured data into a mesh. Here is the command to do that:

```
$ rosrun object_recognition_reconstruction mesh_object --all --
visualize --commit
```

11. You will see the conversion as shown here:

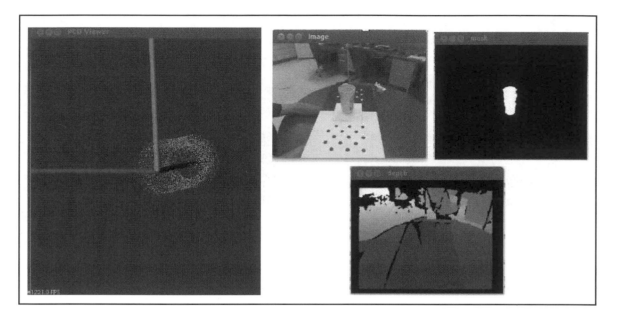

Figure 21: Reconstruction of mesh (with a different object)

12. You can see the point cloud of the captured object and the image during reconstruction. After reconstruction, we can train the models in the database using the following command:

```
$ rosrun object_recognition_core training -c `rospack find
object_recognition_linemod`/conf/training.ork
```

13. You can use different pipelines here for training, such as tod, tabletop, or linemod. Here, we've used the linemod pipeline. Each pipeline has its own merits and demerits.

14. After training, we can check whether the object has been uploaded to the database by going to the following link and checking whether it looks like the screenshot shown after it:

```
http://localhost:5984/_utils/database.html?object_recogn
ition/
```

Figure 22: List of object in database

The next process is recognizing the object using the trained model. Let's discuss how to do that.

Recognizing objects

There are several commands to start recognition using a trained model.

Starting `roscore`:

```
$ roscore
```

Starting the ROS driver for Kinect:

```
$ roslaunch openni_launch openni.launch
```

Setting the ROS parameters for the Kinect driver:

```
$ rosrun dynamic_reconfigure dynparam set /camera/driver
depth_registration True
$ rosrun dynamic_reconfigure dynparam set /camera/driver image_mode 2
$ rosrun dynamic_reconfigure dynparam set /camera/driver depth_mode 2
```

Republishing the depth and RGB image topics using `topic_tools relay`:

```
$ rosrun topic_tools relay /camera/depth_registered/image_raw
/camera/depth/image_raw
$ rosrun topic_tools relay /camera/rgb/image_rect_color
/camera/rgb/image_raw
```

Here is the command to start recognition; we can use different pipelines to perform detection. The following command uses the tod pipeline. This will work well for textured objects.

```
$ rosrun object_recognition_core detection -c `rospack find
object_recognition_tod`/conf/detection.ros.ork --visualize
```

Alternatively, we can use the tabletop pipeline, which can detect objects placed on a flat surface, such as a table itself:

```
$ rosrun object_recognition_core detection -c  `rospack find
object_recognition_tabletop`/conf/detection.object.ros.ork
```

You could also use the linemod pipeline, which is the best for rigid object recognition:

```
$ rosrun object_recognition_core detection -c `rospack find
object_recognition_linemod`/conf/detection.object.ros.ork
```

After running the detectors, we can visualize the detections in Rviz. Let's start Rviz and load the proper display type, shown in the screenshot:

```
$ rosrun rviz rviz
```

Figure 23: Object detection visualized in Rviz

The **Fixed Frame** can be set to `camera_rgb_frame`. Then, we have to add a `PointCloud2` display with the `/camera/depth_registered/points` topic. To detect the object and display its name, you have to add a new display type called `OrkObject`, which is installed along with the object-recognition package. You can see the object being detected, as shown in the previous screenshot.

If it is a tabletop pipeline, it will mark the plane area in which object is placed, as shown in the next screenshot. This pipeline is good for grasping objects from a table, which can work well with the ROS MoveIt! package.

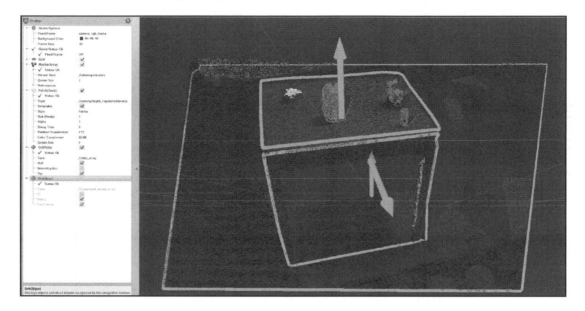

Figure 24: Tabletop detection visualized in Rviz

For visualizing, you need to add `OrkTable` with the `/table_array` topic and `MarkerArray` with the `/tabletop/clusters` topic.

We can add any number of objects to the database; detection accuracy depends on the quality of model, quality of 3D input, and processing power of the PC.

Questions

- What is the main difference between object detection and recognition?
- What is 2D and 3D object recognition?
- What are the main functions of the `find_object_2d` package in ROS?
- What are the main steps involved in detecting 3D objects using an object recognition package in ROS?

Summary

In this chapter, we dealt with object detection and recognition. Both these things are extensively used in robotic applications. The chapter started with a popular ROS package for 2D object detection. The package is called `find_2d_object`, and we covered object detection using a webcam and Kinect. After going through a demo using this package, we discussed 3D object recognition using a ROS package called `object_recognition`, which is mainly for 3D object recognition. We saw methods to build and capture the object model and its training procedure. After training, we discussed the steps to start detecting the object using a depth camera. Finally, we visualized the object recognition in Rviz.

In the next chapter, we will deal with interfacing ROS and Google TensorFlow.

7
Deep Learning Using ROS and TensorFlow

You may have come across *deep learning* many times on the Web. Most of us are not fully aware of this technology, and many people are trying to learn it too. So in this chapter, we are going to see the importance of deep learning in robotics and how we can implement robotics applications using deep learning and ROS.

Here are the main topics we are going to discuss in this chapter:

- Introducing deep learning and its applications
- Deep learning for robotics
- Software frameworks and programming languages for deep learning
- Getting started with Google TensorFlow
- Installing TensorFlow for Python
- Embedding TensorFlow APIs in ROS
- Image recognition using ROS and TensorFlow
- Introduction to scikit-learn
- Implementing SVM using scikit-learn
- Embedding SVM on a ROS node
- Implementing an SVM-ROS application

Introduction to deep learning and its applications

So what actually is deep learning? It is a buzzword in neural network technology. What is a neural network then? An artificial neural network is a computer software model that replicates the behaviour of neurons in the human brain. A neural network is one way to classify data. For example, if we want to classify an image by whether it contains an object or not, we can use this method. There are several other computer software models for classification like logistic regression, **Support Vector Machine** (**SVM**); a neural network is one among them.

So why we are not calling it neural network instead of deep learning? The reason is that in deep learning, we use a large number of artificial neural networks. So you may ask, "So why it was not possible before?" The answer: to create a large number of neural networks (multilayer perceptron), we may need a high amount of computational power. So how has it become possible now? It's because of the availability of cheap computational hardware. Will computational power alone do the job? No, we also need a large dataset to train with.

When we train a large set of neurons, it can learn various features from the input data. After learning the features, it can predict the occurrence of an object or anything we have taught to it.

To teach a neural network, we can either use the supervised learning method or go unsupervised. In supervised learning, we have a training dataset with input and its expected output. These values will be fed to the neural network, and the weights of the neurons will be adjusted in such a way that it can predict which output it should generate whenever it gets a particular input data. So what about unsupervised learning? This type of algorithm learns from an input dataset without having corresponding outputs. The human brain can work like supervised or unsupervised way, but unsupervised learning is more predominant in our case.

The main applications of deep neural networks are in the classification and recognition of objects, such as image recognition and speech recognition.

In this book, we are mainly dealing with supervised learning for building deep learning applications for robots.

Deep learning for robotics

Here are the main robotics areas where we apply deep learning:

- **Deep-learning-based object detector**: Imagine a robot wants to pick a specific object from a group of objects. What could be the first step for solving this problem? It should identify the object first, right? We can use image processing algorithms such as segmentation and Haar training to detect an object, but the problem with those techniques is they are not scalable and can't be used for many objects. Using deep learning algorithms, we can train a large neural network with a large dataset. It can have good accuracy and scalability compared to other methods. Datasets such as ImageNet (`http://image-net.org/`), which have a large collection of image datasets, can be used for training. We also get trained models that we can just use without training. We will look at an ImageNet-based image recognition ROS node in an upcoming section.

- **Speech recognition**: If we want to command a robot to perform some task using our voice, what will we do? Will the robot understand our language? Definitely not. But using deep learning techniques, we can build more a accurate speech recognition system compared to the existing **Hidden Markov Model (HMM)** based recognizer. Companies such as Baidu (`http://research.baidu.com/`) and Google (`http://research.google.com/pubs/SpeechProcessing.html`) are trying hard to create a global speech recognition system using deep learning techniques.

- **SLAM and localization**: Deep learning can be used to perform SLAM and localization of mobile robots, which perform much better than conventional methods.

- **Autonomous vehicles**: The deep learning approach in self-driving cars is a new way of controlling the steering of vehicles using a trained network in which sensor data can be fed to the network and corresponding steering control can be obtained. This kind of network can learn by itself while driving.

- **Deep reinforcement learning**: Do you want to make your robot act like a human? Then use this technique. Reinforcement learning is a kind of machine learning technique that allows machines and software agents to automatically determine the ideal behavior within a specific context, in order to maximize its performance. By combining it with deep learning, robots can truly behave as truly intelligent agents that can solve tasks that are considered challenging by humans.

One of the companies doing a lot in deep reinforcement learning is DeepMind owned by Google. They have built a technique to master the Atari 2600 games to a superhuman level with only the raw pixels and score as inputs (`https://deepmind.com/research/dqn/`). **AlphaGo** is another computer program developed by DeepMind, which can even beat a professional human Go player (`https://deepmind.com/research/alphago/`).

Deep learning libraries

Here are some of the popular deep learning libraries used in research and commercial applications:

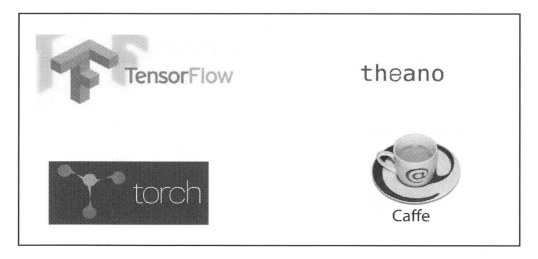

Figure 1: Popular deep learning libraries

- **TensorFlow**: This is an open source software library for numerical computation using data flow graphs. The TensorFlow library is designed for machine intelligence and developed by the Google Brain team. The main aim of this library is to perform machine learning and deep neural network research. It can be used in a wide variety of other domains as well (`https://www.tensorflow.org/`).

- **Theano**: This is an open source Python library (http://deeplearning.net/software/theano/) that enables us to optimize and evaluate mathematical expressions involving multidimensional arrays efficiently. Theano is primarily developed by the machine learning group at the University of Montreal , Canada.
- **Torch**: Torch is again a scientific computing framework with wide support for machine learning algorithms that puts GPUs first. It's very efficient, being built on the scripting language LuaJIT and has an underlying C/CUDA implementation (http://torch.ch/).
- **Caffe**: Caffe (http://caffe.berkeleyvision.org/) is a deep learning library made with a focus on modularity, speed, and expression. It is developed by the **Berkeley Vision and Learning Centre (BVLC)**.

Getting started with TensorFlow

As we discussed, TensorFlow is an open source library mainly designed for fast numerical computing. This library mainly works with Python and was released by Google. TensorFlow can be used as a foundation library to create deep learning models.

We can use TensorFlow both for research and development and in production systems. The good thing about TensorFlow is it can run on a single CPU all the way to a large-scale distributed system of hundreds of machines. It also works well on GPUs and mobile devices.

You can check out the Tensorflow library at the following link:

https://www.tensorflow.org/

Installing TensorFlow on Ubuntu 16.04 LTS

Installing TensorFlow is not a tedious task if you have a fast Internet connection. The main tool we need to have is `pip`. It is a package management system used to install and manage software packages written in Python.

> You may get latest installation instruction for Linux from following link:
> https://www.tensorflow.org/install/install_linux

Here is the command to install `pip` on Ubuntu:

```
$ sudo apt-get install python-pip python-dev
```

After installing `pip`, you have to execute the following command to set a BASH variable called `TF_BINARY_URL`. This is for installing the correct binaries for our configuration. The following variable is for the Ubuntu 64 bit, Python 2.7, CPU only version:

```
$ export
TF_BINARY_URL=https://storage.googleapis.com/tensorflow/linux/cpu/tensorflo
w-0.11.0-cp27-none-linux_x86_64.whl
```

If you have an NVIDIA GPU, you may need a different binary. You may also need to install CUDA toolkit 8.0 cuDNN v5 for installing this:

```
$ export
TF_BINARY_URL=https://storage.googleapis.com/tensorflow/linux/gpu/tensorflo
w-0.11.0-cp27-none-linux_x86_64.whl
```

Installing TensorFlow with NVIDIA acceleration:
`http://www.nvidia.com/object/gpu-accelerated-applications-tens`
`orflow-installation.html`
`https://alliseesolutions.wordpress.com/2016/09/08/install-gpu-`
`tensorflow-from-sources-w-ubuntu-16-04-and-cuda-8-0-rc/`
Installing cuDNN:
`https://developer.nvidia.com/cudnn`
For more Python distributions and other OS configuration, check out the following link:
`https://www.tensorflow.org/versions/r0.11/get_started/os_setup.h`
`tml`

After defining the BASH variable, use the following command to install the binaries for Python 2:

```
$ sudo pip install --upgrade $TF_BINARY_URL
```

If everything works fine, you will get the following kind of output in Terminal:

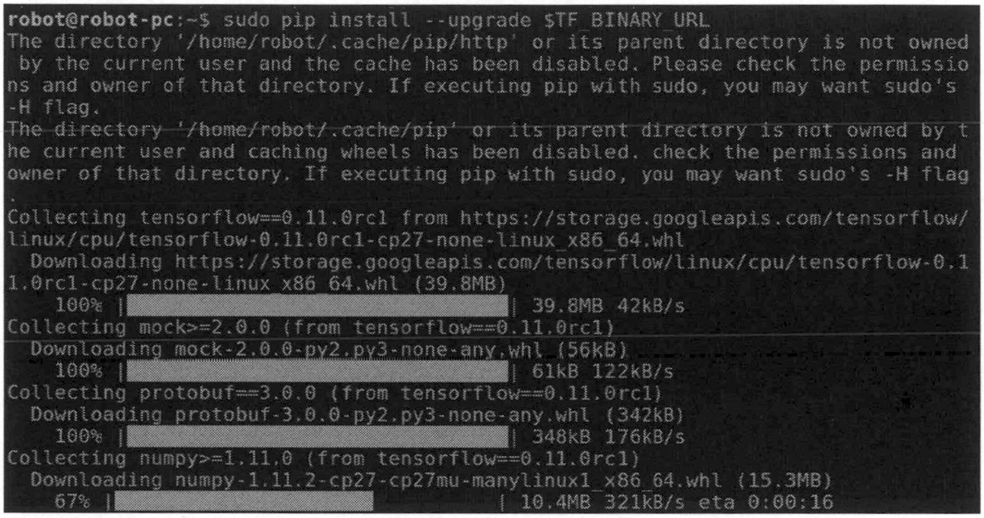

```
robot@robot-pc:~$ sudo pip install --upgrade $TF_BINARY_URL
The directory '/home/robot/.cache/pip/http' or its parent directory is not owned
 by the current user and the cache has been disabled. Please check the permissio
ns and owner of that directory. If executing pip with sudo, you may want sudo's
-H flag.
The directory '/home/robot/.cache/pip' or its parent directory is not owned by t
he current user and caching wheels has been disabled. check the permissions and
owner of that directory. If executing pip with sudo, you may want sudo's -H flag
.
Collecting tensorflow==0.11.0rc1 from https://storage.googleapis.com/tensorflow/
linux/cpu/tensorflow-0.11.0rc1-cp27-none-linux_x86_64.whl
  Downloading https://storage.googleapis.com/tensorflow/linux/cpu/tensorflow-0.1
1.0rc1-cp27-none-linux_x86_64.whl (39.8MB)
    100% |████████████████████████████████| 39.8MB 42kB/s
Collecting mock>=2.0.0 (from tensorflow==0.11.0rc1)
  Downloading mock-2.0.0-py2.py3-none-any.whl (56kB)
    100% |████████████████████████████████| 61kB 122kB/s
Collecting protobuf==3.0.0 (from tensorflow==0.11.0rc1)
  Downloading protobuf-3.0.0-py2.py3-none-any.whl (342kB)
    100% |████████████████████████████████| 348kB 176kB/s
Collecting numpy>=1.11.0 (from tensorflow==0.11.0rc1)
  Downloading numpy-1.11.2-cp27-cp27mu-manylinux1_x86_64.whl (15.3MB)
    67% |████████████████████        | 10.4MB 321kB/s eta 0:00:16
```

Figure 2: Installing TensorFlow on Ubuntu 16.04 LTS

If everything has been properly installed on your system, you can check it using a simple test.

Open a Python Terminal, execute the following lines, and check whether you are getting the results shown in the following screenshot. We will look at an explanation of the code in the next section.

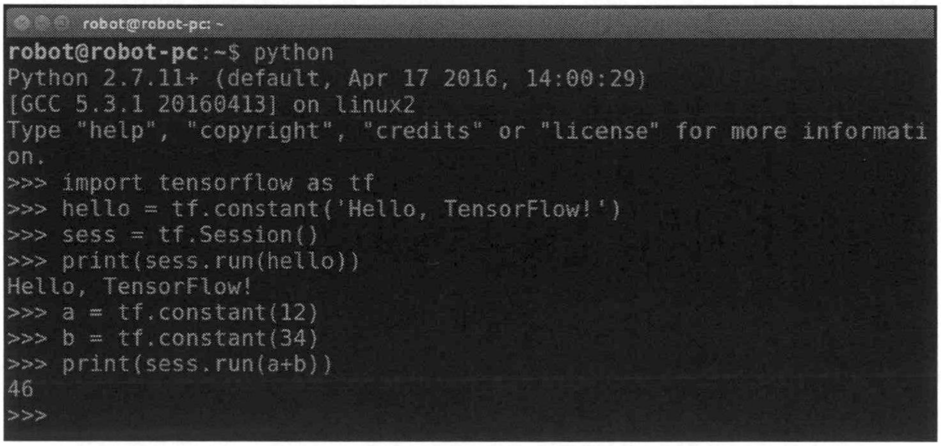

```
robot@robot-pc: ~
robot@robot-pc:~$ python
Python 2.7.11+ (default, Apr 17 2016, 14:00:29)
[GCC 5.3.1 20160413] on linux2
Type "help", "copyright", "credits" or "license" for more informati
on.
>>> import tensorflow as tf
>>> hello = tf.constant('Hello, TensorFlow!')
>>> sess = tf.Session()
>>> print(sess.run(hello))
Hello, TensorFlow!
>>> a = tf.constant(12)
>>> b = tf.constant(34)
>>> print(sess.run(a+b))
46
>>>
```

Figure 3: Testing a TensorFlow installation on Ubuntu 16.04 LTS

Here is our hello world code in TensorFlow

```
import tensorflow as tf
hello = tf.constant('Hello, TensorFlow!')
sess = tf.Session()
print (sess.run(hello))
a = tf.constant(12)
b = tf.constant(34)
print(sess.run(a+b))
```

TensorFlow concepts

Before you start programming using TensorFlow functions, you should understand its concepts. Here is the block diagram of TensorFlow concepts demonstrated using addition operation in Tensorflow.

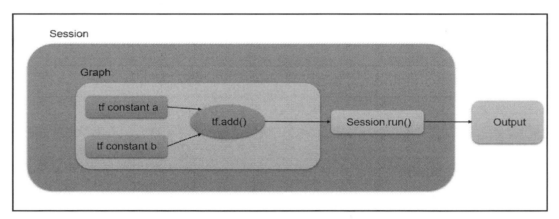

Figure 4: Block diagram of Tensorflow concepts

Let's look at each concepts:

Graph

In TensorFlow, all computations are represented as graphs. A graph consists of nodes. The nodes in a graph are called operations or **ops**. An op or node can take tensors. Tensors are basically typed multi-dimensional arrays. For example, an image can be a tensor. So, in short, the TensorFlow graph has the description of all the computation required.

In the preceding example, the ops of the graphs are as follows:

```
hello = tf.constant('Hello, TensorFlow!')
a = tf.constant(12)
b = tf.constant(34)
```

These `tf.constant()` methods create a constant op that will be added as a node in the graph. You can see how a string and integer are added to the graph.

Session

After building the graph, we have to execute it, right? For computing a graph, we should put it in a session. A `Session` class in TensorFlow places all ops or nodes onto computational devices such as CPU or GPU.

Here is how we create a `Session` object in TensorFlow:

```
sess = tf.Session()
```

For running the ops in a graph, the `Session` class provides methods to run the entire graph:

```
print(sess.run(hello))
```

It will execute the op called `hello` and print "`Hello, TensorFlow`" in Terminal.

Variables

During execution, we may need to maintain the state of the ops. We can do so by using `tf.Variable()`. Let's check out an example declaration of `tf.Variable()`:

This line will create a variable called `counter` and initialize it to scalar value 0.

```
state = tf.Variable(0, name="counter")
```

Here are the ops to assign a value to the variable:

```
one = tf.constant(1)
update = tf.assign(state, one)
```

If you are working with variables, we have to initialize them all at once using the following function:

```
init_op = tf.initialize_all_variables()
```

After initialization, we have to run the graph for putting this into effect. We can run the previous ops using the following code:

```
sess = tf.Session()
sess.run(init_op)
print(sess.run(state))
sess.run(update)
```

Fetches

To fetch the outputs from the graph, we have to execute the run() method, which is inside the Session object. We can pass the ops to the run() method and retrieve the output as tensors:

```
a = tf.constant(12)
b = tf.constant(34)
add = tf.add(a,b)
sess = tf.Sessions()
result = sess.run(add)
print(result)
```

In the preceding code, the value of result will be 12+34.

Feeds

Until now, we have been dealing with constants and variables. We can also feed tensors during the execution of a graph. Here we have an example of feeding tensors during execution. For feeding a tensor, first we have to define the feed object using the tf.placeholder() function. After defining two feed objects, we can see how to use it inside sess.run():

```
x = tf.placeholder(tf.float32)
y = tf.placeholder(tf.float32)

output = tf.mul(input1, input2)

with tf.Session() as sess:
  print(sess.run([output], feed_dict={x:[8.], y:[2.]}))

# output:
# [array([ 16.], dtype=float32)]
```

Writing our first code in TensorFlow

Let's start coding using TensorFlow. We are again going to write basic code that performs matrix operations such as matrix addition, multiplication, scalar multiplication and multiplication with a scalar from *1* to *99*. The code is written for demonstrating basic capabilities of TensorFlow, which we have discussed previously.

Here is the code for all these operations:

```
import tensorflow as tf
import time

matrix_1 = tf.Variable([[1,2,3],[4,5,6],[7,8,9]],name="mat1")
matrix_2 = tf.Variable([[1,2,3],[4,5,6],[7,8,9]],name="mat2")

scalar = tf.constant(5)
number = tf.Variable(1, name="counter")

add_msg = tf.constant("\nResult of matrix addition\n")
mul_msg = tf.constant("\nResult of matrix multiplication\n")
scalar_mul_msg = tf.constant("\nResult of scalar multiplication\n")
number_mul_msg = tf.constant("\nResult of Number multiplication\n")


mat_add = tf.add(matrix_1,matrix_2)
mat_mul = tf.matmul(matrix_1,matrix_2)
mat_scalar_mul = tf.mul(scalar,mat_mul)
mat_number_mul = tf.mul(number,mat_mul)


init_op = tf.initialize_all_variables()
sess = tf.Session()
tf.device("/cpu:0")
sess.run(init_op)

for i in range(1,100):

  print "\nFor i =",i

  print(sess.run(add_msg))
  print(sess.run(mat_add))

  print(sess.run(mul_msg))
  print(sess.run(mat_mul))
  print(sess.run(scalar_mul_msg))
  print(sess.run(mat_scalar_mul))
```

```
        update = tf.assign(number,tf.constant(i))
        sess.run(update)
        print(sess.run(number_mul_msg))
        print(sess.run(mat_number_mul))

        time.sleep(0.1)

    sess.close()
```

As we know, we have to import the `tensorflow` module to access its APIs. We are also importing the `time` module to provide a delay in the loop:

```
import tensorflow as tf
import time
```

Here is how to define variables in TensorFlow. We are defining `matrix_1` and `matrix_2` variables, two 3×3 matrices:

```
matrix_1 = tf.Variable([[1,2,3],[4,5,6],[7,8,9]],name="mat1")
matrix_2 = tf.Variable([[1,2,3],[4,5,6],[7,8,9]],name="mat2")
```

In addition to the preceding matrix variables, we are defining a constant and a scalar variable called `counter`. These values are used for scalar multiplication operations. We will change the value of `counter` from *1* to *99*, and each value will be multiplied with a matrix:

```
scalar = tf.constant(5)
number = tf.Variable(1, name="counter")
```

The following is how we define strings in TF. Each string is defined as a constant.

```
add_msg = tf.constant("\nResult of matrix addition\n")
mul_msg = tf.constant("\nResult of matrix multiplication\n")
scalar_mul_msg = tf.constant("\nResult of scalar multiplication\n")
number_mul_msg = tf.constant("\nResult of Number multiplication\n")
```

The following are the main ops in the graph doing the computation. The first line will add two matrices, second line will multiply those same two, the third will perform scalar multiplication with one value, and the fourth will perform scalar multiplication with a scalar variable.

```
mat_add = tf.add(matrix_1,matrix_2)
mat_mul = tf.matmul(matrix_1,matrix_2)
mat_scalar_mul = tf.mul(scalar,mat_mul)
mat_number_mul = tf.mul(number,mat_mul)
```

If we have TF variable declarations, we have to initialize them using the following line of code:

```
init_op = tf.initialize_all_variables()
```

Here, we are creating a `Session()` object:

```
sess = tf.Session()
```

This is one thing we hadn't discussed earlier. We can perform the computation on any device according to our priority. It can be a CPU or GPU. Here, you can see that the device is a CPU:

```
tf.device("/cpu:0")
```

This line of code will run the graph to initialize all variables:

```
sess.run(init_op)
```

In the following loop, we can see the running of a TF graph. This loop puts each op inside the `run()` method and fetches its results. To be able to see each output, we are putting a delay on the loop:

```
for i in range(1,100):

    print "\nFor i =",i

    print(sess.run(add_msg))
    print(sess.run(mat_add))

    print(sess.run(mul_msg))
    print(sess.run(mat_mul))

    print(sess.run(scalar_mul_msg))
    print(sess.run(mat_scalar_mul))

    update = tf.assign(number,tf.constant(i))
    sess.run(update)
    print(sess.run(number_mul_msg))
    print(sess.run(mat_number_mul))

    time.sleep(0.1)
```

After all this computation, we have to release the `Session()` object to free up the resources:

```
sess.close()
```

The following is the output:

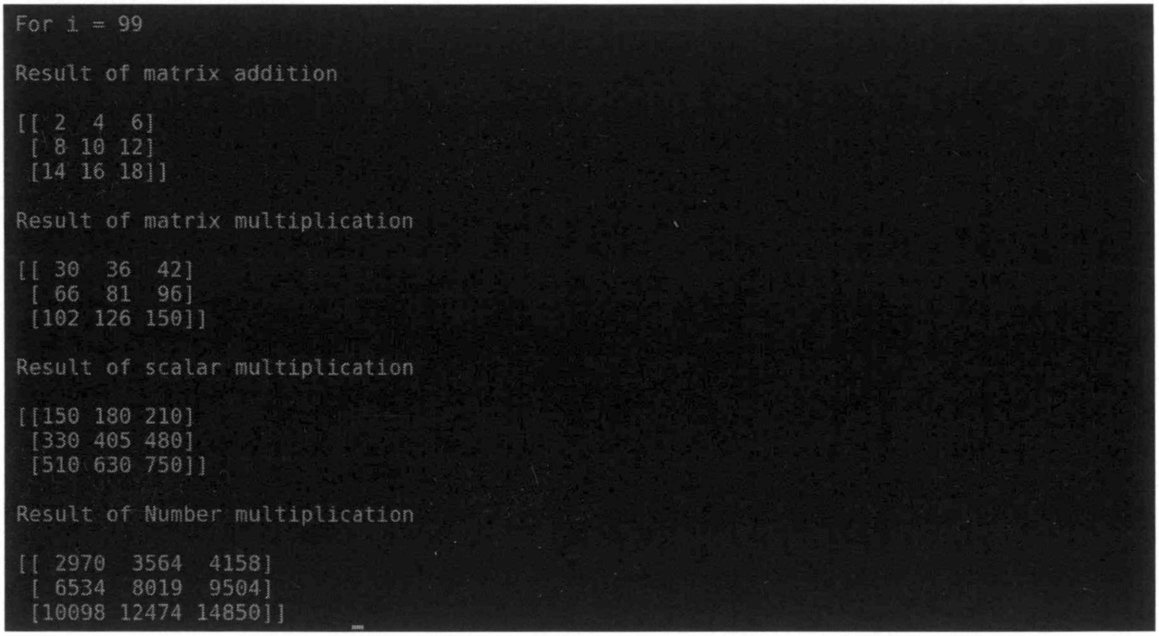

```
For i = 99

Result of matrix addition

[[ 2  4  6]
 [ 8 10 12]
 [14 16 18]]

Result of matrix multiplication

[[ 30  36  42]
 [ 66  81  96]
 [102 126 150]]

Result of scalar multiplication

[[150 180 210]
 [330 405 480]
 [510 630 750]]

Result of Number multiplication

[[ 2970  3564  4158]
 [ 6534  8019  9504]
 [10098 12474 14850]]
```

Figure 5: Output of basic TensorFlow code

Image recognition using ROS and TensorFlow

After discussing the basics of TensorFlow, let's start discussing how to interface ROS and TensorFlow to do some serious work. In this section, we are going to deal with image recognition using these two.

There is a simple package to perform image recognition using TensorFlow and ROS. Here is the ROS package to do this:

```
https://github.com/qboticslabs/rostensorflow
```

This package was forked from `https://github.com/OTL/rostensorflow`. The package basically contains a ROS Python node that subscribes to images from the ROS webcam driver and performs image recognition using TensorFlow APIs. The node will print the detected object and its probability.

 This code was developed using TensorFlow tutorials from the following link:
`https://www.tensorflow.org/versions/r0.11/tutorials/image_recogn ition/index.html`.

The image recognition is mainly done using a model called deep convolution network. It can achieve high accuracy in the field of image recognition. An improved model we are going to use here is Inception-v3 (`https://arxiv.org/abs/1512.00567`).

 This model is trained for the **ImageNet Large Scale Visual Recognition Challenge (ILSVRC)**
(`http://image-net.org/challenges/LSVRC/2016/index`) using data from 2012.

When we run the node, it will download a trained Inception-v3 model to the computer and classify the object according to the webcam images. You can see the detected object's name and its probability in Terminal.

There are a few prerequisites to run this node. Let's go through the dependencies.

Prerequisites

For running a ROS image recognition node, you should install the following dependencies. The first is `cv-bridge`, which helps us convert a ROS image message into OpenCV image data type and vice versa. The second is `cv-camera`, which is one of the ROS camera drivers. Here's how to install them:

```
$sudo apt-get install ros-kinetic-cv-bridge ros-kinetic-cv-camera
```

The ROS image recognition node

You can download the ROS image recognition package from GitHub; it's also available in the book's code bundle. The `image_recognition.py` program can publish detected results in the `/result` topic, which is of the `std_msgs/String` type and is subscribed to image data from the ROS camera driver from the `/image` (`sensor_msgs/Image`) topic.

So how does `image_recognition.py` work?

First take a look at the main modules imported to this node. As you know, `rospy` has ROS Python APIs. The ROS camera driver publishes ROS image messages, so here we have to import `Image` messages from `sensor_msgs` to handle those image messages. To convert a ROS image to the OpenCV data type and vice versa, we need `cv_bridge` and, of course, the `numpy`, `tensorflow`, and `tensorflow imagenet` modules to classify of images and download the Inception-v3 model from tensorflow.org. Here are the imports:

```
import rospy
from sensor_msgs.msg import Image
from std_msgs.msg import String
from cv_bridge import CvBridge
import cv2
import numpy as np
import tensorflow as tf
from tensorflow.models.image.imagenet import classify_image
```

The following code snippet is the constructor for a class called `RosTensorFlow()`:

```
class RosTensorFlow():
    def __init__(self):
```

The constructor call has the API for downloading the trained Inception-v3 model from tensorflow.org:

```
classify_image.maybe_download_and_extract()
```

Now, we are creating a TensorFlow `Session()` object, then creating a graph from a saved `GraphDef` file, and returning a handle for it. The `GraphDef` file is available in the code bundle.

```
self._session = tf.Session()
classify_image.create_graph()
```

This line creates a `cv_bridge` object for the ROS-OpenCV image conversion:

```
self._cv_bridge = CvBridge()
```

Here are the subscriber and publisher handles of the node:

```
self._sub = rospy.Subscriber('image', Image, self.callback,
queue_size=1)
        self._pub = rospy.Publisher('result', String, queue_size=1)
```

Here are some parameters used for recognition thresholding and the number of top predictions:

```
self.score_threshold = rospy.get_param('~score_threshold', 0.1)
self.use_top_k = rospy.get_param('~use_top_k', 5)
```

Here is the image call back in which a ROS image message is converted to OpenCV data type:

```
def callback(self, image_msg):
    cv_image = self._cv_bridge.imgmsg_to_cv2(image_msg, "bgr8")
    image_data = cv2.imencode('.jpg', cv_image)[1].tostring()
```

The following code runs the `softmax` tensor by feeding `image_data` as input to the graph. The `'softmax:0'` part is a tensor containing the normalized prediction across 1,000 labels.

```
softmax_tensor =
    self._session.graph.get_tensor_by_name('softmax:0')
```

The `'DecodeJpeg/contents:0'` line is a tensor containing a string providing JPEG encoding of the image:

```
predictions = self._session.run(
    softmax_tensor, {'DecodeJpeg/contents:0': image_data})
predictions = np.squeeze(predictions)
```

The following section of code will look for a matching object string and its probability and publish it through the topic called `/result`:

```
node_lookup = classify_image.NodeLookup()
top_k = predictions.argsort()[-self.use_top_k:][::-1]
for node_id in top_k:
    human_string = node_lookup.id_to_string(node_id)
    score = predictions[node_id]
    if score > self.score_threshold:
        rospy.loginfo('%s (score = %.5f)' % (human_string,
score))
        self._pub.publish(human_string)
```

The following is the main code of this node. It simply initializes the class and calls the `main()` method inside the `RosTensorFlow()` object. The `main` method will `spin()` the node and execute a callback whenever an image comes into the `/image` topic.

```
def main(self):
     rospy.spin()
if __name__ == '__main__':
    rospy.init_node('rostensorflow')
    tensor = RosTensorFlow()
    tensor.main()
```

Running the ROS image recognition node

Let's go through how we can run the image recognition node.

First, you have to plug a UVC webcam, which we used in Chapter 2, Face Detection and Tracking Using ROS, OpenCV and Dynamixel Servos
Run `roscore`:

$ roscore

Run the webcam driver:

$ rosrun cv_camera cv_camera_node

Run the image recognition node, simply using the following command:

$ python image_recognition.py image:=/cv_camera/image_raw

When we run the recognition node, it will download the inception model and extract it into the `/tmp/imagenet` folder. You can do it manually by downloading inception-v3 from the following link:

http://download.tensorflow.org/models/image/imagenet/inception-2015-12-05.tgz

You can copy this file into the `/tmp/imagenet` folder:

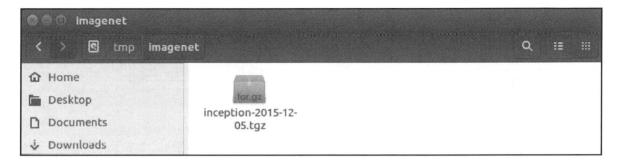

Figure 6: Inception model in the /tmp/imagenet folder

You can see the result by echoing the following topic:

```
$ rostopic echo /result
```

You can view the camera images using following command:

```
$ rosrun image_view image_view image:= /cv_camera/image_raw
```

Here is the output from the recognizer. The recognizer detects the device as a cell phone.

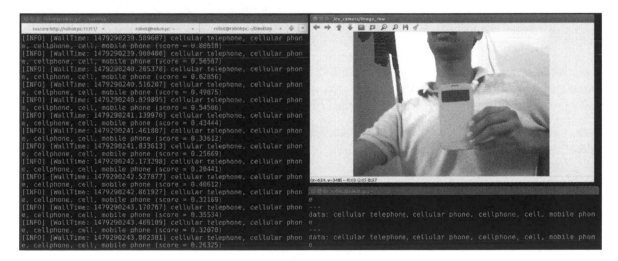

Figure 7: Output from recognizer node

In the next detection, the object is detected as a water bottle:

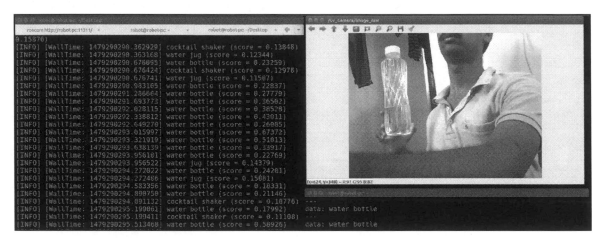

Figure 8: Output from recognizer node detecting a water bottle

Introducing to scikit-learn

Until now, we have been discussing deep neural networks and some of their applications in robotics and image processing. Apart from neural networks, there are a lot of models available to classify data and predict using them.

Generally, in machine learning, we can teach the model using supervised or unsupervised learning. In supervised learning, we training the model against a dataset, but in unsupervised, it discover groups of related observations called clusters instead.

There are lot of libraries available for working with other machine learning algorithms. We'll look at one such library called `scikit-learn`; we can play with most of the standard machine learning algorithms and implement our own application using it.

scikit-learn (`http://scikit-learn.org/`) is one of the most popular open source machine learning libraries for Python. It provides an implementation of algorithms for performing classification, regression, and clustering. It also provides functions to extract features from a dataset, train the model, and evaluate it.

scikit-learn is an extension of a popular scientific python library called **SciPy** (https://www.scipy.org/). scikit-learn strongly binds with other popular Python libraries, such as NumPy and matplotlib. Using NumPy, we can create efficient multidimensional arrays, and using matplotlib, we can visualize the data.

scikit-learn is well documented and has wrappers for performing **Support Vector Machine (SVM)** and natural language processing functions.

Installing scikit-learn on Ubuntu 16.04 LTS

Installing scikit-learn on Ubuntu is easy and straightforward. You can install it either using `apt-get install` or `pip`.

Here is the command to install scikit-learn using `apt-get install`:

```
$ sudo apt-get install python-sklearn
```

We can install it using `pip` using the following command:

```
$ sudo pip install scikit-learn
```

After installing scikit-learn, we can test the installation by doing following commands in Python Terminal.

```
>>> import sklearn
>>> sklearn.__version__
'0.17'
```

Congratulations, you have successfully set up scikit-learn!

Introducing to SVM and its application in robotics

We have set up scikit-learn, so what is next? Actually, we are going to discuss a popular machine learning technique called SVM and its applications in robotics. After discussing the basics, we can implement a ROS application using SVM.

So what is SVM? SVM is a supervised machine learning algorithm that can be used for classification or regression. In SVM, we plot each data item in n-dimensional space along with its value. After plotting, it performs a classification by finding a hyper-plane that separates those data points. This is how the basic classification is done!

SVM can perform better for small datasets, but it does not do well if the dataset is very large. Also, it will not be suitable if the dataset has noisy data.

SVM is widely used in robotics, especially in computer vision for classifying objects and also for classifying various kinds of sensor data in robots.

In the next section, we will see how we can implement SVM using scikit-learn and make an application using it.

Implementing an SVM-ROS application

Following shows the aim of this project.

In this application we are going to classify a sensor data in three ways. The sensor values are assumed to be in between 0 to 30,000 and we are having a dataset which is having the sensor value mapping. For example, for a sensor value, you can assign the value belongs to 1, 2, or 3. To test the SVM, we are making another ROS node called virtual sensor node, which can publish value in between 0 to 30000. The trained SVM model can able to classify the virtual sensor value. This method can be adopted for any kind of sensors for classifying its data.

Before embedding SVM in ROS, here's some basic code in Python using `sklearn` to implement SVM.

The first thing is importing the `sklearn` and `numpy` modules. The `sklearn` module has the `svm` module, which is going to be used in this code, and `numpy` is used for making multi-dimensional arrays:

```
from sklearn import svm
import numpy as np
```

For training SVM, we need an input (predictor) and output (target); here, X is the input and y is the required output:

```
X = np.array([[-1, -1], [-2, -1], [1, 1], [2, 1]])
y = np.array([1, 1, 2, 2])
```

After defining X and y, just create an instance of **SVM Classification (SVC) object**.

Feed X and y to the SVC object for training the model. After feeding X and y, we can feed an input that may not be in X, and it can predict the y value corresponding to the given input:

```
model = svm.SVC(kernel='linear',C=1,gamma=1)
model.fit(X,y)
print(model.predict([[-0.8,-1]]))
```

The preceding code will give an output of 1.

Now, we are going to implement a ROS application that does the same thing. Here, we are creating a virtual sensor node that can publish random values from 0 to 30,000. The ROS-SVM node will subscribe to those values and classify them using the preceding APIs. The learning in SVM is done from a CSV data file.

You can view the complete application package in book code; it's called `ros_ml`. Inside the `ros_ml/scripts` folder, you can see nodes such as `ros_svm.py` and `virtual_sensor.py`.

First, let's take a look at the virtual sensor node. The code is very simple and self-explanatory. It simply generates a random number between 0 and 30,000 and publishes it to the `/sensor_read` topic:

```python
#!/usr/bin/env python
import rospy
from std_msgs.msg import Int32
import random

def send_data():
    rospy.init_node('virtual_sensor', anonymous=True)
    rospy.loginfo("Sending virtual sensor data")
    pub = rospy.Publisher('sensor_read', Int32, queue_size=1)
    rate = rospy.Rate(10) # 10hz

    while not rospy.is_shutdown():
        sensor_reading = random.randint(0,30000)
        pub.publish(sensor_reading)
        rate.sleep()

if __name__ == '__main__':
    try:
        send_data()
    except rospy.ROSInterruptException:
        pass
```

The next node is `ros_svm.py`. This node reads from a data file from a data folder inside the `ros_ml` package. The current data file is named `pos_readings.csv`, which contains the sensor and target values. Here is a snippet from that file:

```
5125,5125,1
6210,6210,1
. . . . . . . . . . . . . .

10125,10125,2
6410,6410,2
5845,5845,2
. . . . . . . . . . . . . .

14325,14325,3
16304,16304,3
18232,18232,3
. . . . . . . . . . . . . . .
```

The `ros_svm.py` node reads this file, trains the SVC, and predicts each value from the virtual sensor topic. The node has a class called `Classify_Data()`, which has methods to read the CSV file and train and predict it using scikit APIs.

We'll step through how these nodes are started:

Start `roscore`:

```
$ roscore
```

Switch to the script folder of `ros_ml`:

```
$ roscd ros_ml/scripts
```

Run the ROS SVM classifier node:

```
$ python ros_svm.py
```

Run the virtual sensor in another Terminal:

```
$ rosrun ros_ml virtual_sensor.py
```

Here is the output we get from the SVM node:

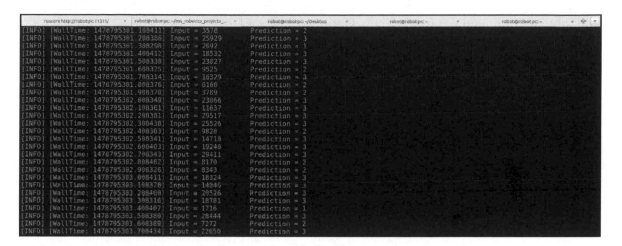

Figure 9: ROS – SVM node output

Questions

- What basically is a neural network?
- What is deep learning?
- Why do we use TensorFlow for deep learning?
- What are the main concepts in TensorFlow?
- Why do we use scikit-learn for machine learning?

Summary

In this chapter, we mainly discussed the various machine learning techniques and libraries that can be interfaced with ROS. We started with the basics of machine learning and deep learning. Then we started working with TensorFlow, which is an open source Python library mainly for performing deep learning. We discussed basic code using TensorFlow and later combined those capabilities with ROS for an image recognition application. After discussing Tensorflow and deep learning, we discussed another Python library called scikit-learn used for machine learning applications. We saw what SVM is and saw how to implement it using scikit-learn. Later, we implemented a sample application using ROS and scikit-learn for classifying sensor data.

In the next chapter, we will discuss ROS on Android and MATLAB.

8
ROS on MATLAB and Android

As you all know, MATLAB is one of the powerful numerical computation tools available for research, education, and commercial applications. Also, we don't need any more explanation of the Android OS, which is one of the most popular mobile operating systems. In this chapter, we will mainly work with the ROS interface of MATLAB and Android.

By combining the capabilities of MATLAB and Android in ROS, we can create powerful robotic projects. Here are the main topics we will discuss in this chapter:

- Getting started with the ROS-MATLAB interface
- Communicating from MATLAB to a ROS network
- Controlling a ROS robot from MATLAB
- Getting started with Android and its ROS interface
- Installing the ROS-Android interface
- Playing with ROS-Android applications
- ROS-Android code walk through
- Creating a basic application using the ROS-Android interface

Getting started with the ROS-MATLAB interface

The ROS-MATLAB interface is a useful interface for researchers and students for prototyping their robot algorithms in MATLAB and testing it on ROS-compatible robots. The robotics system toolbox in MATLAB provides the interface between MATLAB and ROS. We can prototype our algorithm and test it on a ROS-enabled robot or in robot simulators such as Gazebo and V-REP (`http://www.coppeliarobotics.com/downloads.html`). From MATLAB, we can publish or subscribe to a topic, such as a ROS node, and we can make it a ROS master. The MATLAB-ROS interface has most of the ROS functionalities that we need.

Here is a block diagram shows how MATLAB is communicating with a robot which is running on ROS.

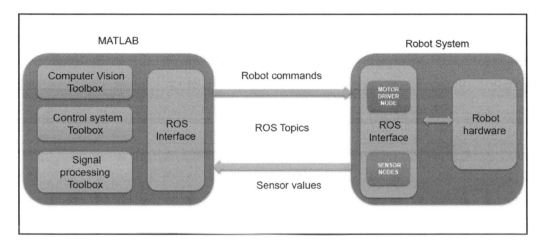

Figure 1: The MATLAB – Robot communication diagram

From the preceding figure, you can understand, MATLAB is equipped with powerful toolboxes such as computer vision, control system and signal processing. We can fetch the data from robot through ROS interface and process using these toolbox. After processing sensor data, we can also send control commands to robot. These communications are all occurs via ROS-MATLAB interface.

Here are some of the main features of the ROS – MATLAB interface:

- It can seamlessly connect to another ROS network and can work with various robot capabilities. We can also visualize the robot sensor data in MATLAB.
- We can create ROS nodes, publishers, and subscribers directly from MATLAB and Simulink.
- We can send and receive topics using ROS messages and ROS custom messages.
- It has full support for ROS services.
- We get ROS functionality from any OS platform (Windows, Linux, or Mac).
- We can make MATLAB the ROS master.
- We can import ROS bag files and analyze, visualize, and post-process logged data.
- It provides full-fledged communication with robot simulators such as Gazebo and V-REP for offline programming.
- We can create standalone ROS C++ nodes from a Simulink model.

Setting Robotics Toolbox in MATLAB

Here is the link to download a trial or purchase the Robotics Toolbox in MATLAB (`https://in.mathworks.com/products/robotics.html`). This toolbox is compatible with MATLAB version 2013 onward. If you don't have MATLAB, you can test the chapter's code using a trial version; if you have it, buy or download a trial version of Robotic Toolbox.

Basic ROS functions in MATLAB

After setting up Robotics Toolbox in MATLAB, we can start working on the important functions of MATLAB that are used to interact with a ROS network. Let's look at them with examples.

Initializing a ROS network

Before running a ROS node, we have to run the `roscore` command, right? The `roscore` command will start a ROS master, and other ROS nodes can find each other through it. In MATLAB, instead of the `roscore` command, we can use the `rosinit` function to start a ROS master.

```
>> rosinit
Initializing ROS master on http://DESKTOP-IOQ6CMI:11311/.
Initializing global node /matlab_global_node_97458 with NodeURI http://DESKTOP-IOQ6CMI:53329/
>>
>>
>>
```

Figure 2 : The rosinit function in MATLAB

The `rosinit` function can start a ROS master and a global node that is connected to the master. Here, we can see that MATLAB itself can act as a ROS master and other nodes can connect to it. We can also connect to a ROS network from MATLAB. We'll cover that in the next section. In such a setup, the ROS master is running on a different system, either on a ROS robot or ROS PC. Let's try some of the ROS commands in MATLAB to list ROS nodes, topics, and all that. The good thing about the MATLAB – ROS interface is that the commands of Robotics Toolbox are similar to the actual ROS bash commands. Let's go through a few commands to list out ROS parameters.

Listing ROS nodes, topics, and messages

The commands to inspect nodes, topics, and messages are similar to ROS bash commands. MATLAB provides a command to start sample ROS nodes that can publish topics. You can just call `exampleHelperROSCreateSampleNetwork` to start these nodes.

```
Command Window
>> exampleHelperROSCreateSampleNetwork
>>
>> rosnode list
/matlab_global_node_97458
/node_1
/node_2
/node_3
>>
>> rostopic list
/pose
/rosout
/scan
>>
```

Figure 3: ROS-MATLAB commands

You can see that the usage of rosnode and rostopic is the same as with real ROS commands. You can even echo the rostopic using rostopic echo /topic_name. Here is one example, in which we are echoing a topic called /pose:

```
Command Window
>> rostopic echo /pose

  Linear
    X :  -1.697815259945545
    Y :   1.457794712253322
    Z :  -2.010832346468831
  Angular
    X :  -5.497355440324553
    Y :   4.095877993429104
    Z :   3.061124697335989
---

  Linear
    X :  -1.690699184539839
    Y :   1.450160062487131
    Z :  -2.020887543487248
  Angular
    X :  -5.532034874430542
    Y :   4.088379517868862
    Z :   3.041723002906606
---
```

Figure 4: ROS topic echo output

You can get the complete list of ROS commands in MATLAB using the `help` command.

Here is the syntax for doing so:

```
>> help robotics.ros
```

This is the screenshot of the list of commands with MATLAB for ROS:

```
Command Window
>> help robotics.ros
  ros (Robot Operating System)
    rosinit            - Initialize the ros system
    rosshutdown        - Shut down the ros system

    rosmessage         - Create a ros message
    rospublisher       - Create a ros publisher
    rossubscriber      - Create a ros subscriber
    rossvcclient       - Create a ros service client
    rossvcserver       - Create a ros service server
    rosactionclient    - Create a ros action client
    rostype            - View available ros message types

    rosaction          - Get information about actions in the ros network
    rosmsg             - Get information about messages and message types
    rosnode            - Get information about nodes in the ros network
    rosservice         - Get information about services in the ros network
    rostopic           - Get information about topics in the ros network

    rosbag             - Open and parse a rosbag log file
    rosparam           - Get and set values on the parameter server
    rosrate            - Execute loop at fixed frequency using ros time
    rostf              - Receive, send, and apply ros transformations

    rosduration        - Create a ros duration object
    rostime            - Access ros time functionality
fx
```

Figure 5: List of ROS-MATLAB commands

Communicating from MATLAB to a ROS network

We have worked with some MATLAB commands and we've understood that we can communicate with ROS from MATLAB. But the previous commands were executed in a MATLAB terminal by making MATLAB the ROS master. But what do we do when we need to communicate with a ROS network or a ROS-based robot? The method is simple.

Assuming your PC has MATLAB and the ROS PC/robot is connected to the same network. It can be connected either through LAN or Wi-Fi. If the PC and robot are connected to the same network, both should have identical IP addresses. The first step is to find each device's IP address.

If your MATLAB installation is in Windows, you can open Command Prompt window by simply searching for cmd in the search window; then, enter the ipconfig command. This will list the network adapters and their details:

```
Wireless LAN adapter Wi-Fi:

    Connection-specific DNS Suffix  . :
    Link-local IPv6 Address . . . . . : fe80::b05d:3405:9b99:8736%9
    IPv4 Address. . . . . . . . . . . : 192.168.1.101
    Subnet Mask . . . . . . . . . . . : 255.255.255.0
    Default Gateway . . . . . . . . . : 192.168.1.1
```

Figure 6: Wi-Fi adapter details and its IP in a MATLAB system

Here you can see that the PC running MATLAB and the ROS system are connected through Wi-Fi, and the IP is marked. If you are using MATLAB from Linux, you can use the ifconfig command instead of ipconfig. You can also get the IP of the ROS-running PC, which could be a Linux PC, using the same command.

```
wlx00177c2e2869 Link encap:Ethernet  HWaddr 00:17:7c:2e:28:69
          inet addr:192.168.1.102  Bcast:192.168.1.255  Mask:255.255.255.0
          inet6 addr: fe80::24f:8bd5:fb19:828f/64 Scope:Link
          UP BROADCAST RUNNING MULTICAST  MTU:1500  Metric:1
          RX packets:953 errors:0 dropped:0 overruns:0 frame:0
          TX packets:391 errors:0 dropped:0 overruns:0 carrier:0
          collisions:0 txqueuelen:1000
          RX bytes:115747 (115.7 KB)  TX bytes:147426 (147.4 KB)
```

Figure 7: Wi-Fi adapter details and IP of ROS system

So in this case, the IP address of the MATLAB system is 192.168.1.101 and that of the ROS system is 192.168.1.102. Here is how the network looks like:

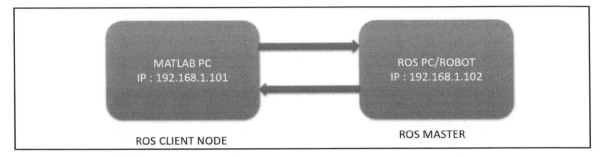

Figure 8: Connecting MATLAB to a ROS network

Connecting from MATLAB to the ROS network is pretty easy. First, we have to set the ROS_MASTER_URI variable, which is the IP of the ROS PC/robot where the ROS master is running. You have to mention the port along with the IP; the default port is 11311.

Before connecting to the ROS network, be sure that you run roscore on the ROS PC/robot. MATLAB can connect to the ROS network if there is a ROS master running on it.

The following command helps us connect to the ROS network:

```
>> setenv('ROS_MASTER_URI','http://192.168.1.102:11311')
>> rosinit
```

```
>> setenv('ROS_MASTER_URI','http://192.168.1.102:11311')
>> rosinit
The value of the ROS_MASTER_URI environment variable, http://192.168.1.102:11311, will be used
Initializing global node /matlab_global_node_75002 with NodeURI http://192.168.1.101:63438/
fx >> |
```

Figure 9: Connecting to ROS network

You can also do this using following command:

```
>> rosinit('192.168.1.102', 'NodeHost', '192.168.1.101')
```

Here, the first argument is the ROS network IP and next one is the IP of the host. If the connection is successful, we will get a message like in preceding screenshot.

After connecting to the network, run an example node on the ROS PC/robot. You can use following node for testing:

```
$ rosrun roscpp_tutorials talker
```

This node basically publishes string data (std_msgs/String) to the /chatter topic. You can see the node output from the following screenshot:

```
robot@robot-pc:~$ rosrun roscpp_tutorials talker
[ INFO] [1481050186.526044121]: hello world 0
[ INFO] [1481050186.626166884]: hello world 1
[ INFO] [1481050186.726160683]: hello world 2
[ INFO] [1481050186.826158292]: hello world 3
[ INFO] [1481050186.926131846]: hello world 4
```

Figure 10: roscpp talker node

Now list the topics in MATLAB and see the magic!

```
>> rostopic list
```

You will see something like the following screenshot:

```
>> rostopic list
/chatter
/rosout
/rosout_agg
fx >>
```

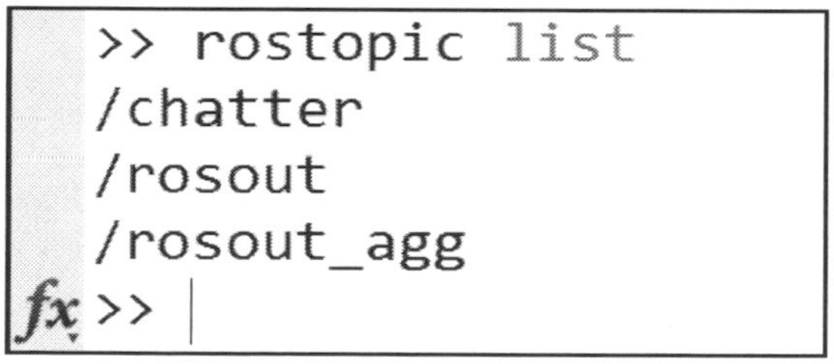

Figure 11: roscpp talker node

We can also publish values from MATLAB to ROS. Let's see how.

This will connect to the ROS network:

```
>>setenv('ROS_MASTER_URI','http://192.168.1.102:11311')
>> rosinit
```

This will create a handle for the ROS publisher. The publisher topic name is `/talker` and message type is `std_msgs/String`.

```
>> chatpub = rospublisher('/talker', 'std_msgs/String');
```

This line will create a new message definition:

```
>> msg = rosmessage(chatpub);
```

Here, we are putting data into the message:

```
>> msg.Data = 'Hello, From Matlab';
```

Now let's send the message through the topic:

```
>> send(chatpub,msg);
```

With this command, we are latching the message to the topic:

```
>> latchpub = rospublisher('/talker', 'IsLatching', true);
```

After executing these commands in MATLAB, check the topic list from the ROS PC and echo it. You will get the same message, like this:

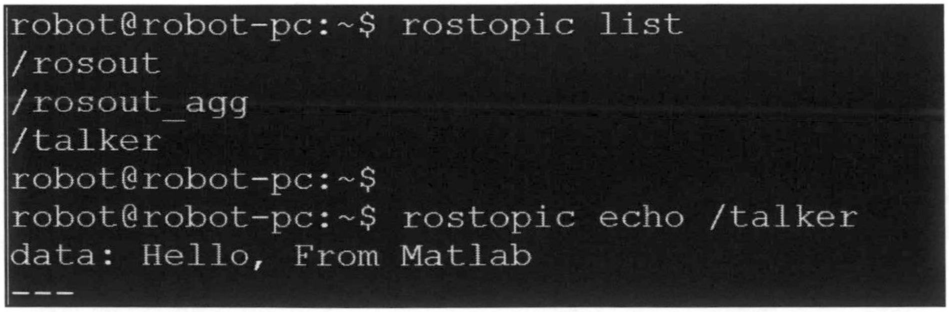

```
robot@robot-pc:~$ rostopic list
/rosout
/rosout_agg
/talker
robot@robot-pc:~$
robot@robot-pc:~$ rostopic echo /talker
data: Hello, From Matlab
---
```

Figure 12: Listing rostopic from MATLAB on a ROS PC

Controlling a ROS robot from MATLAB

Here is an interesting MATLAB GUI application that uses ROS APIs to remotely control a robot. The final application will look like the following:

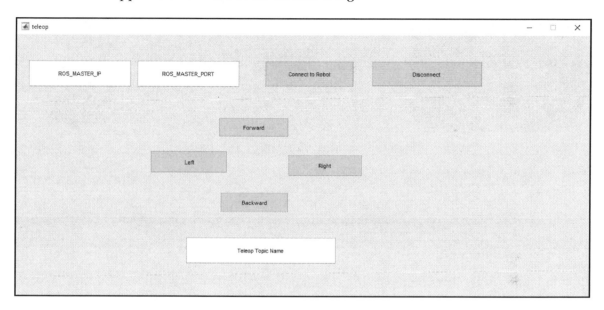

Figure 13: MATLAB-ROS application GUI

In this application, we can put in the ROS master IP, port, and the teleop topic of the robot in its GUI itself. When we press the connect button, the MATLAB application will connect to the ROS network. Now, we can move the robot by pressing the **Forward**, **Backward**, **Left**, and **Right** buttons.

Here is the design block diagram of this application:

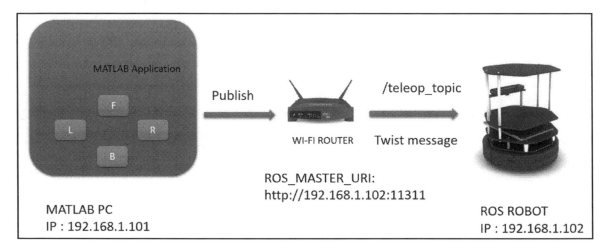

Figure 14: MATLAB-ROS application design block diagram

So let's look at how we can build an application like this.

Here are some of the frequently asking questions in ROS-MATLAB interface

1. How to run multiple ROS nodes in MATLAB?

    Yes, we can run multiple ROS nodes in MATLAB. The following command in MATLAB will give you an example to do it.

```
>>>openExample('robotics/RunMultipleROSNodesToPerformDifferentTasksExample'
)
```

2. Does MATLAB support launch files?

    No, there is no XML kind launch files in MATLAB, but we can start and end nodes in a MATLAB script which will work almost like a launch file.

3. What features exist in both MATLAB and ROS?

    For example plotting data, any recommendations for the use of each?

4. There are plotting tools available in ROS and MATLAB. The tools such as `rqt_gui` help to plot different kind of data which are coming as topics. If you want to play with data and its analysis, MATLAB is the good choice.

Designing the MATLAB GUI application

MATLAB provides easy ways to design a GUI. Here is one popular method to create a GUI using **GUI development environment (GUIDE)** (https://in.mathworks.com/discovery/matlab-gui.html). To start GUIDE in MATLAB, just type `guide` in your MATLAB command line:

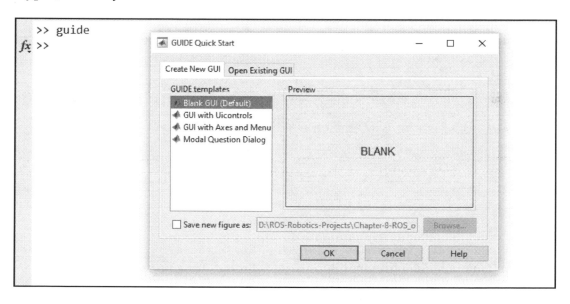

Figure 15: MATLAB GUI wizard

You can select a **Blank GUI** and press **OK**. You will get a blank GUI, and you can add buttons and text boxes according to your requirements. The following figure shows the basic GUI elements in GUIDE. You can see an empty GUI form and toolbox. We can just drag components from the toolbox to the form. For example, if we need a push button and text edit box, we can just drag and drop those items to the empty form and align them on the form:

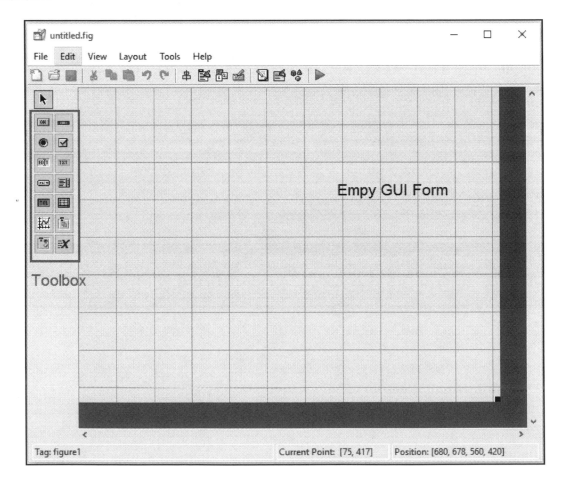

Figure 16: MATLAB GUI empty form

After assigning buttons, we have to generate a callback function for them, which will be executed once the button is pressed (or the text edit box is changed). You can create the callback function from the option highlighted in the following figure. When you save it, you will get a *.m file too. This is the MATLAB code file, in which we are going to write the callback functions.

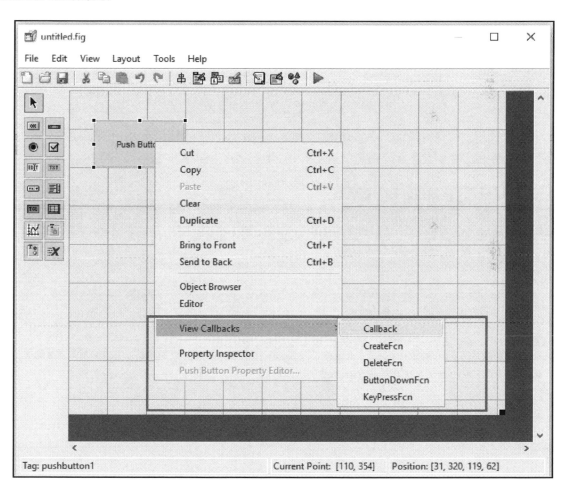

Figure 17: Inserting callback functions

The preceding figure shows how to insert a callback for each button. Right-click on the button and press the **Callback** option. You'll see the empty callback function for this button:

```
% --- Executes on button press in pushbutton1.
function pushbutton1_Callback(hObject, eventdata, handles)
% hObject    handle to pushbutton1 (see GCBO)
% eventdata  reserved - to be defined in a future version of MATLAB
% handles    structure with handles and user data (see GUIDATA)
```

Figure 18: An empty callback function

In the next section, we will discuss the content of each callback of the application.

Explaining callbacks

You can get the complete code from `chapter_8_codes/Matlab/teleop.m`. Let's look at the content and functions of each callback. The first callback we are going to see is for the **ROS MASTER IP** edit box:

```
function edit1_Callback(hObject, eventdata, handles)
global ros_master_ip
ros_master_ip = get(hObject,'String')
```

When we enter an IP address from the ROS network in this edit box, it will store the IP address as a string in a global variable called `ros_master_ip`. If you don't enter the IP, then a default value is loaded, defined outside the callback.

Here are the initial values of `ros_master_ip`, `ros_master_port`, and `teleop topic`.

```
ros_master_ip = '192.168.1.102';
ros_master_port = '11311';
teleop_topic_name = '/cmd_vel_mux/input/teleop';
```

If we don't provide any values in the textbox, these initial values get loaded.

The next GUI element is for obtaining the **ROS MASTER PORT**. This is the callback of this edit box:

```
function edit2_Callback(hObject, eventdata, handles)
global ros_master_port
ros_master_port = get(hObject,'String')
```

In this function too, the port from the edit box is stored as string type in a global variable called `ros_master_port`.

The next edit box is for obtaining the `teleop_topic_name`. Here is its callback function definition:

```
function edit3_Callback(hObject, eventdata, handles)
global teleop_topic_name
teleop_topic_name = get(hObject,'String')
```

Similar to `ros_master_port` and `port`, this too is stored as string in a global variable.

After obtaining all these values, we can press the **Connect to Robot** button for connecting to the ROS robot/ROS PC. If the connection is successful, you can see proper messages in the command line. Here are the callback definitions of the **Connect to Robot** button:

```
function pushbutton6_Callback(hObject, eventdata, handles)

global ros_master_ip
global ros_master_port
global teleop_topic_name
global robot
global velmsg

ros_master_uri =
strcat('http://',ros_master_ip,':',ros_master_port)
setenv('ROS_MASTER_URI',ros_master_uri)

rosinit

robot = rospublisher(teleop_topic_name,'geometry_msgs/Twist');
velmsg = rosmessage(robot);
```

This callback will set the ROS_MASTER_URI variable by concatenating `ros_master_ip` and the port. Then, it initialize the connection by calling `rosinit`. After connecting, it will create a publisher of `geometry_msgs/Twist`, which is for sending the command velocity. The topic name is the name that we give in the edit box.

After successful connection, we can control the robot by pressing keys such as **Forward**, **Backward**, **Left**, and **Right**.

The speeds of linear and angular velocity are initialized as follows:

```
global left_spinVelocity
global right_spinVelocity

global forwardVelocity
global backwardVelocity

left_spinVelocity = 2;
right_spinVelocity = -2;
forwardVelocity = 3;
backwardVelocity = -3;
```

Let's look at the function definition of **Forward** first:

```
function pushbutton4_Callback(hObject, eventdata, handles)
global velmsg
global robot
global teleop_topic_name
global forwardVelocity
velmsg.Angular.Z = 0;
velmsg.Linear.X = forwardVelocity;

send(robot,velmsg);
latchpub = rospublisher(teleop_topic_name, 'IsLatching', true);
```

What it basically does is it publishes a linear velocity and latches it on the topic. In the `Backward` callback, we are providing a negative linear velocity. In the `Left` and `Right` callbacks, we are only providing an angular velocity.

After doing all this, we can save the figure file, which is the `.fig` and `.m` file, which is the MATLAB file.

Running the application

You can load your own application or the application that came along with the book. Here's how to run the application:

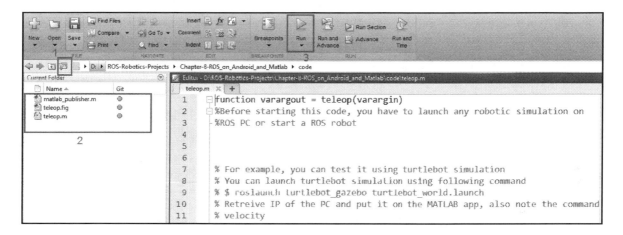

Figure 19: Running MATLAB application

First, you have to click on the **Browse** button, marked **1**, to go to the application folder. If you are in the application folder, you can see the application files listed in the folder marked **2**. After obtaining the files, double-click on the application file, which will pop up in the editor, and click on the **Run** button, marked **3**.

Now, you will get the GUI and can fill the input arguments. After filling it all in, press the Enter key; only then it will give the value to the main code. You can fill the form like shown in the following screenshot. You can see the main GUI entries here.

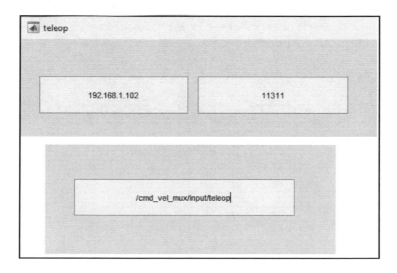

Figure 20: Running the MATLAB application

Before connecting to the ROS robot, confirm whether robot or robot simulation is running on the ROS PC. For doing a test, you can start a TurtleBot simulation on the ROS PC using the following command:

```
$ roslaunch turtlebot_gazebo turtlebot_world.launch
```

The teleop topic of TurtleBot is /cmd_vel_mux/input/teleop, which we have already provided in the application.

After starting the simulation, you can connect to the MATLAB application by pressing the **Connect to Robot** button. If the connection is successful, you can see that the robot is moving when you press the corresponding buttons, as shown here:

Figure 21: Controlling a robot in a ROS network

You can echo the command velocity topic using the following command:

```
$ rostopic echo /cmd_vel_mux/input/teleop
```

After working with the robot, you can press the **Disconnect** button to disconnect from the ROS network.

> You can clone the book code using the following command
> $ git clone https://github.com/qboticslabs/ros_robotics_projects

Getting started with Android and its ROS interface

There exists a cool interface between ROS and Android. As you know, Android is one of most popular operating systems in mobile devices. Just imagine: if we can access all features of a mobile devices on the ROS network, we can build robots using it, right? We can build Android apps with ROS capabilities and can make any kind of robot using it, its scope is unlimited.

The following shows how the communication between android device and ROS robot is happening. The figure shows an example Android-ROS application which can teleoperate robot from an android device. Each android application should inherit from **RosActivity** which is getting from Android-ROS interface, then only we can access ROS API's in our application. We can see more about the API's after this section.

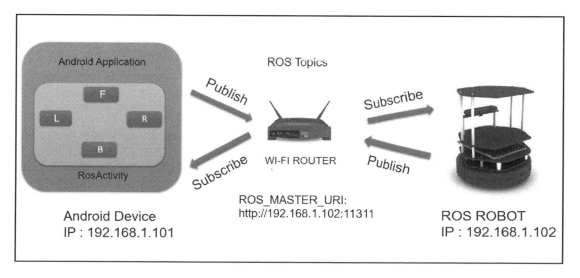

Figure 22: Android – ROS teleop interface

The core backend of the Android ROS library is RosJava (http://wiki.ros.org/rosjava), which is an implementation of ROS in Java. There is also Android core libraries (http://wiki.ros.org/android_core) which are built using RosJava API's. Using Android-ROS APIs we can create ROS nodes and ROS master, but compared to actual ROS API's in C++/Python, the Android-ROS features are less.

So what is the importance of Android-ROS interface? The main reason is, an Android device is like a mini computer, which is having all the sensors and other peripherals. We may can use an android device itself as a robot too. So if there is a ROS interface, we may can expand its capabilities by performing high level functionalities like navigation, mapping and localization. Nowadays, android devices are having high quality cameras, so we can even do image processing application via ROS interface.

Smartphone based robots are already in the market, we can also expand existing robots features by using ROS interface.

In the next section, we are going to see how to set up the ROS-Android interface on your PC and generate the **Android Package Kit** (**APK**) file, which can be directly installed on Android devices. Let's start setting up the ROS-Android interface on Ubuntu.

Before setting up Android, there is a long list of prerequisites that have to be satisfied for compiling and building it. Let's see what they are.

Installing rosjava

As you know, Android is based on Java, so it need rosjava to work.

Here are the methods to install rosjava.

Installing from the Ubuntu package manager

Here is the command to install rosjava from the package manager:

```
$ sudo apt-get install ros-<rosversion_name>-rosjava
```

For example, for Kinetic, use the following command:

```
$ sudo apt-get install ros-kinetic-rosjava
```

For Indigo, you can use the following command:

```
$ sudo apt-get install ros-indigo-rosjava
```

Installing from source code

Here is the procedure to install rosjava from source code:

First, you have to create a catkin workspace folder called rosjava:

```
$ mkdir -p ~/rosjava/src
```

Initialize the workspace and clone the source files using the following command:

```
$ wstool init -j4 ~/rosjava/src
https://raw.githubusercontent.com/rosjava/rosjava/indigo/rosjava.rosinstall
```

If you getting any issues related to wstool, you can install it using the following command:

```
$ sudo apt-get install python-wstool
```

Switch to the rosjava workspace:

```
$ cd ~/rosjava
```

Install the dependencies of the rosjava source files:

```
$ rosdep update
$ rosdep install --from-paths src -i -y
```

After installing the dependencies, build the entire workspace:

```
$ catkin_make
```

After successfully building the repository, you can execute the following command to add the rosjava environment inside bash:

```
$ echo 'source ~/rosjava/devel/setup.bash' >> ~/.bashrc
```

> For more reference, you can check the following link:
> http://wiki.ros.org/rosjava/Tutorials/kinetic/Installation

The next step is to set up `android-sdk` in Ubuntu. We can do it in two ways. One is through the Ubuntu package manager and the other is from the prebuilt binaries we can get from the Android website.

Let's see how to install the `android-sdk` using command line

Installing android-sdk from the Ubuntu package manager

Installing `android-sdk` using a command is pretty simple. Here is the command to install it. It may not be the latest version.

```
$ sudo apt-get install android-sdk
```

Install the latest version of `android-sdk` available on the Android website. For building `android-ros` applications, you only need to install `android-sdk`; an IDE is not mandatory.

Installing android-sdk from prebuilt binaries

Here is the link for downloading latest `android-sdk` version from the website:

`https://developer.android.com/studio/index.html#downloads`

You only need to download the Android tools for building `android-ros` apps:

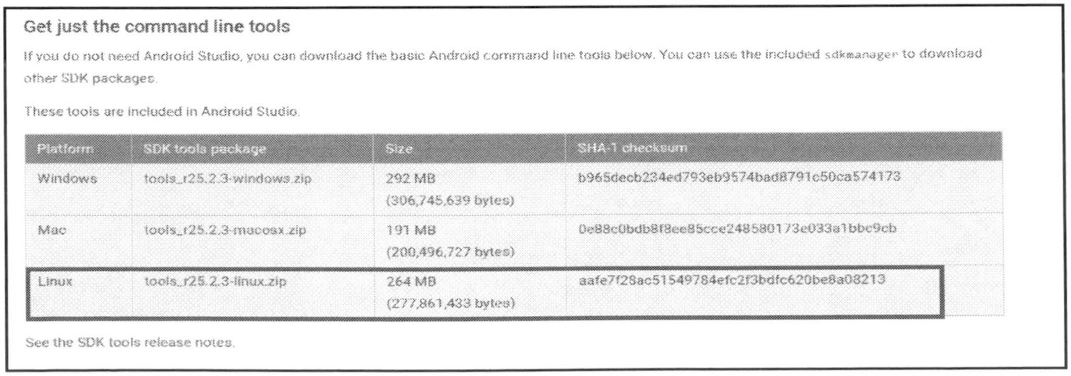

Get just the command line tools

If you do not need Android Studio, you can download the basic Android command line tools below. You can use the included sdkmanager to download other SDK packages.

These tools are included in Android Studio.

Platform	SDK tools package	Size	SHA-1 checksum
Windows	tools_r25.2.3-windows.zip	292 MB (306,745,639 bytes)	b965decb234ed793eb9574bad8791c50ca574173
Mac	tools_r25.2.3-macosx.zip	191 MB (200,496,727 bytes)	0e88c0bdb8f8ee85cce248580173e033a1bbc9cb
Linux	tools_r25.2.3-linux.zip	264 MB (277,861,433 bytes)	aafe7f28ac51549784efc2f3bdfc620be8a08213

See the SDK tools release notes.

Figure 23: Standalone Android SDK

You can download and extract this into the `home` folder, and you have to set up environment variables to access the SDK tools.

Let's look at the variables you have to append on your `.bashrc` file. You can set them using the following commands.

Here is how we set the `ANDROID_HOME` variable, which is required while building `android-ros` applications. You can set your own SDK location here:

```
$ export ANDROID_HOME=~/android-sdk-linux
```

This command will help you access Android commands from bash:

```
$ export PATH=${PATH}:~/android-sdk-linux/tools
$ export PATH=${PATH}:~/android-sdk-linux/platform-tools
```

To run those Android commands, we also need to install the 32-bit Ubuntu libraries. It is required for running most Android tool commands.

We can install it using the following command:

```
$ sudo dpkg --add-architecture i386
$ sudo apt-get update
$ sudo apt-get install libc6:i386 libncurses5:i386 libstdc++6:i386
lib32z1 libbz2-1.0:i386
```

You can also refer to the following instructions to set `android-sdk` in Linux:

`https://developer.android.com/studio/install.html?pkg=tools`

Congratulations, you are almost there!

Now, you can run the following command to start Android SDK manager:

```
$ android
```

From the pop-up window, you have to install the following Android platforms and their build tools to make the ROS-Android interface work:

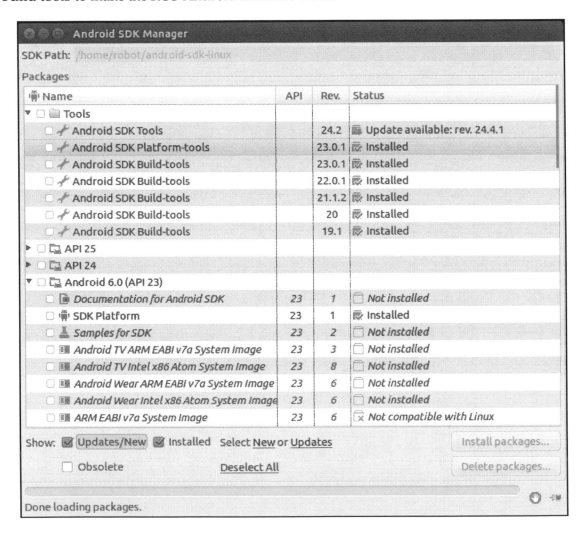

Figure 24: Android SDK manager

Here is the list of things you may need to install in Android SDK manager:

- **SDK Platforms**
  - **Android 2.3.3 (API 10)**
  - **Android 4.0.3 (API 15)**
  - **Android 5.0.1 (API 21)**
  - **Android 6.0 (API 23)**
- **Android SDK Build-tools**
  - **Revision: 19.1**
  - **Revision: 20**
  - **Revision: 21.1.2**
  - **Revision: 22.0.1**
  - **Revision: 23.0.1**
- **Android SDK Platform-tools**
  - **Revision: 23.0.1**
- **Android SDK Tools**
  - **Revision: 24.2**

Your configuration may vary; this was the configuration used to build the apps for this book.

With this, we should have met all the dependencies for the Android-ROS interface.

Let's clone the Android-ROS source code.

Installing the ROS-Android interface

If all the dependencies are satisfied, you can easily build the ROS-Android interface and build a bunch of Android-ROS applications. Here is how we can do that:

Initially, we have to create a workspace folder for the Android interface. We can name it `android_core`:

```
$ mkdir -p ~/android_core
```

After creating this folder, you can initialize the workspace using the following command:

```
wstool init -j4 ~/android_core/src
https://raw.github.com/rosjava/rosjava/indigo/android_core.rosinstall
```

Now switch to the workspace and build the workspace using `catkin_make`:

```
$ cd ~/android_core
$ catkin_make
```

After building the workspace successfully, you can source it by adding it to `.bashrc`:

```
$ echo 'source ~/android_core /devel/setup.bash' >> ~/.bashrc
```

You are now done with setting up the `android_core` package in ROS. So what do you get after building this workspace? You will get a bunch of Android-ROS applications that can be installed on your Android device. You will also get the Android-ROS library, which we can use in our custom application

 For more reference, you can check following link:
`http://wiki.ros.org/android/Tutorials/kinetic.`

Playing with ROS-Android applications

In this section, we will see how to install the ROS-Android application generated from the preceding build process on your Android phone.

Let's take the `android_core` folder and search for `.apk` files; you may get a bunch of applications, as shown in the following figure:

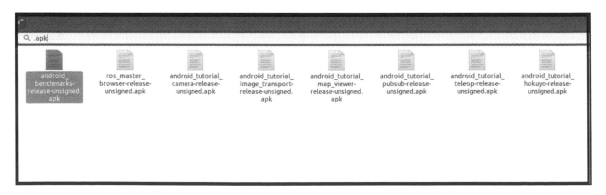

Figure 25: List of generated APK files

You can copy the APK files and install them on your phone.

Troubleshooting

You may get errors while installing these APK files. One of the errors is shown in the following screenshot:

Figure 26: Parse error during installation of APK

Here are the tips to solve this issue:

The first step is to enable installation from **Unknown sources**, as shown in section **1** of the following figure:

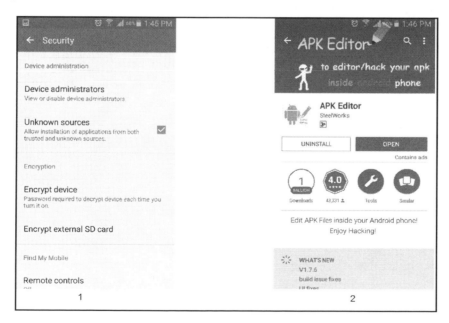

Figure 27: Tips to solve parse error

Install an Android app called **APK Editor**, which can be downloaded from following the link:

`https://play.google.com/store/apps/details?id=com.gmail.heagoo.apkeditor&hl=en`

You can also buy the Pro version, which you may require in the future. Here's the link to the Pro version:

`https://play.google.com/store/apps/details?id=com.gmail.heagoo.apkeditor.pro`

What this app does is enable us to edit the APK that we created and do more stuff with it. For example, the APK that we built was unsigned; using this app, we can sign it. We can also change the minimum and target SDK using the app.

Here is how we can edit the APK and install our APKs:

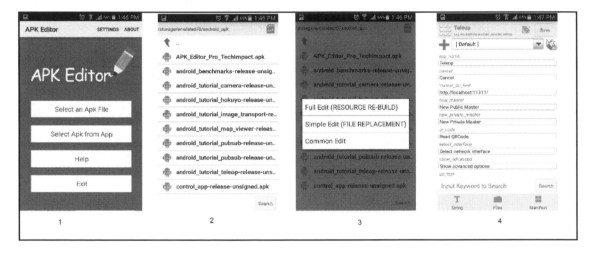

Figure 28: Working with APK Editor

What we need to do with this app is simple. Just choose an APK from this app, click on the **Full Edit** option, and save it. After saving, you can see a wizard that shows an option for installing our app:

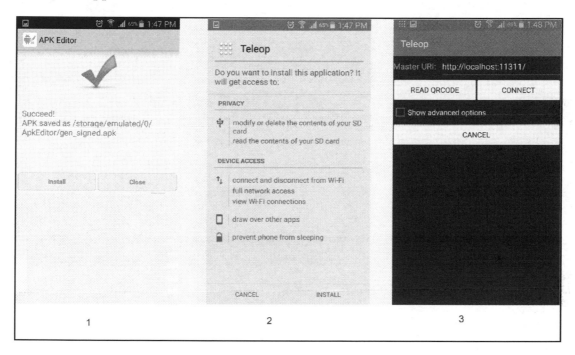

Figure 29: Installing the ROS-Android app

Once you've installed the application successfully, we can work with the ROS-Android examples.

Android-ROS publisher-subscriber application

You can first find the publisher-subscriber application with the name `android_tutorial_pubsub-release.apk`. Install it using the preceding procedure, and let's learn how we can work with it.

You can open the **PubSub Tutorial** application, and you'll see the following window marked **1**:

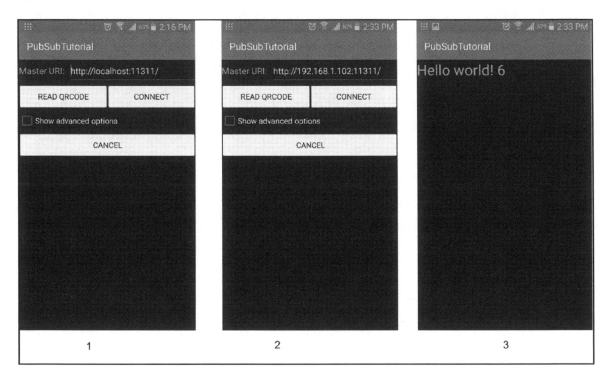

Figure 30: PubSub Tutorial ROS-Android app

Assuming you have connected your Android device and ROS PC over Wi-Fi and in the same network, launch `roscore` on your ROS PC and note its IP too.

In the first window of the app, you have to provide the ROS_MASTER_URI. In that, you can replace the 'localhost' variable with your ROS PC IP address; here, it is 192.168.1.102.

When you press the **Connect** button, the app tries to reach the ROS master, which is running on the ROS PC, and if it is successful, it will start publishing the Hello World message to a topic called /chatter.

Now you can check the ROS PC and list the topics; you'll see the /chatter topic, and you can also echo the topic, as shown in the following screenshot:

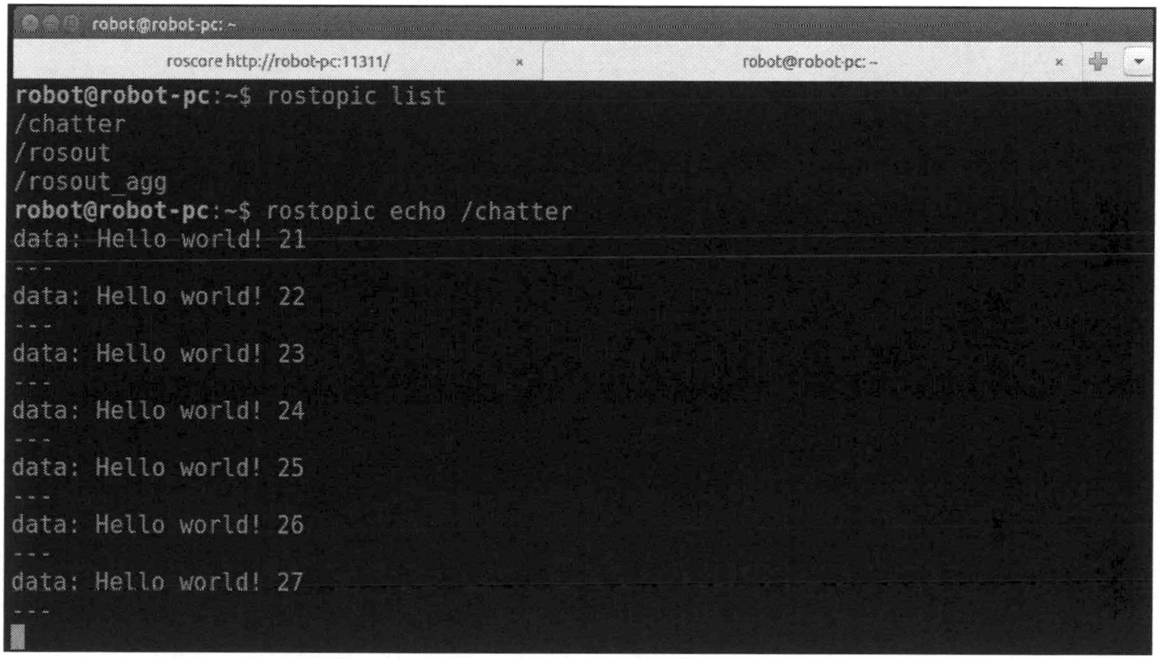

```
robot@robot-pc:~$ rostopic list
/chatter
/rosout
/rosout_agg
robot@robot-pc:~$ rostopic echo /chatter
data: Hello world! 21
---
data: Hello world! 22
---
data: Hello world! 23
---
data: Hello world! 24
---
data: Hello world! 25
---
data: Hello world! 26
---
data: Hello world! 27
---
```

Figure 31: Echoing the /chatter topic on ROS PC

The teleop application

One of the commonly used apps in this list is the Android teleop application. Using this app, you can control the ROS robot from your Android phone.

Like the previous app, the setup is the same, and using a virtual joystick in this app, we can control the movement and rotation of the robot. Here are the screenshots of the app:

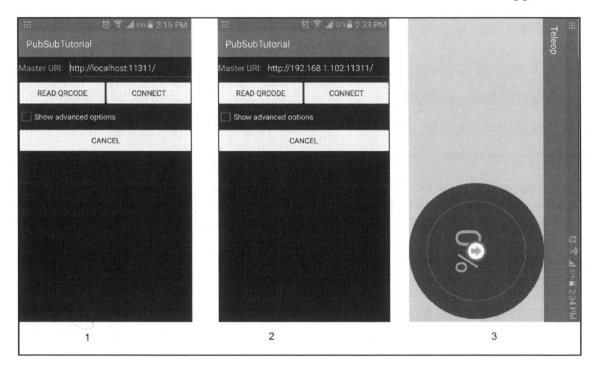

Figure 32: Android teleop application

Here are the topics and output that we may get on the ROS PC or robot. You can see a bunch of topics, actually, which are useful for robot navigation. Now we only need the command velocity topic:

Figure 33: Android teleop application data

The ROS Android camera application

The final application that we are going to check out is the Android-ROS camera application. This application will stream Android phone camera images over ROS topics. You can install the **Camera Tutorial** app on your Android device and try to connect to the ROS master. If the connection is successful, you will see the camera view open up on the mobile device.

Now, check the ROS PC, and you can visualize the camera topic from the phone. Here is the command to perform the visualization:

```
$ rosrun image_view image_view image:=/camera/image
_image_transport:=compressed
```

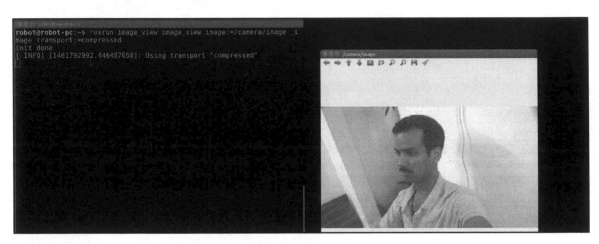

Figure 34: Android-ROS camera app

Making the Android device the ROS master

In the previous test, we made the Android ROS application a ROS node; we can also configure it as a ROS master. Show the advanced option from the app and click on **PUBLIC MASTER**. Now the app itself act as the ROS master. You can connect from your PC to the Android device as a node.

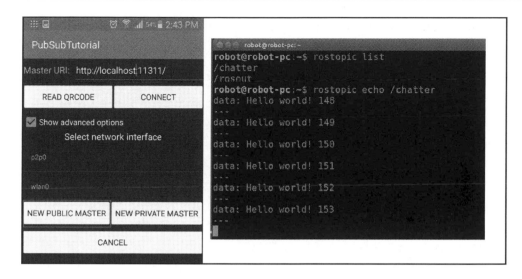

Figure 35: Android-ROS app as ROS MASTER

For listing topics on the ROS PC, you have to set ROS_MASTER_URI inside the .bashrc file:

Here, I have defined ROS_MASTER_URI like this:

```
$ export ROS_MASTER_URI=http://192.168.1.100:11311
```

The IP is the IP address of the Android device.

Code walkthrough

Let's check out the Android-ROS application code for the basic publisher-subscriber app. You can get it from ~/android_core/android_tutorial_pubsub/src. You'll see a file called MainActiviy.java, and now I'll explain the code.

In the beginning of the code, you can see the package name and required Android modules for this application. The important modules are RosActivity and NodeConfiguration. These will help us create a new ROS node in an Android activity (https://developer.android.com/guide/components/activities.html).

```
package org.ros.android.android_tutorial_pubsub;

import android.os.Bundle;
import org.ros.android.MessageCallable;
import org.ros.android.RosActivity;
```

```
import org.ros.android.view.RosTextView;
import org.ros.node.NodeConfiguration;
import org.ros.node.NodeMainExecutor;
import org.ros.rosjava_tutorial_pubsub.Talker;
```

Here is where the Android `MainActivity` starts, which is inherited from `RosActivity`. It is also creates a `Talker` object for publishing topics.

```
public class MainActivity extends RosActivity {

  private RosTextView<std_msgs.String> rosTextView;
  private Talker talker;

  public MainActivity() {
     // The RosActivity constructor configures the notification
title and ticker
     // messages.
     super("Pubsub Tutorial", "Pubsub Tutorial");
  }
```

This is one of the important callback functions whenever an activity is initialized. We have to define the essential components of activities inside this function.

In this code, we are creating a `rosTextView` for `ROS_MASTER_URI` and also performing topic creation and creating a callback for sending the ROS message through the topic:

```
public void onCreate(Bundle savedInstanceState) {
   super.onCreate(savedInstanceState);
   setContentView(R.layout.main);
   rosTextView = (RosTextView<std_msgs.String>)
findViewById(R.id.text);
    rosTextView.setTopicName("chatter");
    rosTextView.setMessageType(std_msgs.String._TYPE);
    rosTextView.setMessageToStringCallable(new
MessageCallable<String, std_msgs.String>() {
     @Override
     public String call(std_msgs.String message) {
        return message.getData();
     }
   });
  }
```

The following function is inherited from `RosActivity`, and what it does is when the `MainActivity` gets initialized, it will run as a thread and query for ROS_MASTER_URI. If it gets the URI, it will start a ROS node itself.

```
protected void init(NodeMainExecutor nodeMainExecutor) {
    talker = new Talker();

    // At this point, the user has already been prompted to either
enter the URI
    // of a master to use or to start a master locally.

    // The user can easily use the selected ROS Hostname in the
master chooser
    // activity.
    NodeConfiguration nodeConfiguration =
NodeConfiguration.newPublic(getRosHostname());
     nodeConfiguration.setMasterUri(getMasterUri());
    nodeMainExecutor.execute(talker, nodeConfiguration);
    // The RosTextView is also a NodeMain that must be executed in
order to
    // start displaying incoming messages.
    nodeMainExecutor.execute(rosTextView, nodeConfiguration);
  }
}
```

You can see more code of ROS-Android applications from the `android_core` package.

Creating basic applications using the ROS-Android interface

We have covered Android – ROS applications provided from the ROS repository. So how can we create our own application using it? Let's take a look.

First, we have to create a separate workspace for our application. Here, it is named `myandroid`:

```
$ mkdir -p ~/myandroid/src
```

Switch to the workspace's `src` folder:

```
$ cd ~/myandroid/src
```

Create a package called `android_foo` that depends on `android_core`, `rosjava_core`, and `std_msg`:

```
$ catkin_create_android_pkg android_foo android_core rosjava_core
std_msgs
```

Switch into `android_foo` and add sample libraries to check whether the project is building properly:

```
$ cd android_foo
$ catkin_create_android_project -t 10 -p
com.github.ros_java.android_foo.bar bar
$ catkin_create_android_library_project -t 13 -p
com.github.ros_java.android_foo.barlib barlib
$ cd ../..
```

And finally, you can build the empty project using `catkin_make`:

```
$ catkin_make
```

If it is building properly, you can add a custom project, such as a `bar` project. The custom project should be inside the `android_foo` folder, and it should be included in the `settings.gradle` file, which is in the `android_foo` folder.

Here is how we can do that. You need to include our app, named `my_ros_app`, in this file to build it. For the application source code, you can modify one of the existing ROS-Android applications' code and write new lines:

```
include 'my_ros_app'
include 'bar'
include 'barlib'
```

Also, inside `my_ros_app`, you should include the ROS Android dependencies in the `build.gradle` file; otherwise, the package will not build properly. Here is a sample `build.gradle` file. You can also mention the minimum SDK, target SDK, and compiled SDK versions in the same file.

```
dependencies {
    compile 'org.ros.android_core:android_10:[0.2,0.3)'
    compile 'org.ros.android_core:android_15:[0.2,0.3)'
}
apply plugin: 'com.android.application'
```

```
android {
   compileSdkVersion 15

  defaultConfig {
    minSdkVersion 15
    applicationId "org.ros.android.my_ros_app"
    targetSdkVersion 21
    versionCode 1
    versionName "1.0"
  }
}
```

If you've entered all this information correctly, you can build your own custom ROS-Android application.

For more reference, you can check the following link:
`http://wiki.ros.org/rosjava_build_tools/Tutorials/indigo/Creatin g%20Android%20Packages`

Troubleshooting tips

There are chances of getting errors while building packages. Errors are mainly because of missing Android platform or build tools. If any platforms are missing, you can install them through the Android SDK manager.

Questions

- What are the main features of MATLAB Robotics Toolbox?
- How to set up MATLAB as a ROS master?
- What is the main backend of the ROS-Android interface?
- How to set up a ROS-Android application as a ROS master?

Summary

In this chapter, we mainly discussed two important interfaces of ROS: MATLAB and Android. Both are very popular platforms, and this chapter will be very useful if you are working on the interfacing of ROS with MATLAB and Android. In MATLAB interfacing, we covered Robotics Toolbox and APIs to connect to ROS networks. Using these APIs, we built a GUI application to teleoperate a ROS robot. In the Android-ROS interfacing section, we saw how to set up and build Android-ROS applications from a Linux PC. After that, we successfully built ROS-Android applications and saw demos of important applications. We also saw the Android-ROS application code and its functions, and finally, we saw how to build a custom Android-ROS application.

Building an Autonomous Mobile Robot

9

An autonomous mobile robot can move from its current position to the goal position autonomously with the help of mapping and localizing algorithms. ROS provides some powerful packages to prototype an autonomous mobile robot from scratch. Some of the packages used in an autonomous robot are the ROS navigation stack, `gmapping`, and `amcl`. Combining these packages, we can build our own autonomous mobile robot. In this chapter, we will see a DIY autonomous mobile robot platform that works using ROS. This project is actually the updated version of the work mentioned in my first book, *Learning Robotics Using Python*, Packt Publishing (`http://learn-robotics.com`). In this chapter, we will mainly go through designing and building the simulation of a robot, then the hardware of robot, and finally the software framework. The chapter will be an abstract of all these things, since explaining everything in a single chapter will be a tedious task.

The following are the main topics we will discuss on this chapter:

- Robot specification and design overview
- Designing and selecting motors and wheels for the robot
- Building a 2D and 3D model of the robot body
- Simulating the robot model in Gazebo
- Designing and building actual robot hardware
- Interfacing robot hardware with ROS
- Setting up the ROS navigation stack and gmapping packages
- Final run

Robot specification and design overview

Here are the main specifications of the robot we are going to design in this chapter:

- A maximum payload of 2 kg
- Body weight of 3 kg
- A maximum speed of 0.35 m/s
- Ground clearance of 3 cm
- Two hours of continuous operation
- Differential drive configuration
- Circular base footprint
- Autonomous navigation and obstacle avoidance
- Low-cost platform

We are going to design a robot that satisfies all these specifications.

Designing and selecting the motors and wheels for the robot

The robot we are going to design should have a differential drive configuration, and from the preceding specification, we can first determine the motor torque values. From the payload value and robot body weight, we can easily compute the motor torque.

Computing motor torque

Let's calculate the torque required to move this robot.

The number of wheels is four, including two caster wheels. The number of wheels undergoing actuation is only two. We can assume the coefficient of friction is 0.6 and of wheel radius is 4.5 cm. We can use the following formula:

Total weight of robot = Weight of robot + Payload

Weight of the robot: 3 x 9.8 ≈ 30 N (W = mg)

Payload: *2 x 9.8 ≈ 20 N*

Total weight: *30 + 20 = 50 N*

This total weight should be split among the four wheels of the robot, so we can write it as $W = 2 \times N1 + 2 \times N2$, where $N1$ is the weight acting on each robot wheel and $N2$ is the weight acting on each caster wheels. The configuration of wheels of the robot is shown in *Figure 1*. The **C1** and **C2** shows the caster wheels of the robot and **M1** and **M2** shows the motor position in which wheels can attach on the slots just near to the motor shaft.

If the robot is stationary, the motors attached to the wheels have to exert maximum torque to get moving. This is the maximum torque equation:

$\mu \times N \times r - T = 0$

Here, μ is the coefficient of friction, N is the average weight acting on each wheel, r is the radius of the wheels, and T is the maximum torque to get moving.

We can write $N = W/2$ since the weight of the robot is equally distributed among all four wheels, but two are only actuated. We are taking $W/2$ as the average weight here.

We can write *0.6 x (50/2) x 0.045 – T = 0*

Hence, $T = 0.675$ *N-m* or *6.88 kg-cm*. We can use a standard value, *10 kg-cm*.

Calculation of motor RPM

From the specification, we get to know that the maximum speed of the robot is 0.35 m/s. We took the wheel radius as 4.5 cm in the preceding section, and one of the other specifications we need to satisfy is ground clearance. The specified ground clearance is 3 cm, so this wheel is satisfying those requirements too. We can find the **rotations per minute (RPM)** of the motors using the following equation:

RPM = ((60 x Speed / (3.14 x Diameter of wheel)

RPM = (60 x 0.35) / (3.14 x 0.09) = 21 / 0.2826 = 74 RPM

We can choose a standard *80 RPM* or *100 RPM* for this robot.

Design summary

After designing, we have the following design values:

- Motor RPM: 80
- Motor torque: 10 kg-cm
- Wheel diameter: 9 cm

Building 2D and 3D models of the robot body

Chassis design is the next step in designing the robot. We can create the 2D drawing of the robot and then draw a 3D model of it. The only specification need to satisfy is that the robot's base footprint should be circular. Here, we are discussing a drawing that is satisfying this condition. If your requirements are different, you may need to modify your design accordingly. Now let's look at some illustrations of the robot's footprint.

The base plate

Following figure shows the base footprint of our robot:

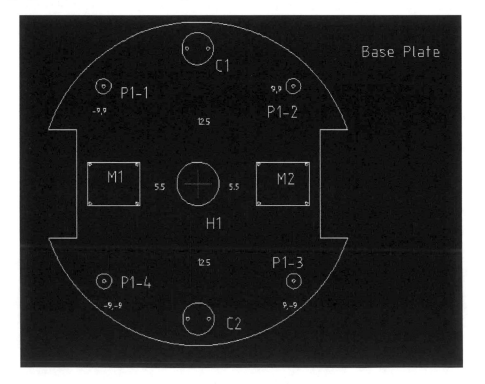

Figure 1: Base plate of the robot

The preceding figure shows the base footprint of our robot. You can see that it is circular and there are two slots on the left and right for attaching motors and wheels. **M1** and **M2** are the positions of the motor body, and the shaft will be in the slots. The motors can be put on the top of the plate or on the bottom. Here, we are attaching the motors to the bottom of this plate. The wheels should be inside these two slots. We have to make sure that the slot length is greater than the wheel diameter. You can see **C1** and **C2**, which are the positions where we are attaching the caster wheels. Caster wheels are freely rotating wheels without any actuation. We can select available caster wheels for this purpose. Some caster wheels may have issues moving on uneven terrain. In that case, we may need to use a caster wheel with spring suspension. This ensures that it always touches the ground even when the terrain is slightly uneven.

You can also see parts such as **P1-1** and **P1-4**, which are the poles from the base plate. If we want to attach an additional layer above the base plate, we can use these poles as the pillars. Poles can be hard plastic or steel, which are fixed to the base plate and have a provision to attach a hollow tube on them. Each poles is screwed on to the base plate.

The center of the base plate is hollow; this will be useful when we have to take wires from the motors. Mainly, we will attach the electronic board required for the robot to this plate.

Here are the dimensions of base plate and each part:

Parts of base plate	Dimensions (length x height) or (radius) in cm
M1 and M2	5 x 4
C1 and C2	Radius = 1.5
S (screw)	0.15
P1-1, P1-2, P1-3, P1-4	Outer radius 0.7, Height 3.5
Left and right wheel section	2.5 x 10
Base plate	Radius = 15

The pole and tube design

The following figure shows how to make a pole and tube for this robot. Again, this design is all up to you. You can design customized poles too:

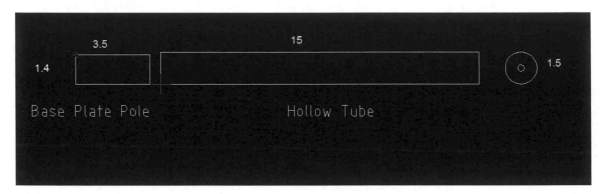

Figure 2: Pole and tube dimension of the robot

From the preceding figure, you can see the dimension of the pole and tube. It's **3.5** cm by **1.4** cm. The poles that we've used here are basically hard plastic. We are using hollow tubes to connect to the poles and extend them for the second layer. The length of the hollow tube is **15** cm, and it has a slightly bigger diameter than the poles, that is, **1.5** cm. Only then will we be able to insert this tube into the pole. A hard plastic piece is inserted at one side of the hollow tube, which helps connect the next layer.

The motor, wheel, and motor clamp design

You can choose a motor and wheels that satisfy the design criteria. Most of the standard motors come with clamps. The motor can be connected to the base plate using this clamp. If you don't have one, you may need to make it. This is the drawing of a standard clamp that goes with one of the motors:

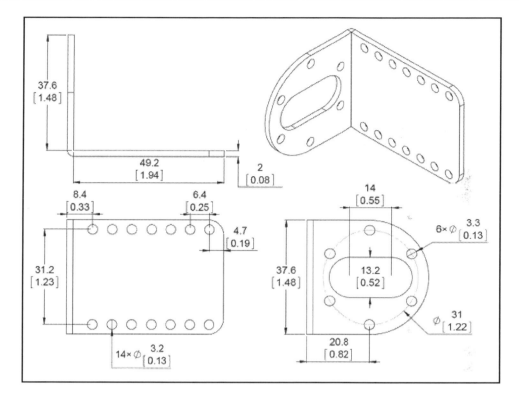

Figure 3: The clamp design

The clamp can be fixed on the base plate, and the motor shaft can be put through the clamp slot which is perpendicular to the clamp base.

The caster wheel design

You can use any caster wheel that can be move freely on the ground. The main use of caster wheels is distributing the weight of the robot and balancing it. If you can use a spring suspension on the caster wheel, it can help you navigate the robot on uneven terrain.

Here are some caster wheels that you can use for this robot:

http://www.robotshop.com/en/robot-wheel.html.

Middle plate and top plate design

If you want a more layers for the robot, you can simply make circular plates and hollow tubes which are compatible with the base plate. Here you can see middle plate design and the tubes used to connect it to the base plate:

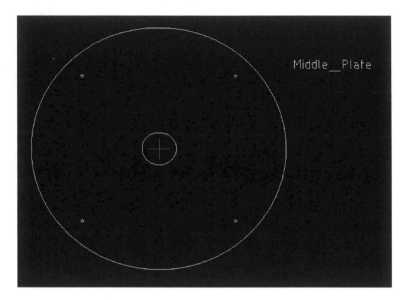

Figure 4: The middle plate design

The middle plate is simply a circular plate having screw holes to connect it to the tubes from the base plate. We can use following kind of hollow tubes to connect the base plate tubes and middle plate.

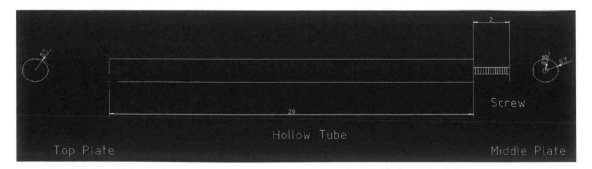

Figure 5: The hollow tube from the second plate

Here you can see that a screw is mounted on one side of the tube; the screw can be used to connect tubes to the base plate. We can mount the top plate on top of the tube too.

The top plate

Here is a diagram of the top plate:

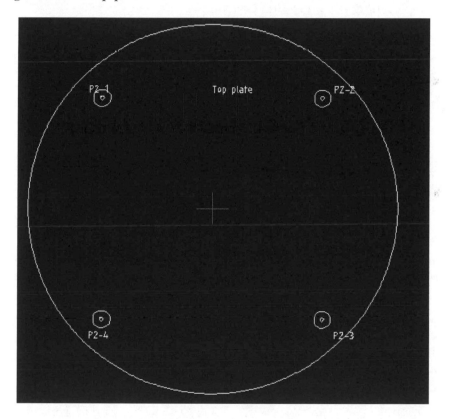

Figure 6: The top plate

The top plate can be placed in a hollow tube. If we want to put anything on top of the robot, we can put it on the top plate. On the middle plate, we can put vision sensors, PC, and so on for processing.

These are the main structural elements that we need for this robot. These drawing can be develop in any CAD software like AutoCAD and LibreCAD. AutoCAD is a proprietary software whereas LibreCAD is free (`http://librecad.org/cms/home.html`). We have used LibreCAD for developing the preceding sketches.

You can simply install LibreCAD in Ubuntu using the following command:

```
$ sudo apt-get install librecad
```

In the next section, we can see how we can model the robot in 3D. The 3D modeling is mainly using for robot simulation.

3D modeling of the robot

The 3D modeling of the robot can be done in any 3D CAD software. You can use popular commercial software such as AutoCAD, SOLIDWORKS, and CATIA or free software such as Blender. The design can be customized according to your specification. Here, you can see a 3D model of the robot built using Blender. Using the 3D model, we can perfect the robot's design without building the actual hardware. We can also create the 3D simulation of the robot using this model. The following screenshot shows the 3D model of a robot designed using Blender:

Figure 7: The 3D model

You can check out this model at `chapter_9_codes/chefbot`.

Simulating the robot model in Gazebo

After modeling the robot, the next stage that we have to do is simulation. The simulation is mainly for mimicking the behavior of designed robot. For the simulation, normally we are putting ideal parameters to the simulated model. When we do the actual robot, there can be some changes from the simulated parameters. We can simulate the robot using Gazebo. Before simulating the robot, it will be good if you understand the mathematical model of a differential robot. The mathematical representation will give you more insight about the working of robot. We are not going to implement the robot controllers from scratch. Instead of that, we are using existing one.

Mathematical model of a differential drive robot

As you may know, robot kinematics is the study of motion without considering the forces that affect the motion, and robot dynamics is the study of the forces acting on a robot. In this section, we will discuss the kinematics of a differential robot.

Typically, a mobile robot or vehicle can have six **degrees of freedom** (**DOF**), which are represented as x, y, z, roll, pitch, and yaw. The x, y, and z degrees are translation, and roll, pitch, and yaw are rotation values. The roll movement of robot is sideways rotation, pitch is forward and backward rotation, and yaw is the heading and orientation of the robot. A differential robot moves along a 2D plane, so we can say it will have only three DOF, such as x, y, and *theta*, where *theta* is the heading of the robot and points along the forward direction of the robot.

The following figure shows the coordinate system of a differential-drive robot:

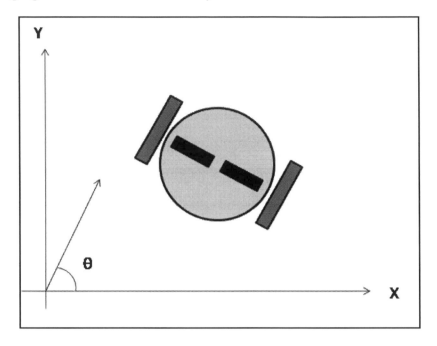

Figure 8: The coordinate system representation of a differential-drive robot

So how to control this robot? It has two wheels, right? So the velocity of each wheel determines the new position of the robot. Let's say V-left and V-right are the respective wheel velocities, (x, y, θ) is the standing position of the robot at time t, and (x', y', θ') is the new position at time $t+ \delta t$, where δt is a small time interval. Then, we can write the standard forward kinematic model of a differential robot like this:

$$
\begin{bmatrix} x' \\ y' \\ \theta' \end{bmatrix} = \begin{bmatrix} \cos(\omega\delta t) & -\sin(\omega\delta t) & 0 \\ \sin(\omega\delta t) & \cos(\omega\delta t) & 0 \\ 0 & 0 & 1 \end{bmatrix} \begin{bmatrix} x - ICC_x \\ y - ICC_y \\ \theta \end{bmatrix} + \begin{bmatrix} ICC_x \\ ICC_y \\ \omega\delta t \end{bmatrix}
$$

Figure 9: Forward kinematics model of a differential drive robot

Here are the unknown variables in the preceding equation:

$R = l/2\ (nl + nr\ )\ /\ (nr - nl\ )$

$ICC = [\ x\text{-}R\ sin\theta,\ y\text{+}R\ cos\theta\ ]$

$\omega\delta t = (nr - nl\ )\ step\ /\ l$

nl and *nr* are encoder counts for left and right wheels. *l* is the length of the wheel axis and *step* is the distance covered by the wheel in each encoder ticks.

ICC stands for **instantaneous center of curvature,** and it is the common point for rotation of the robot wheels.

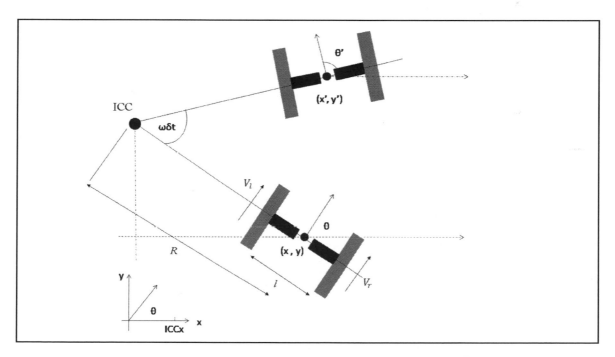

Figure 10: Forward kinematic diagram of differential drive

You can also refer the equations of inverse kinematics of mobile robotics from the following reference.

For more information, check the publication titled *Kinematics Equations for Differential Drive* and *Articulated Steering*, ISSN-0348-0542 and the first author is *Thomas Hellstrom*.

So we've seen the kinematics equations of this robot; the next stage is to simulate the robot.

Simulating Chefbot

The robot in the book is actually designed for carrying food and delivering to the customers in a hotel. It is called Chefbot. Now let's see what are the steps involved for simulating Chefbot. We are using the Gazebo simulator along with ROS for simulating the capabilities of a robot. We'll look at the basic teleoperation of the mapping and localization of a robot in Gazebo.

Building the URDF model of Chefbot

The first step in the simulation is building a robot model compatible with ROS. The URDF (http://wiki.ros.org/urdf) file is the robot model that is compatible with ROS. We are not going to discuss how to write a URDF model; instead, we will see the important sections we have to focus on while creating the URDF of a robot.

Inserting 3D CAD parts into URDF as links

Creating URDF is a time-consuming task; in this section, we will learn how to create a URDF package for a robot and insert 3D CAD models as a robot link in URDF. The first step is to create a robot description package; in this case, `chapter_9_codes/chefbot_code/chefbot_description` is our robot model ROS package. This package contains all the URDF files and 3D mesh files required for a robot. The `chefbot_description/meshes` folder has some 3D models that we designed earlier. These 3D models can be inserted into the URDF file. You can check the existing URDF file from `chefbot_description/urdf`. Here is a snippet that inserts a 3D model into URDF, which can act as a robot link. The code snippet can be found in `urdf/chefbot_base.urdf.xacro`.

```
<joint name="base_joint" type="fixed">
    <origin xyz="0 0 0.0102" rpy="0 0 0" />
    <parent link="base footprint"/>
    <child link="base_link" />
</joint>
 <link name="base_link">
```

```
<visual>
  <geometry>

    <!-- new mesh -->
    <mesh
filename="package://chefbot_description/meshes/base_plate.dae" />
    </geometry>
```

Here, you can see we are inserting the `base_plate.dae` mesh into the URDF file.

Inserting Gazebo controllers into URDF

After inserting the link and assigning joints, we need to insert Gazebo controllers for simulating differential drive and the depth camera plugin, which is done with software models of actual robots. Here is a snippet of the differential drive Gazebo plugin. You can find this code snippet in `urdf/chefbot_base_gazebo.urdf.xacro`.

```
<gazebo>
    <plugin name="kobuki_controller"
filename="libgazebo_ros_kobuki.so">

        <publish_tf>1</publish_tf>
    <left_wheel_joint_name>wheel_left_joint
    </left_wheel_joint_name>
      <right_wheel_joint_name>wheel_right_joint
      </right_wheel_joint_name>
        <wheel_separation>.30</wheel_separation>
        <wheel_diameter>0.09</wheel_diameter>
        <torque>10.0</torque>
        <velocity_command_timeout>0.6</velocity_command_timeout>
        <imu_name>imu</imu_name>
      </plugin>
    </gazebo>
```

In this plugin, we are providing the designed values of the robot, such as motor torque, wheel diameter, and wheel separation. The differential drive plugin that we are using here is `kobuki_controller`, which is used in the TurtleBot simulation.

After creating this controller, we need to create a depth sensor plugin for mapping and localization. Here is the code snippet to simulate the Kinect, a depth sensor. You can find the code snippet from `urdf/chefbot_gazebo.urdf.xacro`.

```
<plugin name="kinect_camera_controller"
filename="libgazebo_ros_openni_kinect.so">
        <cameraName>camera</cameraName>
        <alwaysOn>true</alwaysOn>
```

```
            <updateRate>10</updateRate>
            <imageTopicName>rgb/image_raw</imageTopicName>
            <depthImageTopicName>depth/image_raw
    </depthImageTopicName>
            <pointCloudTopicName>depth/points</pointCloudTopicName>
            <cameraInfoTopicName>rgb/camera_info
                </cameraInfoTopicName>
    <depthImageCameraInfoTopicName>depth/camera_info
     </depthImageCameraInfoTopicName>
            <frameName>camera_depth_optical_frame</frameName>
            <baseline>0.1</baseline>
            <distortion_k1>0.0</distortion_k1>
            <distortion_k2>0.0</distortion_k2>
            <distortion_k3>0.0</distortion_k3>
            <distortion_t1>0.0</distortion_t1>
            <distortion_t2>0.0</distortion_t2>
            <pointCloudCutoff>0.4</pointCloudCutoff>
         </plugin>
```

In the depth sensor plugin, we can provide necessary design values inside it for simulating the same behavior.

You can clone the book code using the following command:
```
$ git clone
https://github.com/qboticslabs/ros_robotics_projects
```

Running the simulation

To simulate the robot, you may need to satisfy some dependencies. The differential robot controller used in our simulation is of Turtlebot. So we have to install Turtlebot packages to get those plugins and run the simulation:

```
$ sudo apt-get install ros-kinetic-turtlebot-simulator ros-kinetic-
turtlebot-navigation ros-kinetic-create-node ros-kinetic-turtlebot-bringup
ros-kinetic-turtlebot-description
```

You can also install ROS packages such as `chefbot_bringup`, `chefbot_description`, `chefbot_simulator` to start the simulation. You can copy these package into your ROS workspace and launch the simulation using the following command:

```
$ roslaunch chefbot_gazebo chefbot_empty_world.launch
```

If everything is working properly, you will get this window, which has the designed robot:

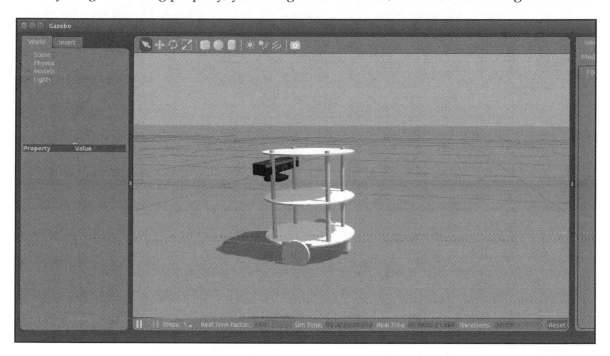

Figure 11: Simulation of Chefbot in Gazebo

You can move the robot around using a teleop node. You can start teleop using the following command:

```
$ roslaunch chefbot_bringup keyboard_teleop.launch
```

You can move the robot with your keyboard, using the keys shown in the following screenshot:

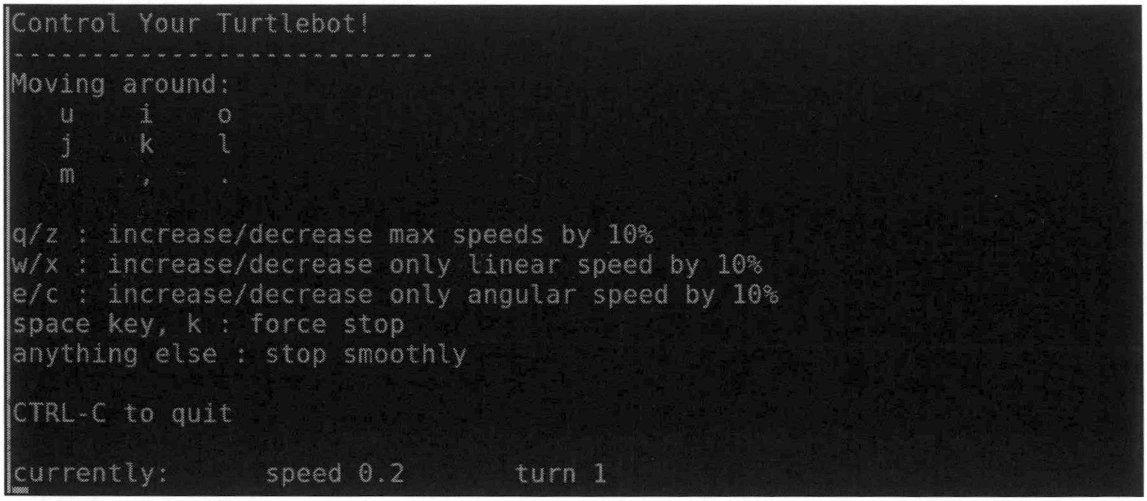

```
Control Your Turtlebot!
- - - - - - - - - - - - - - - - - - - - - - - - - - -
Moving around:
   u    i    o
   j    k    l
   m    ,    .

q/z : increase/decrease max speeds by 10%
w/x : increase/decrease only linear speed by 10%
e/c : increase/decrease only angular speed by 10%
space key, k : force stop
anything else : stop smoothly

CTRL-C to quit

currently:       speed 0.2        turn 1
```

Figure 12: Keyboard teleop

If you can move the robot using teleop, you can now implement its remaining capabilities.

Mapping and localization

Now we can perform mapping and localization of the simulated robot. Mapping is done using the ROS `gmapping` package, which is based on the **Simultaneous Localization and Mapping (SLAM)** algorithm, and localization is done using the `amcl` **Adaptive Monte Carlo Localization (AMCL)** package, which has an implementation of the AMCL algorithm.

In this section, we will launch a new simulated world and see how to map and localize in the world.

Mapping

Here is the command to start the simulated world that has our robot:

```
$ roslaunch chefbot_gazebo chefbot_hotel_world.launch
```

This will launch the world as shown in the following screenshot. The environment is similar to a hotel conference room with tables placed in it:

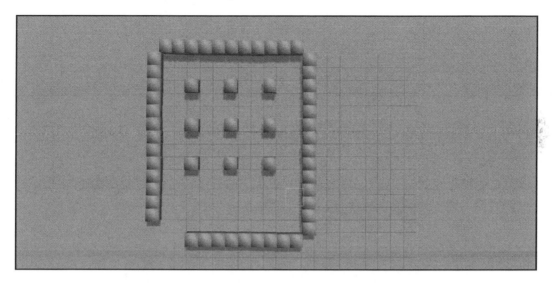

Figure 13: Hotel environment in Gazebo

To start mapping the environment, we can use the following launch file. This will start the gmapping node and finally create the map file.

```
$ roslaunch chefbot_gazebo gmapping_demo.launch
```

After launching gmapping nodes, we can start Rviz for visualizing the map building done by the robot. The following command will start Rviz with necessary settings to view the map file:

```
$ roslaunch chefbot_bringup view_navigation.launch
```

You can start the teleop node and move around the world; this will create a map like the following:

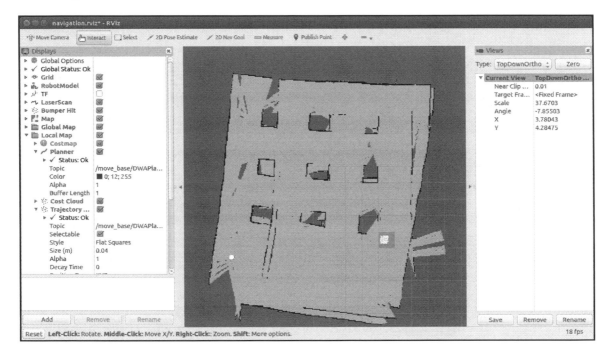

Figure 14: The map visualized in Rviz

After building the map, we can save it using the following command:

```
$ rosrun map_server map_saver -f ~/hotel_world
```

This will save the map in the `home` folder with the name `hotel_world`.

Congratulations; you have successfully built the map of the world and saved it. The next step is to use this map and navigate autonomously around the world. We need the `amcl` package to localize on the map. Combining this with the `amcl` package and ROS navigation, we can autonomously move around the world.

Navigation and localization

Close all the Terminals we have used for mapping, and launch the simulated world in Gazebo using the following command:

```
$ roslaunch chefbot_gazebo chefbot_hotel_world.launch
```

Start localization using the following command:

```
$ roslaunch chefbot_gazebo amcl_demo.launch
map_file:=/home/<user_name>/hotel_world.yaml
```

This will load the saved map and `amcl` nodes. To visualize the robot, we can start Rviz using the following command:

```
$ roslaunch chefbot_bringup view_navigation.launch
```

Now, we can start navigating the robot autonomously. You can click on the **2D Nav Goal** button and click on the map to set the destination. When we set the position, the robot will autonomously move from its starting point to the destination, as shown here:

Figure 15: Visualizing autonomous navigation with AMCL particles

Congratulations! You have successfully set up the robot simulation and performed autonomous navigation using the simulator. Now let's see how can we create the actual robot hardware and program it.

Designing and building actual robot hardware

Let's build the actual hardware of this robot. We need components that satisfy our design values and additional vision sensors to perform SLAM and AMCL. Here is the list::

No	Component name	Link
1	DC gear motor with encoder	`https://www.pololu.com/product/2824`
2	Motor driver	`https://www.pololu.com/product/708`
3	Tiva C 123 or 129 Launchpad	`http://www.ti.com/tool/EK-TM4C123GXL` or `http://www.ti.com/tool/EK-TM4C1294XL`
4	Ultrasonic sensor	`http://www.robotshop.com/en/hc-sr04-ultrasonic-range-finder.html`
5	MPU 6050 (IMU)	`http://www.robotshop.com/en/mpu-6050-6-dof-gyro-accelerometer-imu.html` `http://www.robotshop.com/en/imu-breakout-board-mpu-9250.html`
6	OpenNI compatible depth sensor (Astra Pro)	`https://orbbec3d.com/product-astra-pro/`
7	Intel NUC	`http://www.intel.in/content/www/in/en/nuc/products-overview.html`
8	12V, 10AH battery	Any battery with the specifications provided

Let's discuss the use of each hardware part of the robot.

Motor and motor driver

The motors are controlled using a motor driver circuit. Adjusting the speed of the motors will adjust the speed of the robot. The motor drivers are basically H-bridges that are used to control the speed and direction of the motors. We are using motors and drivers from Pololu. You can check them out from the link in the table.

Motor encoders

Motor encoders are sensors that provide a count corresponding to the speed of the robot wheel. Using the encoder counter, we can compute the distance travelled by each wheel.

Tiva C Launchpad

The Tiva C Launchpad is the embedded controller board used to control the motor and interface with other sensors. The board we are using here is running at 80 MHz and on 256 KB of flash memory. We can program this board using the Arduino language, called **Wiring** (http://wiring.org.co/).

Ultrasonic sensor

The ultrasonic sensor is used to detect nearby obstacles, if any, in front of the robot. This sensor is an optional one; we can enable or disable it in the embedded controller code.

MPU 6050 The IMU of the robot is used improve the odometry data from the robot. The odometry data provides the current robot position and orientation with respect to its initial position. Odometry data is important while building a map using SLAM.

OpenNI depth sensor

To map the environment, we will need a laser scanner or a depth sensor. Laser scanner data is one of the inputs to the SLAM node. One of the latest depth sensors we can use is the Orbbec Astra Pro (https://orbbec3d.com/product-astra-pro/). You can also use a Kinect for this purpose. Using the depthimage_to_laserscan (http://wiki.ros.org/depthimage_to_laserscan) ROS package, we can convert the depth value to laser scan data.

Intel NUC

To run ROS and its packages, we need a computer. A compact PC we can use is the Intel NUC. It can smoothly run all the packages needed for our robot.

Interfacing sensors and motors with the Launchpad

In this section, we will see how to interface each sensor with the Launchpad. The Launchpad can be used to interface motor controllers and also to interface sensors. Here is a block diagram showing how to connect the Launchpad and sensors:

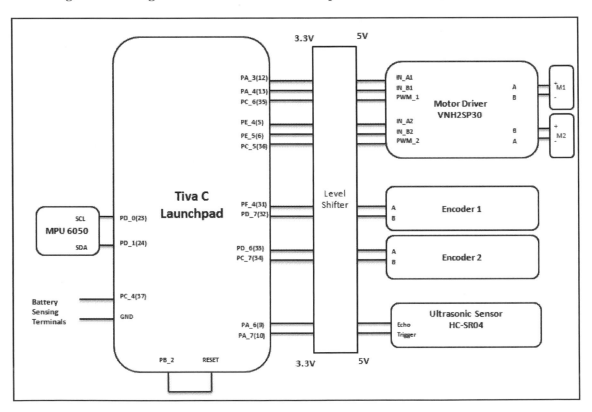

Figure 16: Interconnection between the Launchpad and sensors

The Launchpad works on 3.3V (CMOS) logic, so we may need a logic level shifter to convert from 3.3V to 5V and vice versa. In board like Arduino UNO is having 5V level, so it can directly interface to motor driver without any need of level shifter. Most of the ARM based controller boards are working in 3.3V, so level shifter circuit will be essential while interfacing to a 5V compatible sensor or circuit.

You can clone the book code using the following command:
```
$ git clone
https://github.com/qboticslabs/ros_robotics_projects
```

Programming the Tiva C Launchpad

The programming of the Tiva C Launchpad is done using the Energia IDE, which is the customized version of the Arduino IDE. You can download it from `http://energia.nu/`. As with Arduino, you can choose the serial port of the board and the board name.

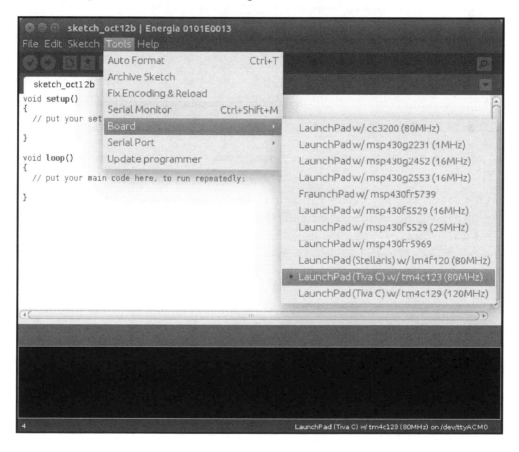

Figure 17: Energia IDE

The embedded code is placed in the `chapter_9_codes/`
`chefbot_code/tiva_c_energia_code_final` folder. Let's look at some important
snippets from the main embedded code.

Here are headers files of the main code. We need to include the following MPU 6050
headers to reading values from it. The `MPU6050` library for Energia is also given along with
the book's code:

```
#include "Wire.h"
#include "I2Cdev.h"
#include "MPU6050_6Axis_MotionApps20.h"
```

The `Messenger` library is used to handle serial data from the PC:

```
#include <Messenger.h>
#include <limits.h>
```

In the following code, the first line is the object of the `MPU6050` class for handling data from
the IMU, and the second one is the object of the `Messenger` library for handling serial
input:

```
MPU6050 accelgyro(0x68);

Messenger Messenger_Handler = Messenger();
```

The following is the main `setup()` function of the code. This will initialize all sensors and
motors of the robot. The `setup()` function will initialize the serial port with a baud rate of
`115200` and initialize encoders, motors, ultrasonic, `MPU6050`, and the messenger object. You
can see the definition of each function in the code itself.

```
void setup()
{
  //Init Serial port with 115200 baud rate
  Serial.begin(115200);
  //Setup Encoders
  SetupEncoders();
  //Setup Motors
  SetupMotors();
  //Setup Ultrasonic
  SetupUltrasonic();
  //Setup MPU 6050
  Setup_MPU6050();
  //Setup Reset pins
  SetupReset();
  //Set up Messenger
  Messenger_Handler.attach(OnMssageCompleted);
```

```
}
```

The following is the main `loop()` function of the code. It will read sensor values and send motor speed commands to the motor driver. The speed commands are received from the PC.

```
void loop()
{

    //Read from Serial port
    Read_From_Serial();
    //Send time information through serial port
    Update_Time();
    //Send encoders values through serial port
    Update_Encoders();
    //Send ultrasonic values through serial port
    Update_Ultra_Sonic();

    //Update motor values with corresponding speed and send speed
  values through serial port
    Update_Motors();


    //Send MPU 6050 values through serial port
    Update_MPU6050();
    //Send battery values through serial port
    Update_Battery();
}
```

We can compile the code and upload it into the board using Energia. If the upload is successful, we can communicate with the board using the `miniterm.py` tool.

Assume that the serial port device is `/dev/ttyACM0`. First, change the permission using following command:

```
$ sudo chmod 777 /dev/ttyACM0
```

We can communicate with the board using the following command:

```
$ miniterm.py /dev/ttyACM0 115200
```

If everything is successful, you will get values like these:

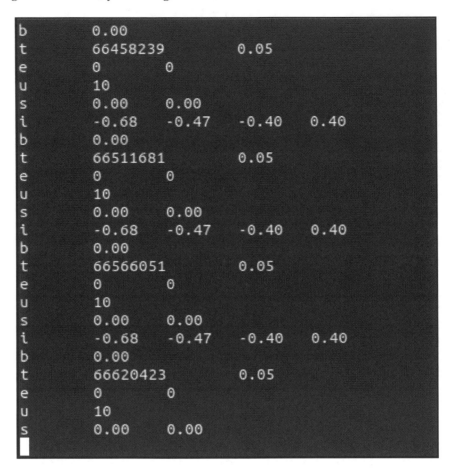

```
b       0.00
t       66458239            0.05
e       0           0
u       10
s       0.00        0.00
i       -0.68       -0.47       -0.40       0.40
b       0.00
t       66511681            0.05
e       0           0
u       10
s       0.00        0.00
i       -0.68       -0.47       -0.40       0.40
b       0.00
t       66566051            0.05
e       0           0
u       10
s       0.00        0.00
i       -0.68       -0.47       -0.40       0.40
b       0.00
t       66620423            0.05
e       0           0
u       10
s       0.00        0.00
```

Figure 18: The serial port values from the board

The messages that you are seeing can be decoded like this: the first letter denotes the device or parameter. Here is what the letters mean:

Letter	Device or parameter
b	Battery
t	Time
e	Encoder
u	Ultrasonic sensor
s	Motor speed
i	IMU value

The serial messages are separated by spaces and tabs so that each value can be decoded easily.

If we are getting serial messages, we can interface the board with ROS.

 The latest ROS Tiva C Launchpad interface can be found here:
`http://wiki.ros.org/rosserial_tivac`.

Interfacing robot hardware with ROS

In this section, we will see how we can interface a robot's embedded controller with ROS. The embedded controller can send speed commands to the motors and obtain speed commands from robot controller nodes. The ROS robot controller nodes receive linear and angular `Twist` command from the ROS navigation stack. The `Twist` command will be subscribed to by the robot controller node and converted into equivalent motor velocity, that is *Vl* and *Vr*.

The robot controller nodes also receive encoder ticks from the embedded controller and calculate the distance traveled by each wheel. Let's take a look at the robot controller nodes.

The Chefbot robot controller nodes are placed in `chefbot_bringup/scripts`. You can check out each node; they're all written in Python.

- `launchpad_node.py`: This is the ROS driver node for handling Launchpad boards. This node will receive serial data from Launchpad and also send data to the board. After running this node, we will get serial data from the board as topics, and we can send data to the board through topics too.
- `SerialDataGateway.py`: This Python module is used to handle serial receive or transmit data in a thread. The `launchpad_node.py` node uses this module to send or receive data to or from the board.
- `Twist_to_motors.py`: This node will subscribe to `Twist` messages from the ROS navigation stack or teleop node and convert them into wheel target velocities.
- `pid_velocity.py`: This is a node that implements the PID controller, which subscribes to the wheel target velocity and converts it into equivalent motor velocity.
- `diff_tf.py`: This node basically subscribes to the encoder data and calculates the distance traversed by the robot. It then publishes as the odometry and **transformation (TF)** topic.

Here is the graph showing the communication between the nodes:

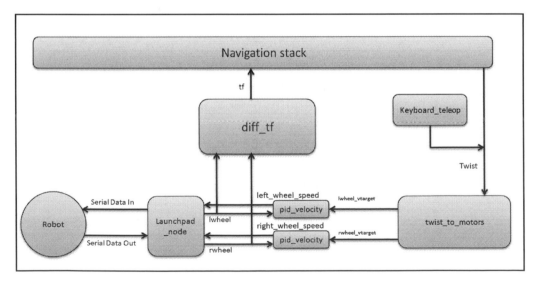

Figure 19: Communication among ROS driver nodes

Here is the list of ROS launch files that we need in order to work with the actual robot. All launch files are placed in the `chefbot_bringup/launch` folder:

- `robot_standalone.launch`: This will launch the ROS driver nodes of Chefbot.
- `model_robot.launch`: This launch file loads the URDF file of Chefbot.
- `view_robot.launch`: This will display the robot model on Rviz.
- `keyboard_teleop.launch`: This will start the keyboard teleop node, which can drive the robot using a keyboard.
- `3dsensor.launch`: This will launch OpenNI to enable depth camera drivers. There may changes to this launch file according to the sensor.
- `gmapping_demo.launch`: This will launch the `gmapping` nodes, which will help us map the robot environment.
- `amcl_demo.launch`: This will launch the AMCL nodes, which help us localize the robot on the map.
- `view_navigation.launch`: This will visualize the map and robot, which helps us command the robot to move to the destination on the map.

Orbbec Astra camera ROS driver:
`http://wiki.ros.org/astra_camera`
`https://github.com/orbbec/ros_astra_camera`

Running Chefbot ROS driver nodes

The following is the block diagram of the connection. Make sure that you are all set with connecting the devices. Make sure you have connected all sensors and the Launchpad board to your PC before running the driver.

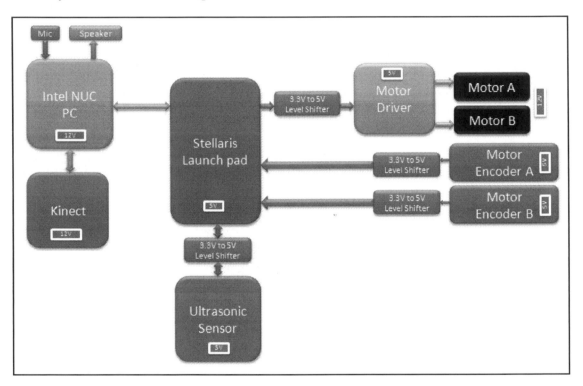

Figure 20: Block diagram of the Chefbot

If we want to launch all driver nodes of the robot, you can simply do it using the following command. Don't forget to change the serial port permission.

```
$ roslaunch chefbot_bringup robot_standalone.launch
```

If everything working fine, you will get the following ROS topics:

```
robot@robot-pc:~$ rostopic list
/battery_level
/cmd_vel_mux/input/teleop
/imu/data
/joint_states
/left_wheel_speed
/lwheel
/lwheel_vel
/lwheel_vtarget
/odom
/qw
/qx
/qy
/qz
/right_wheel_speed
/rosout
/rosout_agg
/rwheel
/rwheel_vel
/rwheel_vtarget
/serial
/tf
/tf_static
/ultrasonic_distance
```

Figure 21: The Chefbot driver topics

You can also visualize the ROS computational graph using `rqt_graph`. Here is the visualization of `rqt_graph`, showing the communication between all nodes:

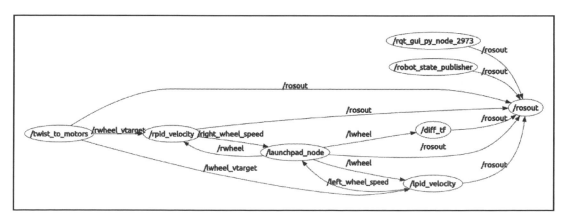

Figure 22: The computation graph view of Chefbot driver nodes

Gmapping and localization in Chefbot

After launching the ROS driver, we can teleop the robot using keyboard teleop. We can use the following command to start keyboard teleoperation:

```
$ roslaunch chefbot_bringup keyboard_teleop.launch
```

If we want to map the robot environment, we can start the gmapping launch file like we did in the simulation:

```
$ roslaunch chefbot_bringup gmapping_demo.launch
```

You can visualize the map building in Rviz using the following command:

```
$ roslaunch chefbot_bringup view_navigation.launch
```

You can build the map by teleoperating the robot around the room. After mapping, save the map as we did in the simulation:

```
$ rosrun map_server map_saver -f ~/test_map
```

After getting the map, launch AMCL nodes to perform final navigation. You have to restart all the launch files and start again.

Let's look at the commands to launch the AMCL nodes.

First, start the ROS driver nodes using the following command:

```
$ roslaunch chefbot_bringup robot_standalone.launch
```

Now start the AMCL nodes:

```
$ roslaunch chefbot_bringup amcl_demo.launch map_file:=~/test_map.yaml
```

Then start Rviz to command the robot on the map:

```
$ roslaunch chefbot_bringup view_navigation.launch
```

You will see Rviz showing something like the following screenshot, in which you can command the robot and the robot can run autonomously:

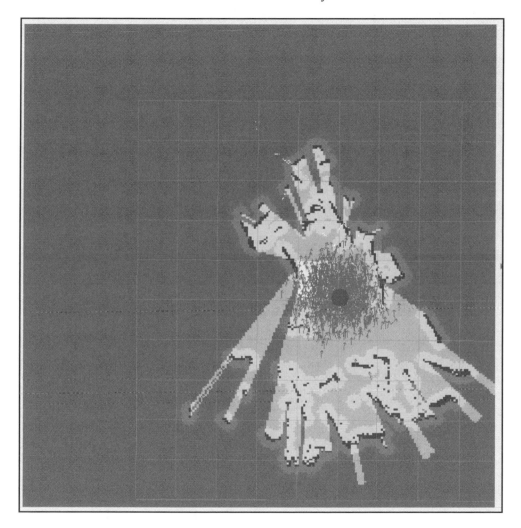

Figure 23: Localization and navigation with Chefbot

The following diagram shows the actual robot hardware. As per our design, we can see circular plate and hollow tubes to add additional layers to the robot. You can also see the **Intel NUC** and **Kinect** camera for robot navigation:

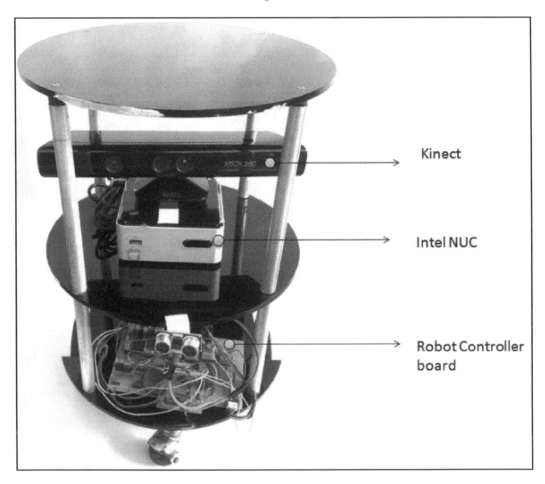

Figure 24: The actual Chefbot prototype

Questions

- How to convert encoder data to estimate the robot's position?
- What is the role of SLAM in robot navigation?
- What is AMCL and why is it used?
- What is the importance of the ROS navigation stack?

Summary

In this chapter, we designed and built an autonomous mobile robot from scratch. The design of the robot started with its specification. From the specification, we designed various parameters of the robot, such as motor torque and speed. After finding out each parameter, we modeled the robot chassis and simulated it using ROS and Gazebo. After simulation, we saw how to create the actual hardware. We selected the components and interconnected the sensors and actuators to the embedded board. We wrote the firmware of the embedded board. The board can communicate with the PC on which the ROS is running. The ROS driver node receives the data from the robot and interfaces with the gmapping and AMCL packages to perform autonomous navigation.

In the next chapter, we will see how to create a self-driving car and interface to Robot Operating System.

10
Creating a Self-Driving Car Using ROS

In this chapter, we will discuss a big technology that is trending in the robotics industry: driverless cars, or self-driving cars. Many of you may have heard about this technology; those who haven't will get an introduction in the first section of the chapter. In this chapter, you can find the following important topics.

- Getting started with self-driving cars
- Software block diagram of a typical self-driving car
- Simulating and interfacing self-driving car sensors in ROS
- Simulating a self-driving car with sensors in Gazebo
- Interfacing a DBW car into ROS
- Introducing the Udacity open source self-driving car project
- Open source self-driving car simulator from Udacity

Creating a self-driving car from scratch is out of the scope of this book, but this chapter may give you an abstract idea of self-driving car components, and tutorials to simulate it.

Getting started with self-driving cars

Just imagine a car driving by itself without the help of anyone. Self-driving cars are robot cars that can think about and decide how to reach the destination. The passenger only needs to specify the destination, and the robot car will take you to the destination safely. To convert an ordinary car into a robotic car, we should add some robotic sensors to it. We know that for a robot, there should be at least three important capabilities. It should be able to *sense*, *plan*, and *act*. Self-driving cars satisfy all these requirements. We'll discuss all the components we need for building a self-driving car. Before discussing the building of self-driving car, let's go through some milestones in self-driving car development.

History of autonomous vehicles

The concept of automating vehicles started long ago. From 1930, people have been trying to automate cars and aircraft, but the hype of self-driving cars increased between 2004 and 2013. To encourage autonomous vehicle technology, the U.S. Department of Defense's research arm, DARPA, conducted a challenge called the Grand DARPA Grand Challenge in 2004. The aim of the challenge was to autonomously drive for 150 miles through a desert roadway. In this challenge, no team was able to complete the goal, so they again challenged engineers in 2007 (http://archive.darpa.mil/grandchallenge/), but this time, the aim was slightly different. Instead of a desert roadway, there was an urban environment spread across 60 miles. In this challenge, four teams were able to finish the goal. The winner of the challenge was Team Taran Racing from Carnegie Mellon University (http://www.tartanracing.org/). The second-place team was Stanford Racing from Stanford University (http://cs.stanford.edu/group/roadrunner/).

Here is the autonomous car that won the DARPA challenge:

Figure 1: Boss, the Tartan autonomous vehicle

After the DARPA Challenge, car companies started working hard to implement autonomous driving capabilities in their cars. Now, almost all car companies have their own autonomous car prototype. In 2009, Google started to develop their self-driving car project, now known as *Waymo* (https://waymo.com/). This project greatly influenced other car companies, and the project was lead by Sebastian Thrun (http://robots.stanford.edu/), the former director of the Stanford Artificial Intelligence Laboratory (http://ai.stanford.edu/).

The car autonomously traveled around 2.7 million kilometers in 2016. Take a look at it:

Source : Google

Figure 2: The Google self-driving car

In 2015, Tesla motors introduced a semi-autonomous autopilot feature in their electric cars. It enables hands-free driving mainly on highways and everything. In 2016, Nvidia introduced their own self-driving car (http://www.nvidia.com/object/drive-px.html), built using their AI car computer called **NVIDIA-DGX-1** (http://www.nvidia.com/object/deep-learning-system.html). This computer was specially designed for the self-driving car and is the best for developing autonomous training driving models.

Other than self-driving cars, there are self-driving shuttles for campus mobility. A lot of startups are building self-driving shuttles now, and one of these startups is called **Auro robotics** (`http://www.auro.ai/`). Here is the shuttle they're building for campuses:

Figure 3: Self-driving shuttle from Auro robotics

There is tremendous progress happening in self-driving car technology. Latest reports say that by the end of 2020, self-driving cars will conquer our roads (`http://www.businessinsider.com/report-10-million-self-driving-cars-will-be-on-the-road-by-2020-2015-5-6?IR=T`). One of the most common terms used when describing autonomous cars is a level of autonomy. Let's go through the different levels of autonomy used when describe an autonomous vehicle.

Levels of autonomy

- **Level 0**: Vehicles having level 0 autonomy are completely manual, with a human driver. Most old cars belong in this category.
- **Level 1**: Vehicles with level 1 autonomy will have a human driver, but they will also have a driver assistance system that can either automatically control the steering system or acceleration/deceleration using information from the environment. All other functions have to be controlled by the driver.
- **Level 2**: In level 2 autonomy, the vehicle can perform both steering and acceleration/deceleration. All other tasks have to be controlled by the driver. We can say that the vehicle is partially automated in this level.
- **Level 3**: In this level, it is expected that all tasks be performed autonomously, but at the same time, it is expected that a human will intervene whenever required. This level is called conditional automation.
- **Level 4**: At this level, there is no need for a driver; everything is handled by an automated system. This kind of autonomous system will work in a particular area under specified weather conditions. This level is called **high automation**
- **Level 5**: This level is called **full automation**. In this level, everything is heavily automated and can work on any road and any weather condition. There is no need for a human driver.

Functional block diagram of a typical self-driving car

The following shows the important components of a self-driving vehicle. The list of parts and their functionalities will be discussed in this section. We'll also look at the exact sensor that was used in the autonomous car for the DARPA Challenge.

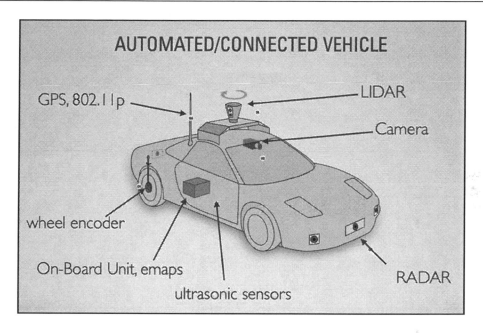

Figure 4: Important components of a self-driving car

GPS, IMU, and wheel encoders

As you know, the **Global Positioning System (GPS)** helps us determine the global position of a vehicle with the help of GPS satellites. The latitude and longitude of the vehicle can be calculated from the GPS data. The accuracy of GPS can vary with the type of sensor; some sensors have an error in the range of meters, and some have less than 1 meter of error. We can find vehicle state by combining GPS, **inertial measurement unit (IMU)** and wheel odometry data, and by using sensor fusion algorithms. This can give better estimate of the vehicle. Let's look at the position estimation modules used for the DARPA Challenge 2007.

POS LV modules from Applanix: This is the module used in the Standford autonomous car, *Junior*. It is a combination of GPS, IMU, and wheel encoders or **distance measurement indicator (DMI)**. You can find it at http://www.applanix.com/products/poslv.html.

Here is what the module looks like:

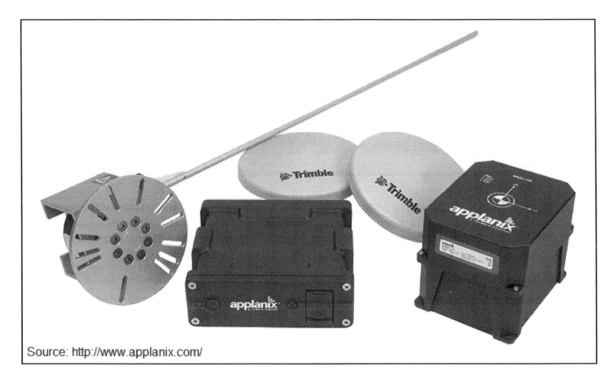

Source: http://www.applanix.com/

Figure 5: Applanix module for autonomous navigation

As you can see from the preceding image, there are wheel encoders, an IMU, and a GPS receiver provided with this package.

OxTS module: This is another GPS/IMU combo module from **Oxford Technical Solution (OxTS)** (`http://www.oxts.com/`). This module was extensively used in the DARPA Challenge in 2007. The module is from the RT 3000 v2 family (`http://www.oxts.com/products/rt3000-family/`). The entire range of GPS modules from OxTS can be found at `http://www.oxts.com/industry/automotive-testing/`. Here is the list of the autonomous vehicles that use these modules: `http://www.oxts.com/customer-stories/autonomous-vehicles-2/`. The following image shows the RT-3000 v2 module:

Figure 6: RT-3000 v2 module

Xsens MTi IMU

The Xsens MTi series has independent IMU modules that can be used in autonomous cars. Here is the link to purchase this product:

```
http://www.xsens.com/products/mti-10-series/
```

Camera

Most autonomous vehicles are deployed with stereo or monocular cameras to detect various things, such as traffic signal status, pedestrians, cyclists, and vehicles. Companies such as MobileEye (http://www.mobileye.com/) which has been acquired by Intel built their **advanced driving assistance system** (**ADAS**) using a sensor fusion of cameras and LIDAR data to predict obstacles and path trajectory.

Other than ADAS, we can also use our own control algorithms by only using camera data. One of the cameras used by the Boss robot car in DARPA 2007 was **Point Grey Firefly (PGF)** (`https://www.ptgrey.com/firefly-mv-usb2-cameras`). These are high dynamic range cameras and have a 45-degree **field of view (FOV)**:

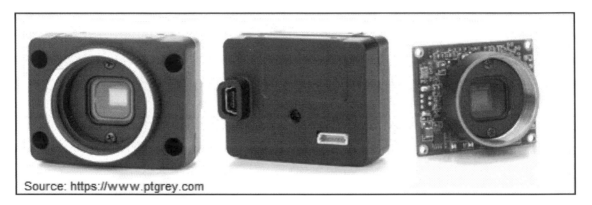

Figure 7: Point Grey Firefly camera

Ultrasonic sensors

In an ADAS system, ultrasonic sensors play an important role in the parking of vehicles, avoiding obstacles in blind spots, and detecting pedestrians. One of the companies providing ultrasound sensors for ADAS systems is Murata (`http://www.murata.com/`). They provide ultrasonic sensors for up to 10 meters, which are optimum for a **parking assistance system (PAS)**. The following diagram shows where ultrasonic sensors are placed on a car:

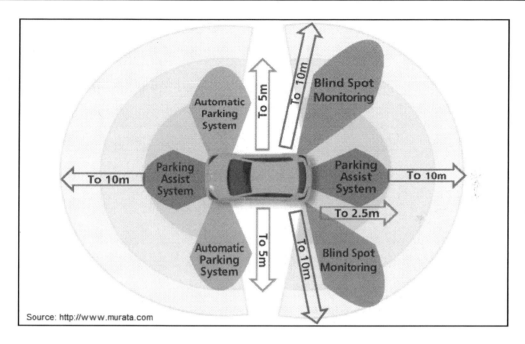

Figure 8: Placement of ultrasonic sensors for PAS

LIDAR and RADAR

The **LIDAR (Light Detection and Ranging)**

(http://oceanservice.noaa.gov/facts/lidar.html) sensors are the core sensors of a self-driving car. A LIDAR sensor basically measures the distance to an object by sending a laser signal and receiving its reflection. It can provide accurate 3D data of the environment, computed from each received laser signal. The main application of LIDAR in autonomous car is mapping the environment from the 3D data, obstacle avoidance, object detection, and so on. Some of the LIDARs used in the DARPA Challenge are will be discussed here.

Velodyne HDL-64 LIDAR

The Velodyne HDL-64 sensor is designed for obstacle detection, mapping, and navigation for autonomous cars. It can give us 360-degree view laser-point cloud data with a high data rate. The range of this laser scan is 80 to 120 m. This sensor is used for almost all the self-driving cars available today. A list of Velodyne sensors available on the market can be found at `http://velodynelidar.com/products.html`.

Here are a few of them:

Figure 9: Some Velodyne sensors

SICK LMS 5xx/1xx and Hokuyo LIDAR

The company SICK (`https://www.sick.com/`) provides a variety of laser scanners that can be used indoor or outdoor. The SICK **Laser Measurement System (LMS)** 5xx and 1xx models are commonly used in autonomous cars for obstacle detection. It provides a scanning range of 180 degrees and has high-resolution laser data. The list of SICK laser scanners available in the market is at `https://www.sick.com/in/en`. Another company, called **Hokuyo** (`http://www.hokuyo-aut.jp/index.html`), also builds laser scanners for autonomous vehicles. Here is the list of laser scanners provided by Hokuyo: `http://www.hokuyo-aut.jp/02sensor/`.

These are two laser scanners by SICK and Hokuyo:

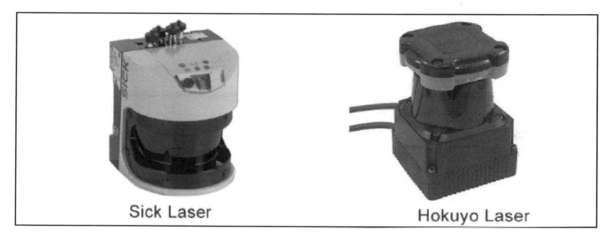

Sick Laser   Hokuyo Laser

Figure 10: SICK and Hokuyo laser scanners

Some of the other LIDARs used in the DARPA Challenge provided given here:
`http://www.conti-online.com/www/industrial_sensors_de_en/`
`https://www.ibeo-as.com/aboutibeo/lidar/`

Continental ARS 300 radar (ARS)

Apart from LIDARs, self-driving cars are also deployed with long-range radars. One of the popular long-range radars is ARS 30X by Continental (`http://www.conti-online.com/www/industrial_sensors_de_en/themes/ars_300_en.html`). It works using the Doppler principle and can measure up to 200 meters. Bosch also manufactures radars suitable for self-driving cars. The main application of radars is collision avoidance. Commonly, radars are deployed at the front of the vehicles.

Delphi radar

Delphi has a new radar for autonomous cars. Here is the link to view the product:

```
http://www.delphi.com/manufacturers/auto/safety/active/electronically-scanning-
radar
```

On-board computer

The onboard computer is the heart of the self-driving car. It may have high-end processors such as Intel Xenon and GPUs to crunch data from various sensors. All sensors are connected to this computer, and it finally predicts the trajectory and sends control commands, such as steering angle, throttle, and braking for the self-driving car.

Software block diagram of self-driving cars

In this section, we will discuss a basic software block diagram of a self-driving car that was in DARPA Challenge:

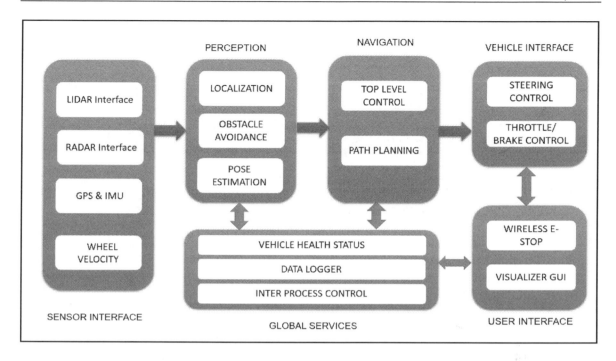

Figure 11: Software block diagram of a self-driving car

Let's learn what each block means. Each block can interact with others using **inter-process communication (IPC)** or shared memory. ROS messaging middleware is a perfect fit in this scenario. In DARPA Challenge, they implemented a publish/subscribe mechanism to do these tasks. One of the IPC library development by MIT for 2006 DARPA challenge was **Lightweight Communications and Marshalling** (LCM). You may can learn more about LCM from the following link (`https://lcm-proj.github.io/`).

- **Sensor interface modules**: As the name of the module indicates, all the communication between the sensors and the vehicle is done in this block. The block enables us to provide the various kinds of sensor data to all other blocks. The main sensors include LIDAR, camera, radar, GPS, IMU, and wheel encoders.
- **Perception modules**: These modules perform processing on perception data from sensors such as LIDAR, camera, and radar and segment the data to find moving and static objects. They also help localize the self-driving car relative to the digital map of the environment.

- **Navigation modules**: This module determines the behavior of the autonomous car. It has motion planners and finite state machines for different behaviors in the robot.

- **Vehicle interface**: After the path planning, the control commands, such as steering, throttle, and brake control, are sent to the vehicle through a **drive-by-wire** (**DBW**) interface. DBW basically works through the CAN bus. Only some vehicles support the DBW interface. Examples are the Lincoln MKZ, VW Passat Wagon, and some models from Nissan.

- **User interface**: The user interface section provides controls to the user. It can be a touch screen to view maps and set the destination. Also, there is an emergency stop button for the user.

- **Global services**: This set of modules helps log the data and has time stamping and message-passing support to keep the software running reliably.

Simulating and interfacing self-driving car sensors in ROS

In the preceding section, we discussed the basic concepts of a self-driving car. That understanding will definitely help in this section too. In this section, we are simulating and interfacing some of the sensors that we are using in self-driving cars. Here is the list of sensors that we are going to simulate and interface with ROS:

- Velodyne LIDAR
- Laser scanner
- Camera
- Stereo camera
- GPS
- IMU
- Ultrasonic sensor

We'll discuss how to set up the simulation using ROS and Gazebo and read the sensor values. This sensor interfacing will be useful when you build your own self-driving car simulation from scratch. So if you know how to simulate and interface these sensors, it can definitely accelerate your self-driving car development.

Simulating the Velodyne LIDAR

The Velodyne LIDAR is becoming an integral part of a self-driving car. Because of high demand, there are enough software modules available for working with this sensor. We are going to simulate two popular models of Velodyne, called **HDL-32E** and **VLP-16**. Let's see how to do it in ROS and Gazebo.

In ROS-Kinetic and Indigo, we can install from a binary package or compile from source code. Here is the command to install Velodyne packages on ROS Kinetic:

```
$ sudo apt-get install ros-kinetic-velodyne-simulator
```

In ROS Indigo, just replace the ROS distribution name:

```
$ sudo apt-get install ros-indigo-velodyne-simulator
```

To install it from source code, just clone the source package to the ROS workspace using the following command:

```
$ git clone https://bitbucket.org/DataspeedInc/velodyne_simulator.git
```

After cloning the package, you can build it using the `catkin_make` command. Here is the ROS wiki page of the Velodyne simulator:

```
http://wiki.ros.org/velodyne_simulator
```

So you are installed the packages. Now it's time to start the simulation of the Velodyne sensor. You can start the simulation using the following command:

```
$ roslaunch velodyne_description example.launch
```

This command will launch the sensor simulation in Gazebo. Note that this simulation will consume a lot of RAM of your system; your system should have at least 8 GB before start the simulation.

You can add some obstacles around the sensor for testing, like this:

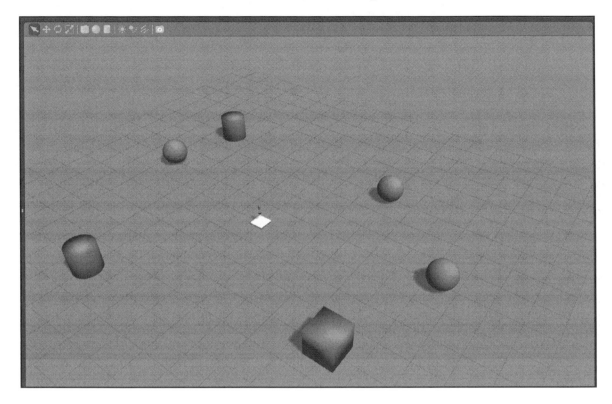

Figure 12: Simulation of Velodyne in Gazebo

You can visualize the sensor data in Rviz by adding display types such as **PointCloud2** and **Robot Model** to visualize sensor data and sensor models. You have to set the **Fixed Frame** to **velodyne**. You can clearly see the obstacles around the sensor in the following figure:

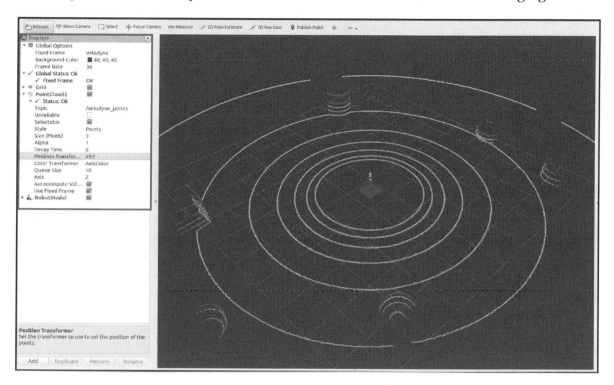

Figure 13: Visualization of a Velodyne sensor in Rviz

Interfacing Velodyne sensors with ROS

We have seen how to simulate a Velodyne sensor; now let's have a look at how we can interface a real Velodyne sensor with ROS.

The following commands are to install the `velodyne` ROS driver package to convert Velodyne data to point cloud data.

ROS Kinetic:

```
$ sudo apt-get install ros-kinetic-velodyne
```

ROS Indigo:

```
$ sudo apt-get install ros-indigo-velodyne
```

These commands will install the ROS Velodyne driver and point cloud converter packages.

This driver supports models such as the HDL-64E, HDL-32E, and VLP-16.

Here are the commands to start the driver nodelets:

```
$ roslaunch velodyne_driver nodelet_manager.launch model:=32E
```

Here, you need to mention the model name along with the launch file to start the driver for a specific model.

The following command will start the converter nodelets to convert Velodyne messages (`velodyne_msgs/VelodyneScan`) to a point cloud (`sensor_msgs/PointCloud2`). Here is the command to perform this conversion:

```
$ roslaunch velodyne_pointcloud cloud_nodelet.launch
  calibration:=~/calibration_file.yaml
```

This will launch the calibration file for Velodyne, which is necessary for correcting noise from the sensor.

We can write all these commands to a launch file, which is shown in the following code block. If you run this launch file, the driver node and point cloud convertor nodelets will start, and we can work with the sensor data:

```
<launch>
  <!-- start nodelet manager and driver nodelets -->
  <include file="$(find
velodyne_driver)/launch/nodelet_manager.launch" />

  <!-- start transform nodelet -->
  <include file="$(find
velodyne_pointcloud)/launch/transform_nodelet.launch">
    <arg name="calibration"
         value="$(find
velodyne_pointcloud)/params/64e_utexas.yaml"/>
```

```
    </include>
  </launch>
```

The calibration files for each model are available in the `velodyne_pointcloud` package.

 Note: The connection procedure of Velodyne to PC is given here:
`http://wiki.ros.org/velodyne/Tutorials/Getting%20Started%20with%20the%20HDL-32E`

Simulating a laser scanner

In this section, we will see how to simulate a laser scanner in Gazebo. We can simulate it by providing custom parameters according to our application. When you install ROS, you also automatically install several default Gazebo plugins, which include Gazebo laser scanner plugin.

We can simply use this plugin and apply our custom parameters. For demonstration, you can use a tutorial package inside `chapter_10_codes` called `sensor_sim_gazebo`. You can simply copy the package to the workspace and build it using the `catkin_make` command. This package contains a basic simulation of the laser scanner, camera, IMU, ultrasonic sensor, and GPS.

Before starting with this package, you should install a package called `hector-gazebo-plugins` using the following command. This package contains Gazebo plugins of several sensors that can be used in self-driving car simulations.

```
$ sudo apt-get install ros-kinetic-hector-gazebo-plugins
```

To start the laser scanner simulation, just use the following command:

```
$ roslaunch sensor_sim_gazebo laser.launch
```

We'll first look at the output of the laser scanner and then dig into the code.

When you launch the preceding command, you will see an empty world with an orange box. The orange box is our laser scanner. You can use any mesh file to replace this shape according to your application. To show laser scanner data, we can place some objects in Gazebo, as shown here. You can add models from Gazebo's top panel.

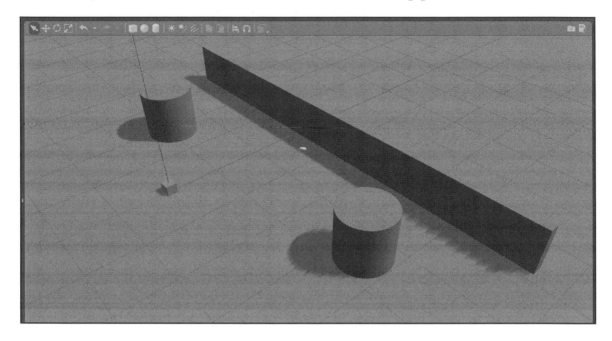

Figure 14: Simulation of a laser scanner in Gazebo

You can visualize the laser data in Rviz, as shown in the next screenshot. The topic to which the laser data is coming is /laser/scan. You can add a **LaserScan** display type to view this data:

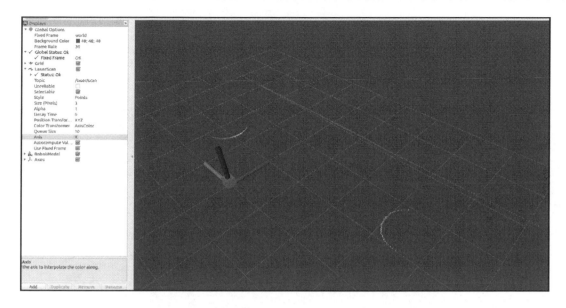

Figure 15: Visualization of laser scanner data in Rviz

You have to set the **Fixed Frame** to a **world** frame and enable the **RobotModel** and **Axes** display types in Rviz.

The following is the list of topics generated while simulating this sensor. You can see the /laser/scan topic.

```
robot@robot-pc:~$ rostopic list
/clicked_point
/clock
/gazebo/link_states
/gazebo/model_states
/gazebo/parameter_descriptions
/gazebo/parameter_updates
/gazebo/set_link_state
/gazebo/set_model_state
/initialpose
/joint_states
/laser/scan
/move_base_simple/goal
/rosout
/rosout_agg
/tf
/tf_static
```

Figure 16: List of topics from the laser scanner simulation

Explaining the simulation code

The `sensor_sim_gazebo` package has the following list of files for simulating all self-driving car sensors. Here is the directory structure of this package:

```
├── CMakeLists.txt
├── include
│   └── sensor_sim_gazebo
├── launch
│   ├── camera.launch
│   ├── gps.launch
│   ├── imu.launch
│   ├── laser.launch
│   ├── sonar.launch
│   └── stereo_camera.launch
├── mesh
│   ├── hokuyo_utm_30lx.dae
│   └── max_sonar_ez4.dae
├── package.xml
├── src
├── urdf
│   ├── camera.xacro
│   ├── gps.xacro
│   ├── imu.xacro
│   ├── laser.xacro
│   ├── sensor.xacro
│   ├── sonar_model.xacro
│   ├── sonar.xacro
│   └── stereo_camera.xacro
```

Figure 17: List of files in sensor_sim_gazebo

To simulate a laser, launch the `laser.launch` file; similarly, to start simulating the IMU, GPS, and camera, launch the corresponding launch files. Inside URDF, you can see the Gazebo plugin definition for each sensor. The `sensor.xacro` file is the orange box definition that you saw in the preceding simulation. It is just a box for visualizing a sensor model. We are using this model for representing all the sensors inside this package. You can use your own model instead of this, too.

The `laser.xacro` file has the Gazebo plugin definition of the laser, as shownhere:

```
<gazebo reference="sensor">
  <sensor type="ray" name="head_hokuyo_sensor">
    <pose>0 0 0 0 0 0</pose>
    <visualize>false</visualize>
    <update_rate>40</update_rate>
    <ray>
      <scan>
```

```
        <horizontal>
          <samples>720</samples>
          <resolution>1</resolution>
          <min_angle>-1.570796</min_angle>
          <max_angle>1.570796</max_angle>
        </horizontal>
      </scan>
      <range>
        <min>0.8</min>
        <max>30.0</max>
        <resolution>0.01</resolution>
      </range>
      <noise>
        <type>gaussian</type>
        <!-- Noise parameters based on published spec for Hokuyo
laser
            achieving "+-30mm" accuracy at range < 10m.  A mean
of 0.0m and
            stddev of 0.01m will put 99.7% of samples within
0.03m of the true
              reading. -->
        <mean>0.0</mean>
        <stddev>0.01</stddev>
       </noise>
    </ray>
    <plugin name="gazebo_ros_head_hokuyo_controller"
 filename="libgazebo_ros_laser.so">
        <topicName>/laser/scan</topicName>
        <frameName>world</frameName>
    </plugin>
   </sensor>
  </gazebo>
```

Here, you can see various parameters of the laser scanner plugin. We can fine-tune these parameters for our custom applications. The plugin we've used here is `libgazebo_ros_laser.so`, and all the parameters are passed to this plugin.

In the `laser.launch` file, we are creating an empty world and spawning the `laser.xacro` file. Here is the code snippet to spawn the model into Gazebo and start a joint-state publisher to start publishing TF data:

```
<param name="robot_description" command="$(find xacro)/xacro --
inorder '$(find sensor_sim_gazebo)/urdf/laser.xacro'" />

<node pkg="gazebo_ros" type="spawn_model" name="spawn_model"
args="-urdf -param /robot_description -model example"/>
```

```
<node pkg="robot_state_publisher" type="robot_state_publisher"
name="robot_state_publisher">
   <param name="publish_frequency" type="double" value="30.0" />
</node>
```

Interfacing laser scanners with ROS

Now that we've discussed the simulation of the laser scanner, let's see how to interface real sensors with ROS.

Here are some links to guide you with setting up Hokuyo and SICK laser scanners in ROS. The complete installation instructions is available.

Hokuyo sensors: http://wiki.ros.org/hokuyo_node

SICK lasers: http://wiki.ros.org/sick_tim

You can install Hokuyo drivers from binary packages using the following commands:

Hokuyo laser scanners.

```
$ sudo apt-get install ros-kinetic-hokuyo3d
```

SICK laser scanners.

```
$ sudo apt-get install ros-kinetic-sick-tim ros-kinetic-lms1xx
```

Simulating stereo and mono cameras in Gazebo

In the previous section, we discussed laser scanner simulation. In this section, we will see how to simulate a camera. A camera is an important sensor for all kinds of robots. We will see how to launch both mono and stereo camera simulations. You can use the following commands to launch the simulations.

Mono camera:

```
$ roslaunch sensor_sim_gazebo camera.launch
```

Stereo camera:

```
$ roslaunch sensor_sim_gazebo stereo_camera.launch
```

You can view the image from the camera either using Rviz or using a tool called image_view.

You can look at the mono camera view using the following command:

```
$ rosrun image_view image_view image:=/sensor/camera1/image_raw
```

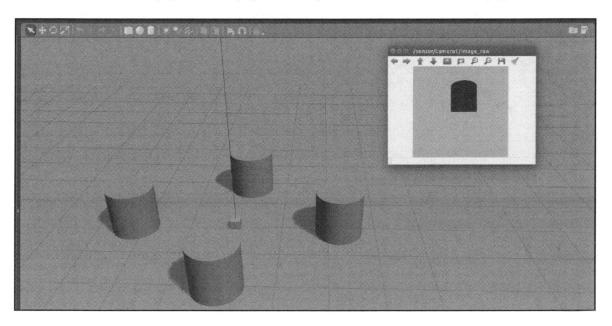

Figure 18: Image from simulated camera

To view images from a simulated stereo camera, use the following commands:

```
$ rosrun image_view image_view image:=/stereo/camera/right/image_raw
$ rosrun image_view image_view image:=/stereo/camera/left/image_raw
```

This commands will display two image windows from each camera of the stereo camera, which is shown here:

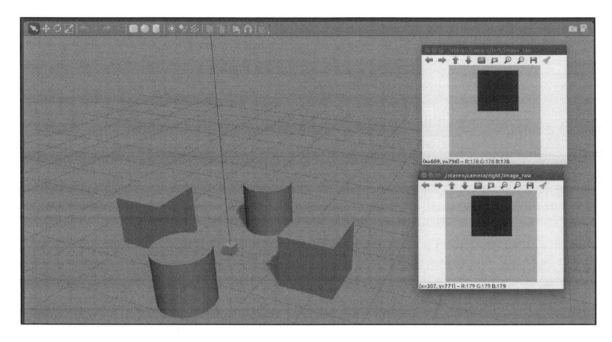

Figure 19: Image from simulated stereo camera

Similar to the laser scanner plugin, we are using a separate plugin for mono and stereo cameras. You can see the Gazebo plugin definition in `sensor_sim_gazebo/urdf/camera.xacro` and `stereo_camera.xacro`.

The `lib_gazebo_ros_camera.so` plugin is used to simulate a mono camera, and `libgazebo_ros_multicamera.so` for a stereo camera.

Interfacing cameras with ROS

In this section, we will see how to interface an actual camera with ROS. There are a lot of cameras available in the market. We'll look at some of the commonly used cameras and how to interface with them.

There are some links to guide you with setting up each driver in ROS.

For the **Point Grey** camera, you can refer to the following link:
`http://wiki.ros.org/pointgrey_camera_driver`

If you are working with a Mobileye sensor, you may get ROS drivers by contacting the company. All details of the driver and its SDK are available at the following link:

`https://autonomoustuff.com/product/mobileye-camera-dev-kit`

If you are working on IEEE 1394 digital cameras, the following drivers can be used to interface with ROS:

`http://wiki.ros.org/camera1394`

One of the latest stereo cameras available is the ZED camera (`https://www.stereolabs.com/`). The ROS drivers of this camera are available at the following link:

`http://wiki.ros.org/zed-ros-wrapper`

If you are working with some normal USB web camera, the
`usb_cam`
driver package will be best for interfacing with ROS:

`http://wiki.ros.org/usb_cam`

Simulating GPS in Gazebo

In this section, we will see how to simulate a GPS sensor in Gazebo. As you know, GPS is one of the essential sensors in a self-driving car. You can start a GPS simulation using the following command:

```
$ roslaunch sensor_sim_gazebo gps.launch
```

Now, you can list out the topic and find the GPS topics published from the Gazebo plugin. Here is a list of topics from the GPS plugin:

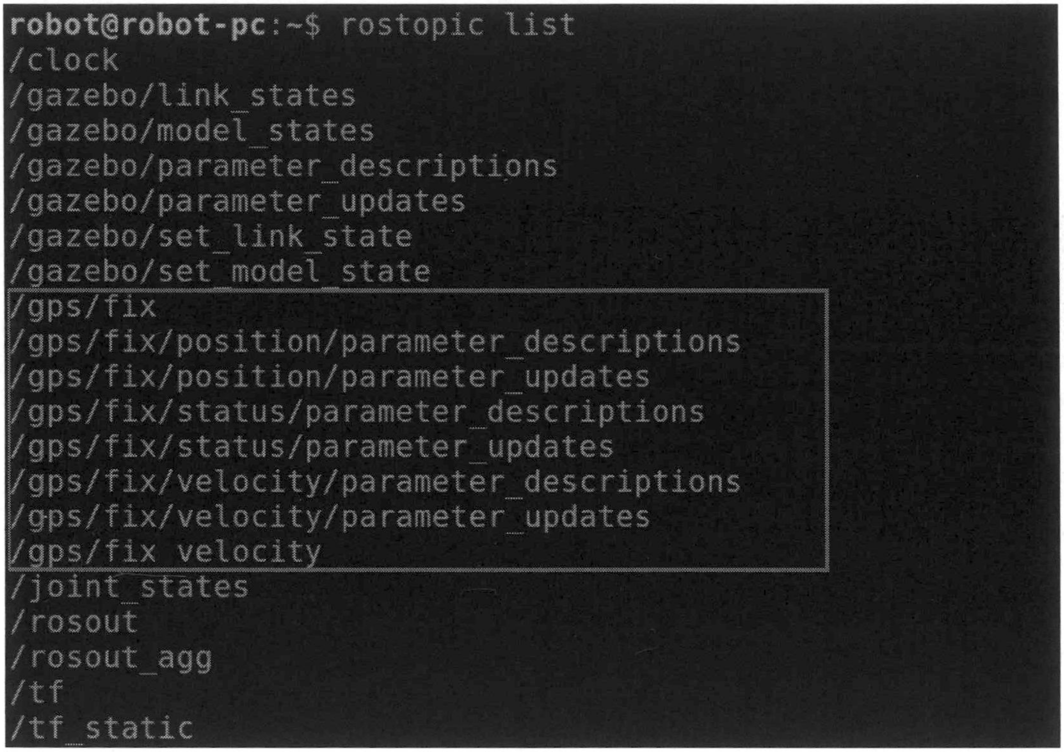

```
robot@robot-pc:~$ rostopic list
/clock
/gazebo/link_states
/gazebo/model_states
/gazebo/parameter_descriptions
/gazebo/parameter_updates
/gazebo/set_link_state
/gazebo/set_model_state
/gps/fix
/gps/fix/position/parameter_descriptions
/gps/fix/position/parameter_updates
/gps/fix/status/parameter_descriptions
/gps/fix/status/parameter_updates
/gps/fix/velocity/parameter_descriptions
/gps/fix/velocity/parameter_updates
/gps/fix_velocity
/joint_states
/rosout
/rosout_agg
/tf
/tf_static
```

Figure 20: List of topics from the Gazebo GPS plugin

You can echo the /gps/fix topic to confirm that the plugin is publishing the values correctly.

You can use the following command to echo this topic:

```
$ rostopic echo /gps/fix
```

```
robot@robot-pc:~$ rostopic echo /gps/fix
header:
  seq: 161
  stamp:
    secs: 40
    nsecs: 500000000
  frame_id: sensor
status:
  status: 0
  service: 0
latitude: -30.0602249716
longitude: -51.17391374
altitude: 9.960587315
position_covariance: [0.0025010000000000006, 0.0, 0.0, 0.0, 0.002501000000
6, 0.0, 0.0, 0.0, 0.0025010000000000006]
position_covariance_type: 2
```

Figure 21: Values published to the /gps/fix topic

If you look at the code in `sensor_sim_gazebo/urdf/gps.xacro`, you will find `<plugin name="gazebo_ros_gps" filename="libhector_gazebo_ros_gps.so">`; these plugins belong to the `hector_gazebo_ros_plugins` package, which we installed at the beginning of the sensor interfacing. We can set all parameters related to GPS in this plugin description, and you can see the test parameters values in the `gps.xacro` file. The GPS model is visualized as a box, and you can test the sensor values by moving this box in Gazebo.

Interfacing GPS with ROS

In this section, we will see how to interface some popular GPS modules with ROS. One of the popular GPS modules we discussed earlier was **Oxford Technical Solutions (OxTS)**. You can find GPS/IMU modules at `http://www.oxts.com/products/`. The ROS interface of this module can be found at `http://wiki.ros.org/oxford_gps_eth`. The Applanix GPS/IMU ROS module driver can be found at the following links:

`http://wiki.ros.org/applanix_driver`

`http://wiki.ros.org/applanix`

Simulating IMU on Gazebo

Similar to GPS, we can start the IMU simulation using the following command:

```
$ roslaunch sensor_sim_gazebo imu.launch
```

You will get orientation values, linear acceleration, and angular velocity from this plugin. After launching this file, you can list out the topics published by the `imu` plugin. Here is the list of topics published by this plugin:

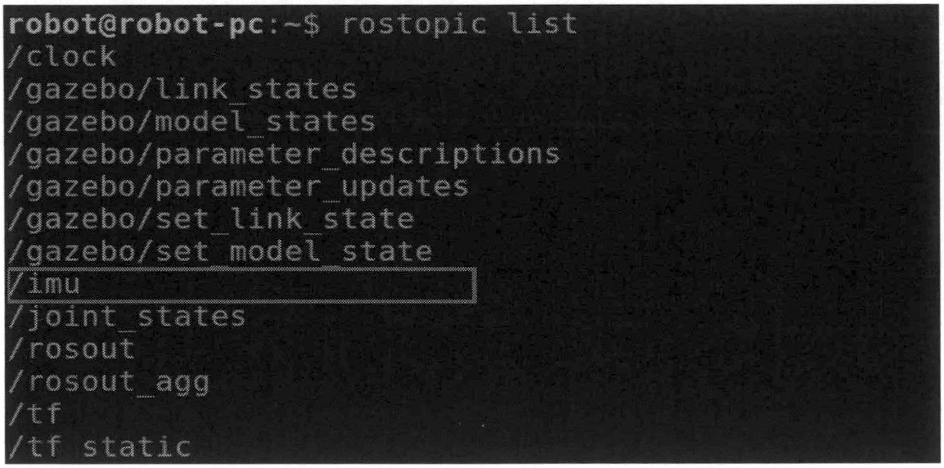

```
robot@robot-pc:~$ rostopic list
/clock
/gazebo/link_states
/gazebo/model_states
/gazebo/parameter_descriptions
/gazebo/parameter_updates
/gazebo/set_link_state
/gazebo/set_model_state
/imu
/joint_states
/rosout
/rosout_agg
/tf
/tf_static
```

Figure 22: List of topics published from the imu ROS plugin

We can check out the `/imu` topic by echoing the topic. You can find orientation, linear acceleration, and angular velocity data from this topic. The values are shown here:

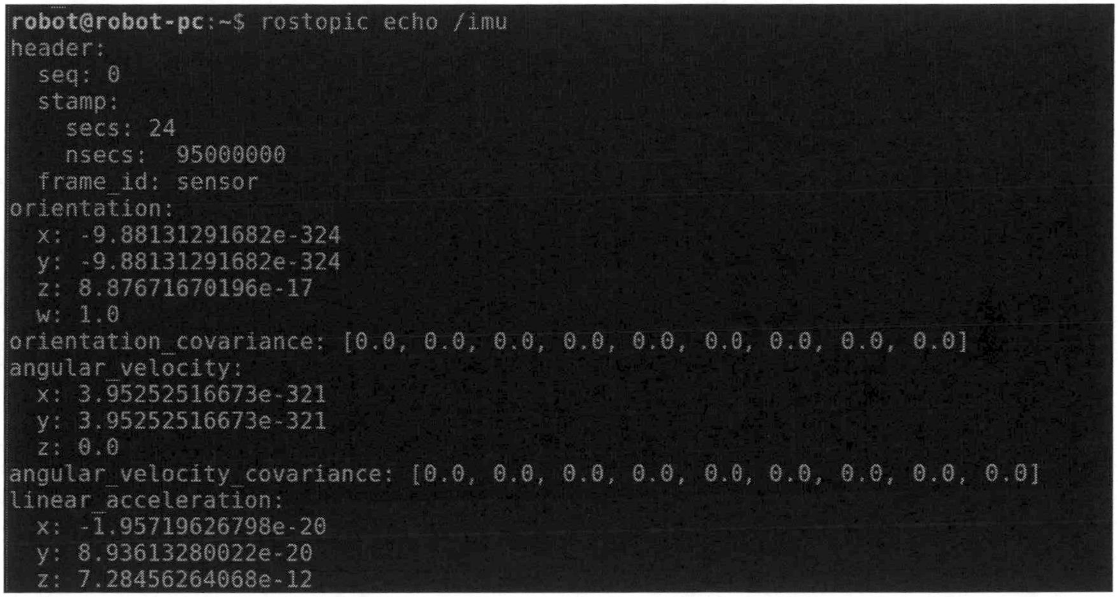

```
robot@robot-pc:~$ rostopic echo /imu
header:
  seq: 0
  stamp:
    secs: 24
    nsecs:  95000000
  frame_id: sensor
orientation:
  x:  -9.88131291682e-324
  y:  -9.88131291682e-324
  z:  8.87671670196e-17
  w:  1.0
orientation_covariance: [0.0, 0.0, 0.0, 0.0, 0.0, 0.0, 0.0, 0.0, 0.0]
angular_velocity:
  x:  3.95252516673e-321
  y:  3.95252516673e-321
  z:  0.0
angular_velocity_covariance: [0.0, 0.0, 0.0, 0.0, 0.0, 0.0, 0.0, 0.0, 0.0]
linear_acceleration:
  x:  -1.95719626798e-20
  y:  8.93613280022e-20
  z:  7.28456264068e-12
```

Figure 23: Data from the /imu topic

If you look at the IMU plugin definition code from
`sensor_sim_gazebo/urdf/imu.xacro`, you can find the name of the plugin and its
parameters.

The name of the plugin is mentioned in the following code snippet:

```
<gazebo>
  <plugin name="imu_plugin" filename="libgazebo_ros_imu.so">
    <alwaysOn>true</alwaysOn>
    <bodyName>sensor</bodyName>
    <topicName>imu</topicName>
    <serviceName>imu_service</serviceName>
    <gaussianNoise>0.0</gaussianNoise>
    <updateRate>20.0</updateRate>
  </plugin>
</gazebo>
```

The plugin's name is `libgazebo_ros_imu.so`, and it is installed along with a standard
ROS installation.

You can also visualize IMU data in Rviz. Choose the Imu display type to view it. The IMU is visualized as a box itself, so if you move the box in Gazebo, you can see an arrow moving in the direction of movement. The Gazebo and Rviz visualizations are shown here:

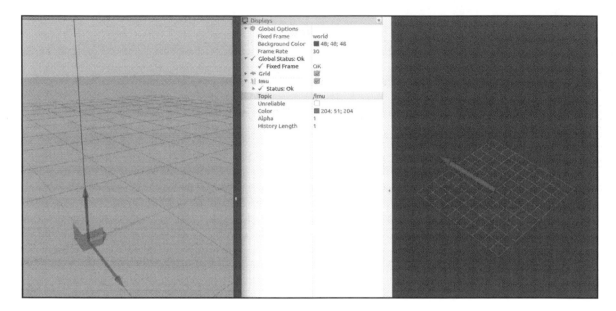

Figure 24: Visualization of the /imu topic

Interfacing IMUs with ROS

Most self-driving cars use integrated modules for GPS, IMU, and wheel encoders for accurate position prediction. In this section, we will look at some popular IMU modules that you can use if you want to use IMU alone.

I'll point you to a few links for ROS drivers used to interface with it. One of the popular IMUs is the MicroStrain 3DM-GX2 (`http://www.microstrain.com/inertial/3dm-gx2`):

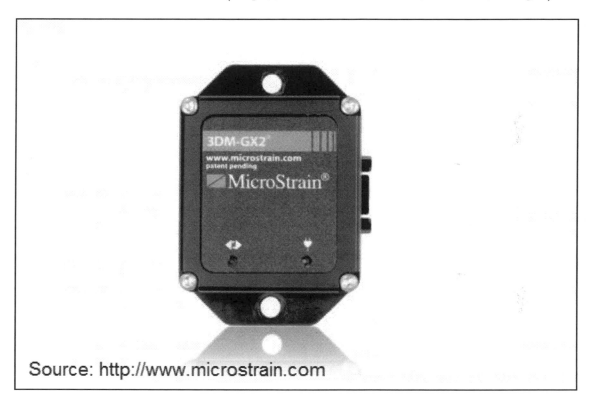

Figure 25: Microstrain-3DM-GX2 IMU

Here are the ROS drivers for this IMU series:

`http://wiki.ros.org/microstrain_3dmgx2_imu`

`http://wiki.ros.org/microstrain_3dm_gx3_45`

Other than that, there are IMUs from Phidget (`http://wiki.ros.org/phidgets_imu`) and popular IMUs such as InvenSense MPU 9250, 9150, and 6050 models (`https://github.com/jeskesen/i2c_imu`). Another IMU sensor series called MTi from Xsens and its drivers can be found at `http://wiki.ros.org/xsens_driver`.

Simulating an ultrasonic sensor in Gazebo

Ultrasonic sensors also play a key role in self-driving cars. We've already seen that range sensors are widely used in parking assistant systems. In this section, we are going to see how to simulate a range sensor in Gazebo. The range sensor Gazebo plugin is already available in the `hector` Gazebo ROS plugin, so we can just use it in our code.

Like we did in earlier demos, we will first see how to run the simulation and watch the output.

The following command will launch the range sensor simulation in Gazebo:

```
$ roslaunch sensor_sim_gazebo sonar.launch
```

In this simulation, we are taking the actual 3D model of the sonar, and it's very small. You may need to zoom in Gazebo to view the model. We can test the sensor by putting an obstacle in front of it. We can start Rviz and can view the distance using the **Range** display type. The topic name is `/distance` and the **Fixed Frame** is **world**.

Here is the range sensor value when the obstacle is far away:

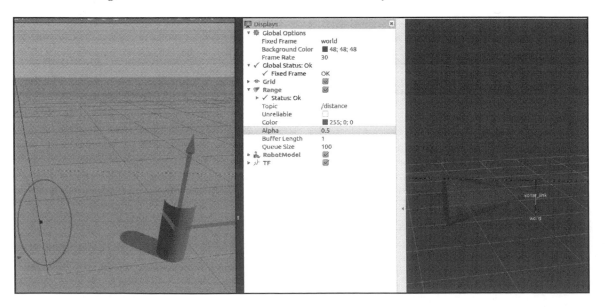

Figure 26: Range sensor value when the obstacle is far away

You can see that the marked point is the ultrasonic sound sensor, and on the right, you can view the Rviz range data as a cone-shaped structure. If we move the obstacle near the sensor, we can see what happens to the range sensor data:

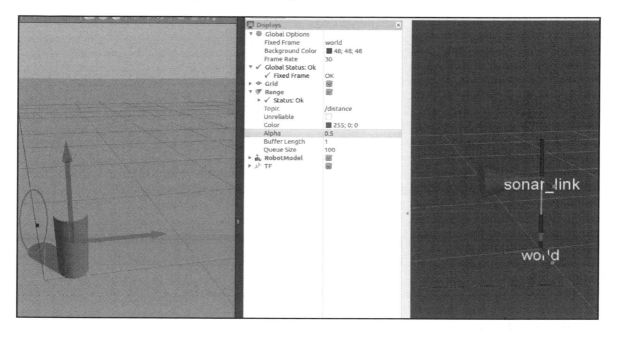

Figure 27: Range sensor value when the obstacle is near

When the obstacle is too near the sensor, the cone size is reduced, which means the distance to the obstacle is very low.

Open the Gazebo sonar plugin definition from `sensor_sim_gazebo/urdf/sonar.xacro`. This file includes a reference to another file called `sonar_model.xacro`, which has the complete sonar plugin definition.

We are using the `libhector_gazebo_ros_sonar` plugin to run this simulation, which is given in the following code snippet from `sonar_mode.xacro`:

```
<plugin name="gazebo_ros_sonar_controller"
filename="libhector_gazebo_ros_sonar.so">
```

Low-cost LIDAR sensors

This is an add-on section for hobbyists. If you are planning to build a miniature model of a self-driving car, you can use the following LIDAR sensors.

Sweep LIDAR

The Sweep 360-degree rotating LIDAR (`http://scanse.io/`) has a range of 40 meters. Compared to high-end LIDARs such as Velodyne, it is very cheap and good for research and hobby projects:

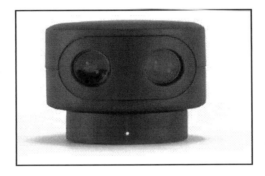

Figure 28: Sweep LIDAR

There is a good ROS interface available for this sensor. Here's the link to the Sweep sensor ROS package: `https://github.com/scanse/sweep-ros`. Before building the package, you need to install some dependencies:

```
$ sudo apt-get install ros-kinetic-pcl-conversions ros-kinetic-
pointcloud-to-laserscan
```

Now you can simply copy the `sweep-ros` package to your Catkin workspace and build it using the `catkin_make` command.

After building the package, you can plug the LIDAR to your PC through a serial-to-USB converter. If you plug this converter into a PC, Ubuntu will assign a device called `/dev/ttyUSB0`. First, you need to change the permission of the device using the following command:

```
$ sudo chmod 777 /dev/ttyUSB0
```

After changing the permission, we can start launching any of the launch files to view the laser's /scan point cloud data from the sensor.

The launch file will display the laser scan in Rviz:

```
$ roslaunch sweep_ros view_sweep_laser_scan.launch
```

The launch file will display the point cloud in Rviz:

```
$ roslaunch sweep_ros view_sweep_pc2.launch
```

Here is the visualization of the Sweep LIDAR:

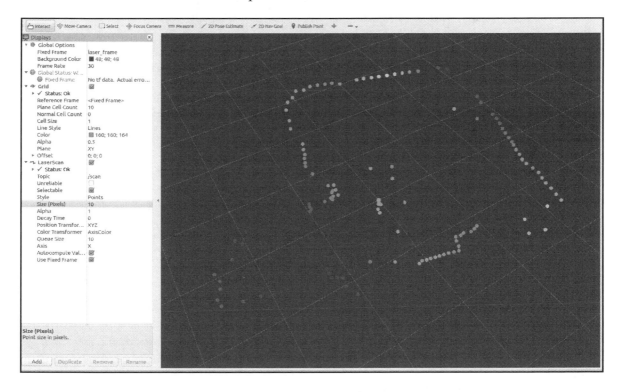

Figure 29: Sweep LIDAR visualization in Rviz

RPLIDAR

Similar to the Sweep LIDAR, RPLIDAR (`http://www.slamtec.com/en/lidar`) is another low-cost LIDAR for hobby projects. RPLIDAR and Sweep have the same applications: SLAM and autonomous navigation:

Figure 30: RPLIDAR

There is a ROS driver for interfacing the RPLIDAR with ROS. The ROS package is at `http://wiki.ros.org/rplidar`. The GitHub link of the package is `https://github.com/robopeak/rplidar_ros`.

Simulating a self-driving car with sensors in Gazebo

In this section, we are going to discuss an open-source self-driving car project done in Gazebo. In this project, we will learn how to implement a robot car model in Gazebo and how to integrate all sensors into it. Also, we will move the robot around the environment using a keyboard, and finally, we will build a map of the environment using SLAM.

Installing prerequisites

This project is fully compatible with ROS Indigo, but some packages are yet to be released in ROS Kinetic. Let's take a look at the prerequisites for setting up packages in ROS Indigo.

The commands given here will install the ROS Gazebo controller manager:

```
$ sudo apt-get install ros-indigo-controller-manager
$ sudo apt-get install ros-indigo-ros-control ros-indigo-ros-
controllers
$ sudo apt-get install ros-indigo-gazebo-ros-control
```

After installing this, we can install the Velodyne simulator packages in Indigo using the following command:

```
$ sudo apt-get install ros-indigo-velodyne
```

This project uses SICK laser scanners, so we have to install the SICK ROS toolbox packages:

```
$ sudo apt-get install ros-indigo-sicktoolbox ros-indigo-sicktoolbox-
wrapper
```

After installing all these dependencies, we can clone the project files into a new ROS workspace. Use these commands:

```
$ cd ~
$ mkdir -p catvehicle_ws/src
$cd catvehicle_ws/src
$ catkin_init_workspace
```

We have created a new ROS workspace, and now it's time to clone the project files to the workspace. The following commands will do this:

```
$ cd ~/catvehicle_ws/src
$ git clone https://github.com/sprinkjm/catvehicle.git
$ git clone https://github.com/sprinkjm/obstaclestopper.git
$ cd ../
$ catkin_make
```

If all packages have compiled successfully, you can add the following line to the `.bashrc` file:

```
$ source ~/catvehicle_ws/devel/setup.bash
```

You can launch the vehicle simulation using the following command:

```
$ roslaunch catvehicle catvehicle_skidpan.launch
```

This command will only start simulation in the command line.

In another Terminal window, run the following command:

```
$ gzclient
```

Figure 31: Robot car simulation in Gazebo

You can see the Velodyne scan in front of the vehicle. We can list out all ROS topics from the simulation using the `rostopic` command. Here are the main topics generated in the simulation:

```
/catvehicle/cmd_vel
/catvehicle/cmd_vel_safe
/catvehicle/distanceEstimator/angle
/catvehicle/distanceEstimator/dist
/catvehicle/front_laser_points
/catvehicle/front_left_steering_position_controller/command
/catvehicle/front_right_steering_position_controller/command
/catvehicle/joint1_velocity_controller/command
/catvehicle/joint2_velocity_controller/command
/catvehicle/joint_states
/catvehicle/lidar_points
/catvehicle/odom
/catvehicle/path
/catvehicle/steering
/catvehicle/vel
/clock
/gazebo/link_states
/gazebo/model_states
/gazebo/parameter_descriptions
/gazebo/parameter_updates
/gazebo/set_link_state
/gazebo/set_model_state
/rosout
/rosout_agg
/tf
/tf_static
```

Figure 32: Main topics generated by robotic car simulation

Visualizing robotic car sensor data

We can view each type of sensor data from the robotic car in Rviz. Just run Rviz and open the `catvehicle.rviz` configuration from `chapter_10_codes`. You can see the Velodyne points and robot car model from Rviz, as shown here:

Figure 33: Complete robot car simulation in Rviz

You can also add a camera view in Rviz. There are two cameras, on the left and right side of the vehicle. We have added some obstacles in Gazebo to check whether the sensor is detecting obstacles. You can add more sensors, such as SICK laser and IMU, to Rviz.

Moving a self-driving car in Gazebo

Okay, so we are done with simulating a complete robotic car in Gazebo; now, let's move the robot around the environment. We can do this using a keyboard teleop node.

We can launch an existing TurtleBot teleop node using the following command:

```
$ roslaunch turtlebot_teleop keyboard_teleop.launch
```

The TurtleBot teleop node is publishing Twist messages to /cmd_vel_mux/input/teleop, and we need to convert them into /catvehicle/cmd_vel.

The following command can do this conversion:

```
$ rosrun topic_tools relay /cmd_vel_mux/input/teleop
/catvehicle/cmd_vel
```

Now, you can move the car around the environment using the keyboard. This will be useful while we perform SLAM.

Running hector SLAM using a robotic car

After moving the robot around the world, let's do some mapping of the world. There are launch files present to start a new world in Gazebo and start mapping. Here is the command to start a new world in Gazebo:

```
$ roslaunch catvehicle catvehicle_canyonview.launch
```

This will launch the Gazebo simulation in a new world. You can enter the following command to view Gazebo:

```
$ gzclient
```

The Gazebo simulator with a new world is shown here:

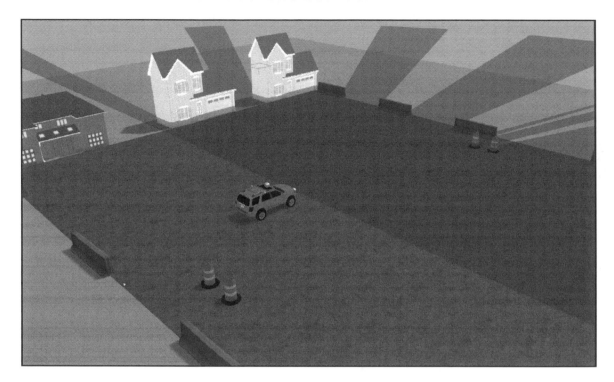

Figure 34: Visualization of a robotic car in an urban environment

You can start the teleoperation node to move the robot, and the following command will start the hector SLAM:

```
$ roslaunch catvehicle hectorslam.launch
```

To visualize the map generated, you can start Rviz and open the configuration file called `catvehicle.rviz`.

You will get the following kind of visualization in Rviz:

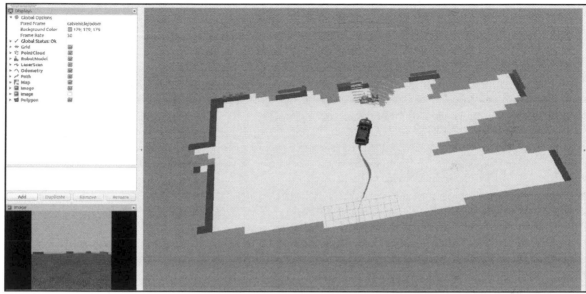

Figure 35: Visualization of a map in Rviz using a robotic car

After completing the mapping process, we can save the map using the following command:

```
$ rosrun map_server map_saver -f map_name
```

The preceding command will save the current map as two files, called `map_name.pgm` and `map_name.yaml`.

For more details of this project, you can check the following link:
http://cps-vo.org/group/CATVehicleTestbed

Interfacing a DBW car with ROS

In this section, we will see how to interface a real car with ROS and make it autonomous. As we discussed earlier, the DBW interface enables us to control a vehicle's throttle, brake, and steering using the CAN protocol.

There's an existing open source project that is doing this job. The project is owned by a company called Dataspeed Inc. (http://dataspeedinc.com/). Here is the list of projects related to self-driving cars from Dataspeed:

https://bitbucket.org/DataspeedInc/

We are going to discuss Dataspeed's ADAS vehicle development project.

First, we will see how to install the ROS packages of this project and look at the functionality of each package and node.

Installing packages

Here are the complete instructions to install these packages. We only need a single command to install all these packages.

We can install this on ROS Indigo and ROS Kinetic using the following command:

```
    bash <(wget -q -O -
https://bitbucket.org/DataspeedInc/dbw_mkz_ros/raw/default/dbw_mkz/scripts/
ros_install.bash)
```

You will get other methods of installation from the following link:

http://wiki.ros.org/dbw_mkz

Visualizing the self-driving car and sensor data

The previous packages help you interface a DBW car with ROS. If we don't have a real car, we can work with ROS bag files, visualize data, and process it offline.

The following command helps you visualize the URDF model of a self-driving car:

```
    $ roslaunch dbw_mkz_description rviz.launch
```

You will get following model when you execute it:

Figure 36: Visualization of a self-driving car

If we want to visualize the Velodyne sensor data, other sensors such as GPS and IMU, and control signal such as steering commands, brake, and acceleration, you can use the following commands:

Use this command to download the ROS bag file:

```
$ wget
https://bitbucket.org/DataspeedInc/dbw_mkz_ros/downloads/mkz_20151207_extra
.bag.tar.gz
```

You will get a compressed file from the preceding command; extract it to your home folder.

Now you can run the following command to read data from the bag file:

```
$ roslaunch dbw_mkz_can offline.launch
```

The following command will visualize the car model:

```
$ roslaunch dbw_mkz_description rviz.launch
```

And finally, we have to run the bag file:

```
$ rosbag play mkz_20151207.bag -clock
```

To view the sensor data in Rviz, we have to publish a static transform:

```
$ rosrun tf static_transform_publisher 0.94 0 1.5 0.07 -0.02 0
base_footprint velodyne 50
```

This is the result:

Figure 37: Visualization of a self-driving car

You can set **Fixed Frame** as the `base_footprint` and view the car model and Velodyne data.

The following commands can helps to communicate using ROS with DBW-based cars.

This is the command to do so:

```
$ roslaunch dbw_mkz_can dbw.launch
```

Now you can test the car using a joystick. Here is the command to launch its nodes:

```
$ roslaunch dbw_mkz_joystick_demo joystick_demo.launch sys:=true
```

Data provided by *Dataspeed Inc*, located in *Rochester Hills, Michigan*. For more information please visit `http://dataspeedinc.com`.

Communicating with DBW from ROS

In this section, we will see how we can communicate from ROS with DBW-based cars.

This is the command to do so:

```
$ roslaunch dbw_mkz_can dbw.launch
```

Now you can test the car using a joystick. Here is the command to launch its nodes:

```
$ roslaunch dbw_mkz_joystick_demo joystick_demo.launch sys:=true
```

Introducing the Udacity open source self-driving car project

There is another open source self-driving car project by Udacity (`https://github.com/udacity/self-driving-car`) that was created for teaching their Nanodegree self-driving car program. The aim of this project is to create a complete autonomous self-driving car using deep learning and using ROS as middleware for communication. The project is split into a series of challenges, and anyone can contribute to the project and win a prize. The project is trying to train a **convolution neural network** (**CNN**) from a vehicle camera dataset to predict steering angles. This approach is a replication of end-to-end deep learning from NVIDIA (`https://devblogs.nvidia.com/parallelforall/deep-learning-self-driving-cars/`), used in their self-driving car project called DAVE-2.

The following is the block diagram of DAVE-2. DAVE-2 stands for DARPA Autonomous Vehicle-2, which is inspired by the DAVE project by DARPA.

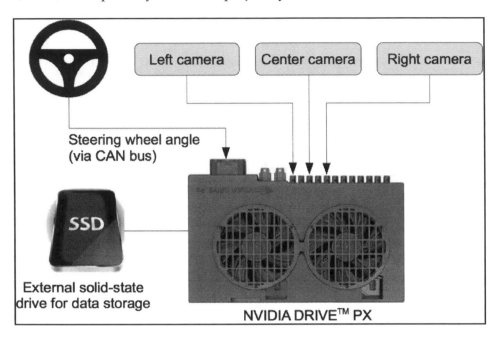

Figure 38: DAVE-2 block diagram

This system basically consists of three cameras and an NVIDIA supercomputer called NVIDIA PX. This computer can train images from this camera and predict the steering angle of the car. The steering angle is fed to the CAN bus and controls the car.

The following are the sensors and components used in the Udacity self-driving car:

- **2016 Lincoln MKZ**: This is the car that is going to be made autonomous. In the previous section, we saw the ROS interfacing of this car. We are using that project here too.
- **Two Velodyne VLP-16 LiDARs**
- **Delphi radar**
- **Point Grey Blackfly cameras**
- **Xsens IMU**
- **Engine control unit (ECU)**

This project uses the `dbw_mkz_ros` package to communicate from ROS to the Lincoln MKZ. In the previous section, we set up and worked with the `dbw_mkz_ros` package. Here is the link to obtain a dataset for training the steering model:
`https://github.com/udacity/self-driving-car/tree/master/datasets`. You will get a ROS launch file from this link to play with these bag files too.

Here is the link to get an already trained model that can only be used for research purposes: `https://github.com/udacity/self-driving-car/tree/master/steering-models`. There is a ROS node for sending steering commands from the trained model to the Lincoln MKZ. Here, `dbw_mkz_ros` packages act as an intermediate layer between the trained model commands and the actual car.

Open source self-driving car simulator from Udacity

Udacity also provides an open source simulator for training and testing self-driving deep-learning algorithms. The simulator project is available at `https://github.com/udacity/self-driving-car-sim`. You can also download the precompiled version of a simulator for Linux, Windows, and Mac from the same link.

Here are the screenshots of this simulator. We can discuss the working of the simulator along with the screenshots.

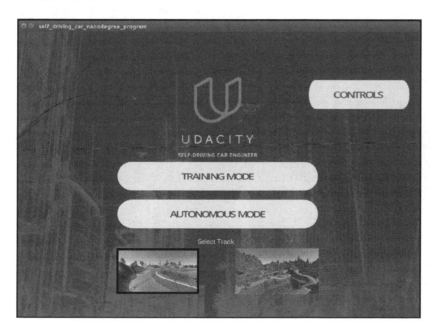

Figure 39: Udacity self-driving car simulator

You can see two options in the simulator; the first is for training and the second is for testing autonomous algorithms. We can also select the **Track** in which we have to drive the vehicle. When you click on the **Training Mode** button, you will get a racing car on the selected track. You can move the car using the WASD key combination, like a game. Here is a screenshot of the training mode.

Figure 40: Udacity self-driving car simulator in training mode

You can see a **RECORD** button in the top-right corner, which is used to capture the front camera images of the car. We can browse to a location, and those captured images will be stored in that location.

After capturing the images, we have to train the car using deep-learning algorithms to predict steering angle, acceleration, and braking. We are not discussing the code, but I'll provide a reference for you to write it. The complete code reference to implement the driving model using deep learning and the entire explanation for it are at `https://github.com/thomasantony/sdc-live-trainer`. The `live_trainer.py` code helps us train the model from captured images.

After training the model, we can run `hybrid_driver.py` for autonomous driving. For this mode, we need to select autonomous mode in the simulator and execute the `hybrid_driver.py` code.

Figure 41: Udacity self-driving car simulator in autonomous mode

You can see the car moving autonomously and manually override the steering control at any time.

This simulator can be used to test the accuracy of the deep learning algorithm we are going to use in a real self-driving car.

MATLAB ADAS toolbox

MATLAB also providing toolbox for working with ADAS and autonomous system. You can design, simulate, and test ADAS and autonomous driving systems using this toolbox. Here is the link to check the new toolbox.

```
https://in.mathworks.com/products/automated-driving.html
```

Questions

- What is the level of autonomy of a self-driving car?
- What are the different levels of autonomy?
- What are the important block diagrams of a self-driving car?
- List down five important sensors used in a self-driving car.

Summary

This chapter was a deep discussion of self-driving cars and their implementation. The chapter started by discussing the basics of self-driving car technology and its history. Afterward, we discussed the core blocks of a typical self-driving car. We also discussed the concept of autonomy levels in self-driving cars. Then, we took a look at different sensors and components commonly used in a self-driving car. We discussed how to simulate such a car in Gazebo and interfacing it with ROS. After discussing all sensors, we saw an open-source self-driving car project that incorporates all sensors and simulated the car model itself in Gazebo. We visualized its sensor data and moved the robot using a teleoperation node. We also mapped the environment using hector SLAM. The next project was from Dataspeed Inc., in which we saw how to interface a real DBW-compatible vehicle with ROS. We visualized the offline data of the vehicle using Rviz. Finally, we took a look at the Udacity self-driving car project and its simulator.

In the next chapter, we will see how to teleoperate a robot using the VR headset and Leap motion.

11
Teleoperating a Robot Using a VR Headset and Leap Motion

The term **virtual reality** is gaining popularity nowadays, even though it started long ago. The concept of virtual reality began in the 1950s as science fiction, but it took 60 years to become more popular and acceptable. Why it is more popular now? The answer is the availability of cheap computing. Before, a virtual reality headset was very expensive. Now, we can build one for $5. You may have heard about Google Cardboard, which is the cheapest virtual reality headset available currently, and there are many upcoming models based on it. Now we only need a good smartphone and cheap **virtual reality (VR)** headset to get the virtual reality experience. There are also high-end VR headsets such as the Oculus Rift and HTC Vive that have a high frame rate and response.

In this chapter, we will discuss a ROS project in which we can control a robot using a Leap Motion sensor and experience the robot environment using a virtual reality headset. We will demonstrate this project using a TurtleBot simulation in Gazebo and control the robot using Leap Motion. To visualize the robot environment, we will use a cheap VR headset along with an Android smartphone.

Here are the main topics we will discuss in this chapter:

- Getting started with a VR headset and Leap Motion
- Project prerequisites
- Design and working of the project
- Installing the Leap Motion SDK on Ubuntu
- Playing with the Leap Motion visualizer tool

- Installing ROS packages for Leap Motion
- Visualizing Leap Motion data in Rviz
- Creating a teleoperation node for Leap Motion
- Building and installing the ROS-VR Android application
- Working with the ROS-VR application and interfacing with Gazebo
- Working with the TurtleBot simulation in VR
- Troubleshooting the ROS-VR application
- Integrating the ROS-VR application and Leap Motion teleoperation

Getting started with a VR headset and Leap Motion

This section is for beginners who haven't worked with VR headsets and Leap Motion yet. A (**VR**) headset is a head-mounted display in which we can either put a smartphone or that has an inbuilt display that can be connected to HDMI or some other display port. A VR headset can create a virtual 3D environment by mimicking human vision, that is, stereo vision. Human vision works like this: we have two eyes and get two separate and slightly different images in each eye. The brain then combines these two images and generates a 3D image of the surroundings. Similarly, VR headsets have two lenses and a display. The display can be inbuilt or a smartphone. This screen will show a separate view of the left and right image, and when we put the smartphone or inbuilt display into the headset, it will focus and reshape using two lenses and will simulate 3D stereoscopic vision. In effect, we can explore a 3D world inside this headset. Rather than just visualizing the world, we can also control the event in the 3D world and hear sound too. Cool, right?

Here is the internal structure of a Google Cardboard VR headset:

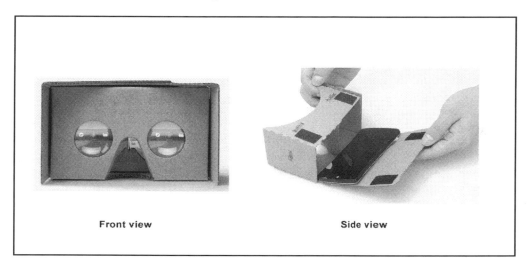

Figure 1: Google Cardboard VR headset

There is a variety of models of VR headsets available in addition to the high-end models such as Oculus Rift, HTC Vive, and so on. The following is one of the VR headsets, which we will use in this chapter. It works based on the same principle of Google Cardboard, but instead of cardboard, it uses a plastic body:

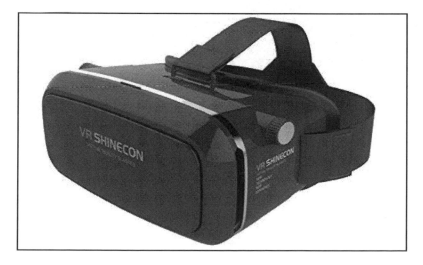

Figure 2: VR-SHINECON headset

You can test the VR feature by downloading Android VR applications from Google Play Store.

 You can search for `Cardboard` in Google Play Store to get the Google VR application. You can use it for testing VR on your smartphone.

The next device we are using in this project is the Leap Motion controller (`https://www.leapmotion.com/`). The Leap Motion controller is basically an input device like a PC mouse in which we can control everything using hand gestures. The Leap can accurately track the hands of a user and map the position and orientation of each finger joint accurately. It has two IR cameras and several IR projectors facing upward. The user can position their hand above the device and move their hand. The position and orientation of hands and fingers can be accurately retrieved from their SDK.

Here is the Leap Motion controller and how we can interact with it:

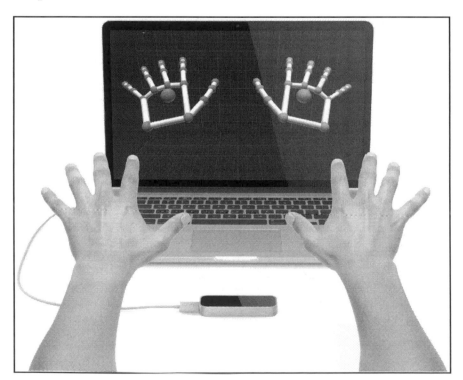

Figure 3: Interacting with the Leap Motion controller

Project prerequisites

So let's start discussing the project. The following are the software and hardware prerequisites of this project:

No	Component/software	Link
1	Low-cost VR headset	`https://vr.google.com/cardboard/get-cardboard/`
2	Leap Motion controller	`https://www.leapmotion.com/`
3	Wi-Fi router	Any router can connect to a PC or Android phone
4	Ubuntu 14.04.5 LTS	`http://releases.ubuntu.com/14.04/`
5	ROS Indigo	`http://wiki.ros.org/indigo/Installation/Ubuntu`
6	Leap Motion SDK	`https://www.leapmotion.com/setup/linux`

This project has been tested on ROS Indigo, and the code is compatible with ROS Kinetic too, but the Leap Motion SDK is still in development for Ubuntu 16.04 LTS. So here the code is tested using Ubuntu 14.04.5 and ROS Indigo. If you are ready with the components, let's look at the design of the project and how it works.

Design and working of the project

This project can be divided into two sections: teleoperation using **Leap Motion** and streaming images to an Android phone to get a VR experience inside a VR headset. Before going to discuss each design aspect, let's see how we have to interconnect these devices.

The following figure shows how the components are interconnected for this project:

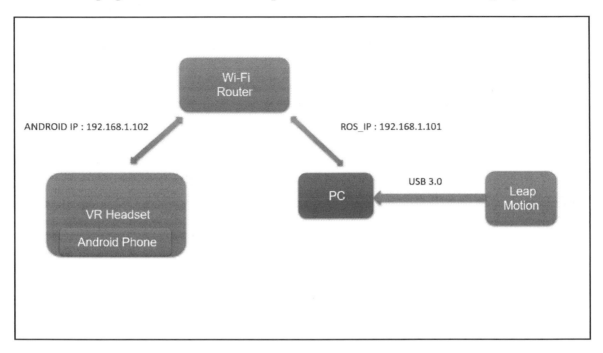

Figure 4: Hardware components and connection

You can see that each device (that is, PC and Android phone) is connected to a Wi-Fi router, and the router has assigned an IP to each device. Each device communicates using these IP addresses. You will see the importance of these addresses in the upcoming sections.

Next, we will see how we can teleoperate a robot in ROS using Leap Motion. We will be controlling it while wearing the VR headset. So, we don't need to press any buttons to move the robot; rather, we can just move it with our hands.

The basic operation involved here is converting the Leap Motion data into ROS Twist messages. Here, we are only interested in reading the orientation of the hand. We are taking roll, pitch, and yaw and mapping them into ROS Twist messages. Here is how:

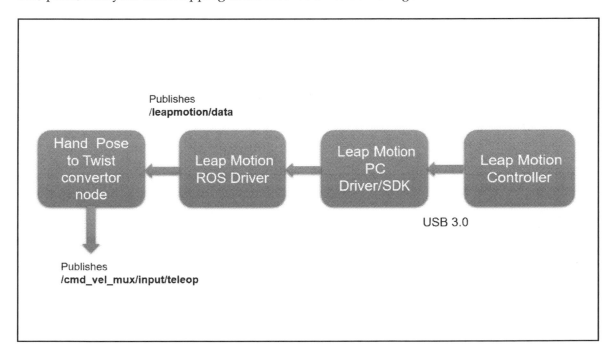

Figure 5: Leap Motion data to ROS command velocity

The preceding figure shows how Leap Motion data is manipulated into ROS Twist messages. The **Leap Motion PC Driver/SDK** interfaces the controller with Ubuntu, and the **Leap Motion ROS Driver**, which works on top of this driver/SDK, fetches the hand and finger position and publishes it as ROS topics. The node we are going to write can convert the hand position to Twist data, which will subscribe to the Leap Motion data topic called /leapmotion/data, convert it into corresponding command velocities, and publish to the topic called /cmd_vel_mux/input/teleop. The conversion algorithm is based on comparing the hand orientation value. If the value is in a particular range, we will publish a particular Twist value.

Here is the simple algorithm that converts Leap Motion orientation data into Twist messages:

1. Take the orientation values of hand, such as yaw, pitch, and roll, from the Leap Motion ROS driver.
2. The roll movement of the hand corresponds to robot rotation. If the hand rotates anticlockwise, then the robot will be triggered to rotate anticlockwise by sending a command velocity. This will be the opposite case of a roll of the hand in the clockwise direction.
3. If the hand is pitched down, the robot will move forward, and if the hand is pitched up, the robot will move backward.
4. If there is no hand movement, the robot will stop.

This is a simple algorithm to move a robot using Leap Motion. Okay, let's start with setting up a Leap Motion controller in Ubuntu and working with its ROS interface.

Installing the Leap Motion SDK on Ubuntu 14.04.5

In this project, we have chosen Ubuntu 14.04.5 LTS and ROS Indigo because the Leap Motion SDK will smoothly work with this combination. The Leap Motion SDK is not fully supported by Ubuntu 16.04 LTS; if there are any further fixes from the company, this code will work on Ubuntu 16.04 LTS with ROS Kinetic.

The Leap Motion SDK is the core of the Leap Motion controller. The Leap Motion controller has two IR cameras facing upwards and also has several IR projectors. This is interfaced with a PC, and the Leap SDK runs on the PC, which has drivers for the controller. It also has algorithms to process the hand image to produce the joint values of each finger joint.

Here is the procedure to install the Leap Motion SDK in Ubuntu:

1. Download the SDK from `https://www.leapmotion.com/setup/linux`; you can extract this package and you will find two DEB files that can be installed on Ubuntu.

2. Open Terminal on the extracted location and install the DEB file using the following command (for 64-bit PCs):

   ```
   $ sudo dpkg -install Leap-*-x64.deb
   ```

   If you are installing it on a 32-bit PC, you can use the following command:

   ```
   $ sudo dpkg -install Leap-*-x86.deb
   ```

3. If you can install this package without any errors, then you are done with installing the Leap Motion SDK and driver.

 There are more detailed installation and debugging tips are given on the following website:
https://support.leapmotion.com/hc/en-us/articles/223782608-Linux
-Installation

Visualizing Leap Motion controller data

If you successfully installed the Leap Motion driver/SDK, we can start the device by following these steps:

1. Plug the Leap Motion controller into a USB port; you can plug it into USB 3.0, but 2.0 is fine too.
2. Open Terminal and execute the dmesg command to verify that the device is properly detected on Ubuntu:

   ```
   $ dmesg
   ```

3. It may give you the following result if it's detected properly.

```
[10010.420978] usb 2-1.2: new high-speed USB device number 8 using ehci-pci
[10010.513671] usb 2-1.2: New USB device found, idVendor=f182, idProduct=0003
[10010.513682] usb 2-1.2: New USB device strings: Mfr=1, Product=2, SerialNumber=0
[10010.513688] usb 2-1.2: Product: Leap Dev Kit
[10010.513692] usb 2-1.2: Manufacturer: Leap Motion
[10010.514270] uvcvideo: Found UVC 1.00 device Leap Dev Kit (f182:0003)
lentin@lentin-Aspire-4755:~$ 
```

Figure 6: Kernel message when plugging in Leap Motion

If you are getting this message, you're ready to start the Leap Motion controller manager.

Playing with the Leap Motion visualizer tool

You can invoke the Leap Motion controller manger by executing the following command:

```
$ sudo LeapControlPanel
```

If you want to start just the driver, you can use the following command:

```
$ sudo leapd
```

Use this command to restart the driver:

```
$ sudo service leapd stop
```

If you are running the Leap control panel, you can see an additional menu on the left-hand side of the screen. Select the **Diagnostic Visualizer** to view the data from Leap Motion:

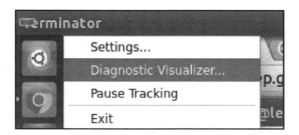

Figure 7: Leap Motion control panel

When you click on this option, a window will pop up in which you can see your hand, and figures get tracked when you put your hand over the device. You can also see the two IR camera views from the device. Here is the screenshot of the Visualizer application.

You can quit the driver from the same drop-down menu, too:

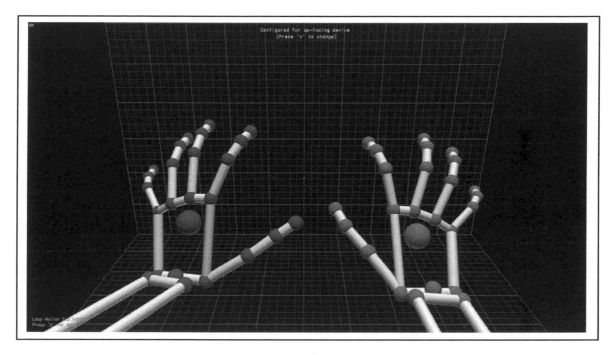

Figure 8: Leap Motion controller Visualizer application

You can interact with the device and visualize the data here. If everything is working well, we can proceed to the next stage: installing ROS driver for the Leap Motion.

> You can get more shortcuts to Visualizer from the following link:
> https://developer.leapmotion.com/documentation/cpp/supplements/L
> eap_Visualizer.html

Installing the ROS driver for the Leap Motion controller

To interface the Leap Motion with ROS, we will need the ROS driver for it. Here is the link to get the ROS driver for Leap Motion; you can clone it using the command:

```
$ git clone https://github.com/ros-drivers/leap_motion
```

Before installing the `leap_motion` driver package, we have to do a few things to have it properly compiled.

The first step is to set the path of the Leap Motion SDK in the `.bashrc` file. Assuming that the Leap SDK is in the user's `home` folder with the name `LeapSDK`, we have to set the path variable in `.bashrc` as follows.

```
$ export LEAP_SDK=$LEAP_SDK:$HOME/LeapSDK
```

This environment variable is needed for compiling the code of the ROS driver, which has Leap SDK APIs.

We also have to add the path of the Python extension of the Leap Motion SDK to `.bashrc`. Here is the command used to do it:

```
export PYTHONPATH=$PYTHONPATH:$HOME/LeapSDK/lib:$HOME/LeapSDK/lib/x64
```

This will enable Leap Motion SDK APIs in Python. After going through the preceding steps, you can save `.bashrc` and take a new Terminal, so that we will get the preceding variables in the new Terminal.

The final step is to copy the `libLeap.so` file to `/usr/local/lib`. Here is how we do it:

```
$ sudo cp $LEAP_SDK/lib/x64/libLeap.so /usr/local/lib
```

After copying, execute `ldconfig`:

```
$ sudo ldconfig
```

Okay, you are finished with setting the environment variables. Now you can compile the `leap_motion` ROS driver package. You can create a ROS workspace or copy the `leap_motion` package to an existing ROS workspace and use `catkin_make`.

You can use the following command to install the `leap_motion` package:

```
$ catkin_make install --pkg leap_motion
```

This will install the `leap_motion` driver; check whether the ROS workspace path is properly set.

Testing the Leap Motion ROS driver

If everything has been installed properly, we can test it using a few commands.

First, launch the Leap Motion driver or control panel using the following command:

```
$ sudo LeapControlPanel
```

After launching the command, you can verify that the device is working by opening the Visualizer application. If it's working well, you can launch the ROS driver using the following command:

```
$ roslaunch leap_motion sensor_sender.launch
```

If it's working properly, you will get topics with this:

```
$ rostopic list
```

```
lentin@lentin-Aspire-4755:~$ rostopic list
/leapmotion/data
/rosout
/rosout_agg
```

Figure 9: Leap ROS driver topics

If you can see `rostopic/leapmotion/data` in the list, you can confirm that the driver is working. You can just echo the topic and see that the hand and finger values are coming in, as shown in the following screenshot:

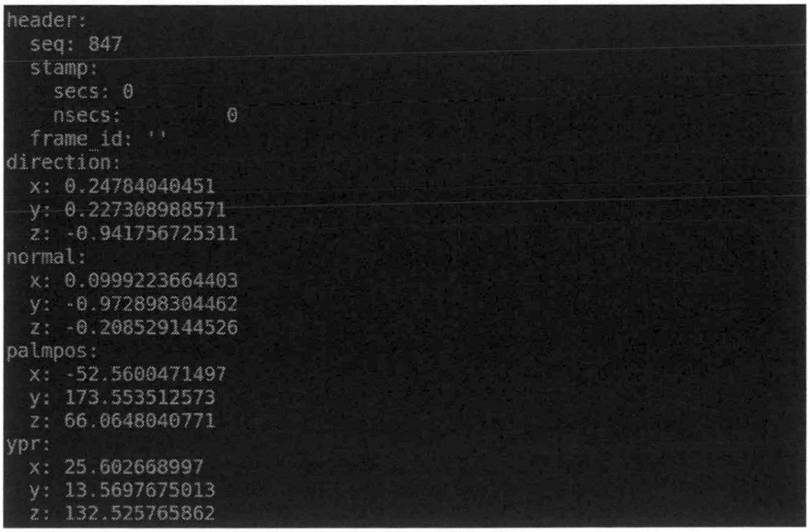

```
header:
  seq: 847
  stamp:
    secs: 0
    nsecs:          0
  frame_id: ''
direction:
  x: 0.24784040451
  y: 0.227308988571
  z: -0.941756725311
normal:
  x: 0.0999223664403
  y: -0.972898304462
  z: -0.208529144526
palmpos:
  x: -52.5600471497
  y: 173.553512573
  z: 66.0648040771
ypr:
  x: 25.602668997
  y: 13.5697675013
  z: 132.525765862
```

Figure 10: Data from the Leap ROS driver topic

Visualizing Leap Motion data in Rviz

We can visualize Leap Motion data in Rviz too. There is a ROS package called
leap_client (https://github.com/qboticslabs/leap_client). You can install this
package by setting the following environment variable in .bashrc:

```
export LEAPSDK=$LEAPSDK:$HOME/LeapSDK
```

Note that, when we add new variables in .bashrc, you may need to open new Terminal or
type bash in the existing Terminal.

Now, we can clone the code in a ROS workspace and build the package using
catkin_make.

Let's play around with this package. To launch nodes, we have to start LeapControlPanel:

```
$ sudo LeapControlPanel
```

Then start the ROS Leap driver launch file:

```
$ roslaunch leap_motion sensor_sender.launch
```

Now launch the leap_client launch file to start the visualization nodes. This node will
subscribe to the leap_motion driver and convert it into visualization markers in Rviz.

```
$ roslaunch leap_client leap_client.launch
```

Now, you can open Rviz using the following command and select the
leap_client/launch/leap_client.rviz configuration file to visualize the markers
properly:

```
$ rosrun rviz rviz
```

If you load the leap_client.rviz configuration, you may get hand data like the
following (you have to put your hand over the Leap):

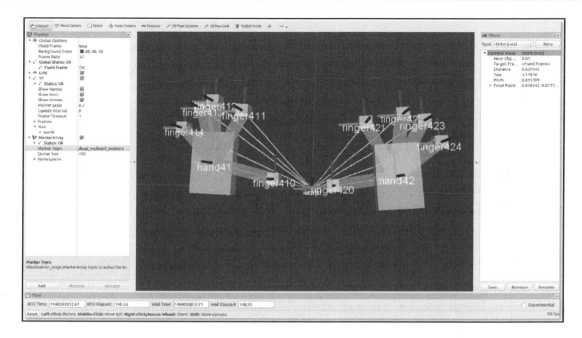

Figure 11: Data from the Leap ROS driver topic

Creating a teleoperation node using the Leap Motion controller

In this section, we can see how to create a teleoperation node for a robot using Leap Motion data. The procedure is very simple. We have to create a ROS package for this node. The following is the command to create a new package. You can also find this package from chapter_11_codes/vr_leap_teleop.

```
$ catkin_create_pkg vr_leap_teleop roscpp rospy std_msgs
visualization_msgs geometry_msgs message_generation visualization_msgs
```

After creation, you can use catkin_make. Now, let's create the node to convert Leap Motion data to Twist. You can create a folder called scripts inside the vr_leap_teleop package. Now you can copy the node called vr_leap_teleop.py from the existing package. Let's see how this code works.

We need the following Python modules in this node. Here, we require message definitions from the leap_motion package, which is the driver package.

```
import rospy
from leap_motion.msg import leap
from leap_motion.msg import leapros
from geometry_msgs.msg import Twist
```

Now we have to set some range values, in which we have to check whether the current hand value is within range. We are also defining the teleop topic name here.

```
teleop_topic = '/cmd_vel_mux/input/teleop'


low_speed = -0.5
stop_speed = 0
high_speed = 0.5

low_turn = -0.5
stop_turn = 0
high_turn = 0.5

pitch_low_range = -30
pitch_high_range = 30

roll_low_range = -150
roll_high_range = 150
```

Here is the main code of this node. In this code, you can see that the topic from the Leap Motion driver is being subscribed to here. When a topic is received, it will call the `callback_ros()` function:

```
def listener():
    global pub
    rospy.init_node('leap_sub', anonymous=True)
    rospy.Subscriber("leapmotion/data", leapros, callback_ros)
    pub = rospy.Publisher(teleop_topic, Twist, queue_size=1)

    rospy.spin()


if __name__ == '__main__':
    listener()
```

The following is the definition of the `callback_ros()` function. What it basically does is that it will receive the Leap Motion data and extract the orientation components of the palm only. So we will get yaw, pitch, and roll from this function. We are also creating a `Twist()` message to send the velocity values to the robot.

```
def callback_ros(data):
```

```
global pub

msg = leapros()
msg = data
yaw = msg.ypr.x
pitch = msg.ypr.y
roll = msg.ypr.z


twist = Twist()

twist.linear.x = 0; twist.linear.y = 0; twist.linear.z = 0
twist.angular.x = 0; twist.angular.y = 0; twist.angular.z = 0
```

We are performing a basic comparison with the current roll and pitch values again within the following ranges. Here are actions we've assigned for each movement of the robot:

Hand gesture	Robot movement
Hand pitch low	Move forward
Hand pitch high	Move backward
Hand roll anticlockwise	Rotate anticlockwise
Hand roll clockwise	Rotate clockwise

Here is a code snippet taking care of one condition. So in this case, if the pitch is low, then we are providing a high value for linear velocity in the x direction for moving forward.

```
if(pitch > pitch_low_range and pitch < pitch_low_range + 30):
  twist.linear.x = high_speed; twist.linear.y = 0;
  twist.linear.z = 0
    twist.angular.x = 0; twist.angular.y = 0; twist.angular.z = 0
```

Okay, so we have built the node, and we can test it at the end of the project. In the next section, we will see how to implement VR in ROS.

Building a ROS-VR Android application

In this section, we will see how to create a virtual reality experience in ROS, especially in robotics simulators such as Gazebo. Luckily, we have an open source Android project called ROS Cardboard (`https://github.com/cloudspace/ros_cardboard`). This project is exactly what we want we want for this application. This application is based on ROS-Android APIs, which help us visualize compressed images from a ROS PC. It also does the splitting of the view for the left and right eye, and when we put this on a VR headset, it will feel like 3D.

Here is a figure that shows how this application works:

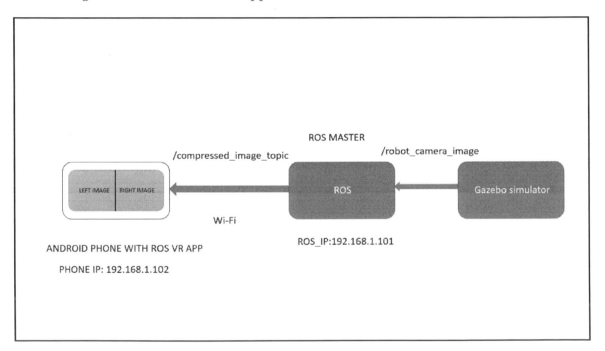

Figure 12: Communication between a ROS PC and Android phone

From the preceding figure, you can see that the image topic from Gazebo can be accessed from a ROS environment, and the compressed version of that image is sent to the ROS-VR app, which will split the view into left and right to provide 3D vision. Setting the `ROS_IP` variable on PC is important for the proper working of the VR application. The communication between PC and phone happens over Wi-Fi, both on same network.

Building this application is not very tough; first, you can clone this app into some folder. You need to have all of the Android development environment and SDK installed. To do so, you can refer to Chapter 8, *ROS on MATLAB and Android*. Just clone it and you can simply build it using the following instructions:

Plug your Android device into Ubuntu and execute the following command to check whether the device is detected on your PC:

```
$ adb devices
```

The **adb** command, which stands for **Android Debug Bridge**, will help you communicate with an Android device and emulator. If this command lists out the devices, then you are done; otherwise, do a Google search to find out how to make it work. It won't be too difficult.

After getting the device list, clone the ROS Cardboard project using the following command. You can clone into home or desktop.

```
$ git clone https://github.com/cloudspace/ros_cardboard.git
```

After cloning, enter the folder and execute the following command to build the entire package and install it on the device:

```
$ ./gradlew installDebug
```

You may get an error saying the required Android platform is not available; what you need is to simply install it using the Android SDK GUI. If everything works fine, you can able install the APK on an Android device. If you are unable to build the APK, you can also find it in chapter_11_codes/ros_cardboard. If installing the APK to the device directly failed, you can find the generated APK from ros_cardboard/ros_cardboard_module/build/outputs/apk. You can copy this APK to the device and try to install it. If you have any difficulty installing it, you can use the APK editor app, mentioned in Chapter 8, *ROS on MATLAB and Android*.

Working with the ROS-VR application and interfacing with Gazebo

The new APK will be installed with a name such as ROSSerial; before starting this app, we need to set a few things up on the ROS PC.

The next step is to set the ROS_IP variable in the .bashrc file. Execute the ifconfig command and retrieve the Wi-Fi IP address of the PC, as shown here:

```
wlan0     Link encap:Ethernet  HWaddr 94:39:e5:4d:7d:da
          inet addr:192.168.1.101  Bcast:192.168.1.255  Mask:255.255.255.0
          inet6 addr: fe80::9639:e5ff:fe4d:7dda/64 Scope:Link
          UP BROADCAST RUNNING MULTICAST  MTU:1500  Metric:1
          RX packets:1303 errors:0 dropped:0 overruns:0 frame:0
          TX packets:1127 errors:0 dropped:0 overruns:0 carrier:0
          collisions:0 txqueuelen:1000
          RX bytes:1136655 (1.1 MB)  TX bytes:243000 (243.0 KB)
```

Figure 13: PC Wi-Fi adapter IP address

For this project, the IP address was 192.168.1.101, so we have to set the ROS_IP variable as the current IP in .bashrc. You can simply copy the following line to the .bashrc file:

```
$ export ROS_IP=192.168.1.101
```

We need to set this; only then will the Android VR app work.

Now start the roscore command on the ROS PC:

```
$ roscore
```

The next step is to open the Android app, and you will get a window like the following. Enter ROS_IP in the edit box and click on the **CONNECT** button.

Figure 14: ROS-VR application

If the app is connected to the ROS master on the PC, it will show up as connected and show a blank screen with a split view. Now list out the topics on the ROS PC:

```
lentin@lentin-Aspire-4755:~$ rostopic list
/rosout
/rosout_agg
/usb_cam/image_raw/compressed
lentin@lentin-Aspire-4755:~$
```

Figure 15: Listing ROS-VR topics on PC

You can see topics such as /usb_cam/image_raw/compressed or /camera/image/compressed in the list, and what we want to do is feed a compressed image to whatever image topic the app is going to subscribe to. If you've installed the usb_cam (https://github.com/bosch-ros-pkg/usb_cam) ROS package already, you can launch the webcam driver using the following command:

```
$ roslaunch usb_cam usb_cam-test.launch
```

This driver will publish the camera image in compressed form to the /usb_cam/image_raw/compressed topic, and when there is a publisher for this topic, it will display it on the app also. If you are getting some other topics from the app, say, /camera/image/compressed, you can use topic_tools (http://wiki.ros.org/topic_tools) for remapping the topic to the app topic. You can use the following command:

```
$ rosrun topic_tools relay /usb_cam/image_raw/compressed
/camera/image/compressed
```

Now, you can see the camera view in the VR app like this:

Figure 16: ROS-VR app

This is the split view that we are getting in the application. We can also display images from Gazebo in the similar manner. Simple, right? Just remap the robot camera compressed image to the app topic. In the next section, we will learn how to view Gazebo images in the VR app.

Working with TurtleBot simulation in VR

We can start a TurtleBot simulation using the following command:

```
$ roslaunch turtlebot_gazebo turtlebot_playground.launch
```

You will get the TurtleBot simulation in Gazebo like this:

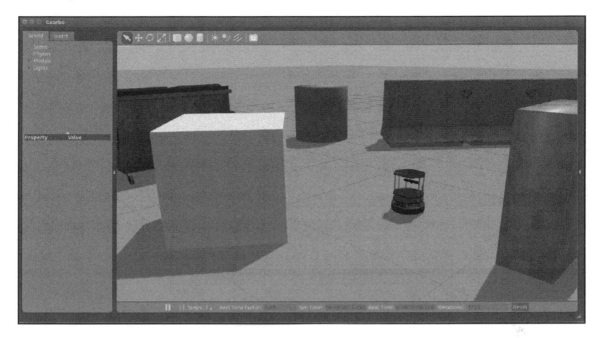

Figure 17: TurtleBot simulation in Gazebo

You can move the robot by launching the teleop node with the following command:

```
$ roslaunch turtlebot_teleop keyboard_teleop.launch
```

You can now move the robot using the keyboard. Launch the app again and connect to the ROS master running on the PC. Then, you can remap the Gazebo RGB image compressed data into an app image topic, like this:

```
$ rosrun topic_tools relay /camera/rgb/image_raw/compressed
/usb_cam/image_raw/compressed
```

Now, what happens is that the robot camera image is visualized in the app, and if you put the phone into a VR headset, it will simulate a 3D environment. The following screenshot shows the split view of the images from Gazebo:

Figure 18: Gazebo image view in ROS-VR app

You can move the robot using a keyboard as of now. In the next section, we can see the possible issues and the solutions that you may encounter when you work with the application.

Troubleshooting the ROS-VR application

You may get issues working with ROS-VR applications. One of the issues may be the size of the image. The left and right image size can vary according to the device screen size and resolution. This project was tested on a full-HD 5-inch screen, and if you have a different screen size or resolution, you may need to hack the application code. You can go to the app's project folder and open the code: `ros_cardboard/ros_cardboard_module/src/main/java/com/cloudspace/cardboard/CardboardOverlayEyeView.java`. You can change the `final float imageSize = 1.0f` value to `1.8f` or `2f`; this will stretch the image and fill the screen, but we might lose some part of the image. After this change, build it again and install it.

One of the other issues associated with the working of this app is that the app will not work until we set the ROS_IP value on the PC. So you should check whether ROS_IP is set.

If you want to change the topic name of the app, then go to ros_cardboard/ros_cardboard_module/src/main/java/com/cloudspace/cardboard/CardboardViewerActivity.java and change this line:

```
mOverlayView.setTopicInformation("/camera/image/compressed",
CompressedImage._TYPE);
```

If you want to work with other high-end VR headsets such as Oculus and HTC Vive, you can follow these links:
https://github.com/OSUrobotics/ros_ovr_sdk
https://github.com/robosavvy/vive_ros
http://wiki.ros.org/oculus_rviz_plugins

In the next section, we will combine the power of the VR headset and Leap Motion robot controller node.

Integrating ROS-VR application and Leap Motion teleoperation

In this section, we are going to replace the keyboard teleoperation with Leap Motion-based teleoperation. When we roll our hand to the anticlockwise direction, the robot also rotate anticlockwise, and vice versa. If we pitch our hand down, the robot will move forward, and if we pitch it up, it will move backward. So we can start the VR application and Turtlebot simulation like the previous section and, instead of keyboard teleop, run the Leap teleop node.

So before starting the Leap teleop node, launch the PC driver and ROS driver using the following commands:

```
$ sudo LeapControlPanel
```

Start the ROS driver using the following command:

```
$ roslaunch leap_motion sensor_sender.launch
```

Now launch Leap Motion on the Twist node using the following command:

```
$ rosrun vr_leap_teleop vr_leap_teleop.py
```

Now you can put the VR headset on your head and control the robot using your hand.

Questions

- How does a virtual reality headset work?
- How does the Leap Motion controller work?
- What is the algorithm to map from hand coordinates to Twist commands?
- We have installed PC driver for Leap Motion and for working with ROS, we have installed ROS driver. What is the difference between a ROS driver and PC driver?

Summary

This chapter was about creating a project to teleoperate a robot using a Leap Motion controller and VR headset. The basic aim of the chapter was to teleoperate the robot with hand gestures using a Leap Motion controller. After that, we visualized the robot camera image in a VR headset with the help of an Android phone. We started with discussing the general idea of VR and the Leap Motion controller, and then we switched to the design of the project. Then, we discussed the Leap Motion interface with PC and the driver installation. Later, we saw how to build a ROS node to control the robot using our hand. After building a teleop node, we saw how to create a VR app for ROS and then integrated both the app and the teleop node to experience 3D control of the robot using our hands.

12
Controlling Your Robots over the Web

Until now, we have been controlling and interacting with robots from the command line. What about creating a frontend GUI? If your robot is in a distant location and you want to visualize and control it through the web, this chapter can help you. This is the final chapter of this book, and deals with building a cool interactive web application based on ROS and controlling a robot using it. The projects in this chapter can be mainly used for creating a frontend robot commander in your browser. We'll discuss a few projects using the ROS web framework. Here is a list of the projects and topics we are going to cover in this chapter:

- Getting started with ROS web packages
- Setting up ROS web packages
- Teleoperating and visualizing a robot from a web browser
- Controlling robot joints from a web browser
- Robot surveillance application
- Web-based speech-controlled robot application

Getting started with ROS web packages

ROS offers several powerful and very useful packages to communicate over the Web and interact with robots from web browsers . In the first section, we will discuss some of the open source modules and packages for building cool robot web applications. The packages that we will discuss here are developed and maintained by the ROS web tools community (http://robotwebtools.org/). After discussing the basic web frameworks, we can start discussing projects that use it.

rosbridge_suite

If we want to interact with the ROS framework from our web browser, there should be some system that can convert the web browser commands to the ROS topics/services. `rosbridge` provides a JSON interface to ROS, allowing any client to send JSON commands (`http://www.json.org/`) to publish or subscribe to ROS topics, call ROS services, and more. `rosbridge` supports a variety of transport layers, including WebSockets (`https://en.wiki pedia.org/wiki/WebSocket`) and TCP.

The `rosbridge_suite` (`http://wiki.ros.org/rosbridge_suite`) is a meta-ROS package having an implementation of the `rosbridge` protocol. The JSON commands are converted to ROS topics/services using a node called `rosbridge_server`. This node can send or receive JSON commands from web browsers to ROS over web sockets. The `rosbridge_server` is the intermediate layer between the ROS system and web browser. The complete description of the rosbridge and `rosbridge_suit` can be found at `https://g ithub.com/RobotWebTools/rosbridge_suite`.

The following figure shows how the communication between the rosbridge server and web browser happens:

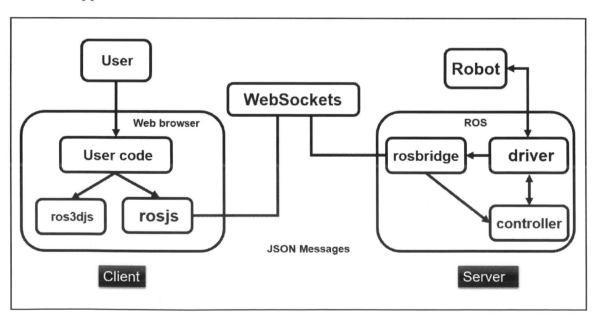

Figure 1: rosbridge_suite connection diagram

The rosbridge server can communicate with the ROS nodes. It can be a robot controller or ROS nodes. The rosbridge can also receive data from ROS which can send to web browser.

The `rosbridge_suite` collection consists of three packages:

- `rosbridge_library`: This package contains Python APIs to convert JSON messages to ROS messages and vice versa.
- `rosbridge_server`: This package has the WebSocket implementation of the `rosbridge` library. We have to start this tool for communicating with the web browser.
- `rosapi`: This provides service calls to fetch meta-information from ROS, such as a list of ROS topics and ROS parameters.

In the web browser, we can see rosbridge client. A rosbridge client is a program that communicates with rosbridge using its JSON API. In the preceding figure, we are using `roslibjs` as the client. Let's understand the main capabilities of these clients.

roslibjs, ros2djs, and ros3djs

In the previous section we have discussed about rosbridge, rosbridge server and rosbridge clients. In this section, we can see a list of rosbridge clients which can be used to send JSON commands from web browsers. Each client is used in different scenario.

Using **roslibjs** (`http://wiki.ros.org/roslibjs`), we can implement basic functionalities of ROS topics, services, actionlib, TF support, URDF, and many more ROS features–using this module.

The **ros2djs** (`http://wiki.ros.org/ros2djs`) is built on top of `roslibjs`. This library provides a 2D visualization manager for ROS. Using this library, we can visualize 2D maps in a web browser.

The **ros3djs** (`http://wiki.ros.org/ros3djs`) library is another cool JavaScript library that can visualize 3D data, such as URDF, TF, interactive markers, and maps. We can create a web-based Rviz instance using its APIs. We will look at some interesting projects using these libraries in the upcoming sections.

The tf2_web_republisher package

The `tf2_web_republisher` (http://wiki.ros.org/tf2_web_republisher) is a useful tool for interacting with robots via web browser. The main function of this package is to precompute TF data and send it via `rosbridge_server` to a `ros3djs` client. The TF data is essential to visualizing the posture and movement of the robot in a web browser.

Setting up ROS web packages on ROS Kinetic

In this section, we are going to see how to set up the previously mentioned libraries on our PC.

Installing rosbridge_suite

We can install `rosbridge_suite` using `apt-get` or build from the source code. First, let's see how to install it via `apt-get`.

Here are the commands to install it:

```
$ sudo apt-get update
```

On ROS Kinetic:

```
$ sudo apt-get install ros-kinetic-rosbridge-suite
```

On ROS Indigo:

```
$ sudo apt-get install ros-indigo-rosbridge-suite
```

If you are looking for the latest package, you can clone it and install it.

You can switch to your catkin workspace's `src` folder and clone the source code using the following command:

```
$ git clone https://github.com/RobotWebTools/rosbridge_suite
```

After cloning the folder, you can use `catkin_make`:

```
$ catkin_make
```

If you encounter any dependency issues, install that package too.

Now we can work with the rosbridge client libraries `roslibjs`, `ros2djs`, and `ros3djs`.

Setting up rosbridge client libraries

To store all these library files, you can create a folder called `ros_web_ws`. Actually, there is no need to create a catkin workspace because we don't need to build the modules. You will get the prebuilt modules once you download it from the repositories.

Switch to the `ros_web_ws` folder and run the following commands to clone each ROS JavaScript library:

For `roslibjs`:

```
$ git clone https://github.com/RobotWebTools/roslibjs.git
```

For `ros2djs`:

```
$ git clone https://github.com/RobotWebTools/ros2djs
```

For `ros3djs`:

```
$ git clone https://github.com/RobotWebTools/ros3djs
```

If you check out the `ros3djs` folder, you will see the following:

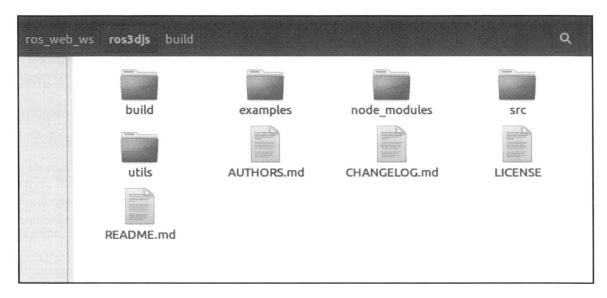

Figure 2: The ros3d_js module folder

The `build` folder contains the `ros3djs.js` modules, which can be used in our web application, and in the `examples` folder, you can find starter web applications. Similar to `ros3djs`, you can also find examples from `roslibjs` and `ros2djs`.

This is the API list of these three modules:

`roslibjs` APIs: `http://robotwebtools.org/jsdoc/roslibjs/current/`

`ros2djs` APIs: `http://robotwebtools.org/jsdoc/ros2djs/current/`

`ros3djs` APIs: `http://robotwebtools.org/jsdoc/ros3djs/current/`

Installing tf2_web_republisher on ROS Kinetic

We can install the `tf2_web_republisher` package by following these steps:

First, switch to your ROS catkin workspace and clone the package code using the following command:

```
$ git clone https://github.com/RobotWebTools/tf2_web_republisher
```

After cloning the code, install the following package, which may be required to build the preceding package:

```
$ sudo apt-get install ros-kinetic-tf2-ros
```

After installing the dependent package, you can install `tf2_web_republisher`, by using the `catkin_make` command from the workspace.

 If you are getting an error regarding message generation, you can add the following line of code to `package.xml`:
`<build_depend>message_generation</build_depend>`

Teleoperating and visualizing a robot on a web browser

This is the first project in this chapter. As we have seen in the other chapters, we are starting with a simple project. This web application can teleoperate the robot from the web browser itself using a keyboard. Along with the teleoperation, we can also visualize the robot in the browser itself. Here is the working block diagram of this project:

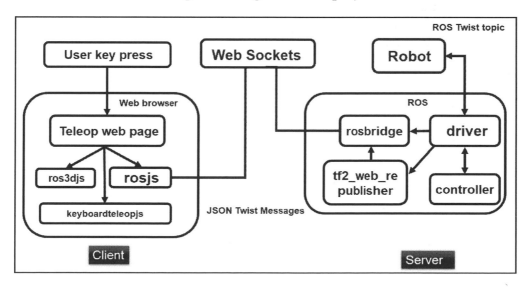

Figure 3: Working of web-based robot keyboard teleoperation project

Working of the project

In this section, we can see the basic working of this project. Imagine that a Turtlebot simulation is running on your PC. We have to control the robot from the web based teleoperation, so when we press a button from web browser, the key press is detected using JavaScript code and map each key press to ROS Twist message. This is done by using rosbridge clients. The rosbridge client sends Twist message as JSON command to the rosbridge server. The communication is happening over WebSockets as shown in the preceding image. When ROS system receives this topic, it can feed to the robot.

At the same time, the TF data and robot description are sending to the rosbridge client for visualizing the robot movement inside the browser. This is done by `tf2_web_republisher`.

We are using a ROS package called `keyboardteleopjs` (`http://wiki.ros.org/keyboardteleopjs`), which can send Twist messages from a web browser according to the key press. Along with that, we are using `ros3djs` to visualize the robot model in the browser. Upon getting the JSON Twist command, the rosbridge server will convert it into the corresponding ROS topic. You find web keyboard teleoperation application `keyboardteleop.html` from `chapter_12_code/ros_web_ws`.

Before running the application, let's discuss the code. Open `keyboardteleop.html` in a text editor, and let's now look at the use of each section of the code.

Basically, web applications are written in HTML/CSS and JavaScript. Similar to other programming languages, initially we have to include the CSS/JS modules that we are going to use in the HTML code. We can call the APIs of these modules and use them in our code. Let's go through the various modules we are using in this code.

The following code snippet includes a CSS file and standard jQuery (`https://jquery.com/`) modules into this code:

```
<link rel="stylesheet" type="text/css"
href="http://ajax.googleapis.com/
ajax/libs/jqueryui/1.8/themes/base/jquery-ui.css" /><script
src="https://ajax.googleapis.com/
ajax/libs/jquery/1.8.0/jquery.min.js"></script><script
src="https://ajax.googleapis.com/
ajax/libs/jqueryui/1.8.23/jquery-ui.min.js"></script>
```

The following code snippet loads JavaScript modules required for loading mesh files into the web browser. We can load mesh files such as STL and COLLADA files, primarily.

```
<script src="http://cdn.robotwebtools.org/
threejs/current/three.js"></script><script
src="http://cdn.robotwebtools.org/
threejs/current/ColladaLoader.js"></script><script
src="http://cdn.robotwebtools.org/   threejs/current/STLLoader.js">
</script><script src="http://cdn.robotwebtools.org/
ColladaAnimationCompress/current/ColladaLoader2.js"></script>
```

The following JS modules are importing `roslibjs` and `ros3djs`. The `roslibjs` and `ros3djs` are imported from the `build` folder.

```
<script src="http://cdn.robotwebtools.org/
EventEmitter2/current/eventemitter2.min.js"></script>
<script src="../build/roslib.js"></script>
<script src="../build/ros3d.js"></script>
```

We can also include this from web resources:

```
<script src="http://cdn.robotwebtools.org/
roslibjs/current/roslib.js"></script>
<script src="http://cdn.robotwebtools.org/
 ros3djs/current/ros3d.min.js"></script>
```

The following script will help you to perform keyboard teleoperation from a web browser. The script is actually got by downloading the `keyboardteleop` ROS package:

```
<script src="../build/keyboardteleop.js"></script>
```

Alternatively, we can use the following line from the web resource:

```
<script src="http://cdn.robotwebtools.org/
keyboardteleopjs/current/keyboardteleop.js"></script>
```

So we are done with including necessary modules for this application. Next, we have to add JavaScript code inside this HTML code. Following are the main section of the code, which is doing tasks such as connecting to the WebSocket, creating a handler for sending Twist messages, creating a handler for keyboard teleoperation, and creating a new 3D viewer, URDF, and TF client. Let's go through each section one by one.

Connecting to rosbridge_server

The whole initialization of this project is written inside a single function called init().
Let's take a look at all the things inside this function.

The first part of the code connects to rosbridge_server if it is running. The following
code snippet does this:

```
var ros = new ROSLIB.Ros({
  url : 'ws://localhost:9090'
});
```

As you can see, we are creating an object of ROSLIB.Ros for communicating with
rosbridge_server. When this code runs, it will connect to rosbridge_server, which is
listening on ws://localhost:9090. Instead of running both on the same system, we can
provide the IP address of the system that is running ROS and rosbridge_server.

Initializing the teleop

In this section, we'll see how to initialize keyboard teleoperation. We've already discussed a
JS module to handle keyboard teleoperation. The following code shows the initialization of
that module:

```
var teleop = new KEYBOARDTELEOP.Teleop({
  ros : ros,
  topic : teleop_topic
});
```

This will create a handler of the KEYBOARDTELEOP.Teleop class with the given topic name.
The topic name is already defined in the beginning of the code. We also need to pass the
ROS node object we created earlier.

Creating a 3D viewer inside a web browser

In this section, we will see how to create a 3D viewer for visualizing URDF models inside a
web browser. We can define properties of the viewer and the HTML ID for displaying the
viewer in the corresponding area:

```
var viewer = new ROS3D.Viewer({
  background : 000,
  divID : 'urdf',
  width : 1280,
```

```
    height : 600,
    antialias : true

});
```

The following line of code will add a 3D grid into the 3D viewer:

```
viewer.addObject(new ROS3D.Grid());
```

Creating a TF client

The following code creates a TF client, which can subscribe to the TF data from the tf2_web_republisher package and update the 3D viewer according to it. Here, we have to mention the fixed frame name, such as Rviz. The fixed frame is already defined in the beginning of our code. For a TurtleBot simulation, it will be odom.

```
var tfClient = new ROSLIB.TFClient({
  ros : ros,
  fixedFrame : base_frame,
  angularThres : 0.01,
  transThres : 0.01,
  rate : 10.0
});
```

Creating a URDF client

This section of code creates a URDF client, which is responsible for loading the robot's URDF file. For proper working of the URDF client, we should provide a ROS node object, TF client object, base URL for COLLADA files to load, and the 3D viewer scene object to render the URDF file. To load the meshes into the 3D viewer, we may have to use a mesh loader such as ROS3D.COLLADA_LOADER from Three.js, which is included in the beginning of the code. This loader can retrieve the COLLADA file from the robot_description parameter:

```
var urdfClient = new ROS3D.UrdfClient({
  ros : ros,
  tfClient : tfClient,
  path : 'http://resources.robotwebtools.org/',
  rootObject : viewer.scene,
  loader : ROS3D.COLLADA_LOADER
});
```

After the `init()` function, we can see two other functions. One is for handling the slider, which can set the speed of the robot, and next function is `submit_values()`, which will execute when the **Submit** button is clicked on. This function retrieves the teleop topic and base frame name from the input text box and calls the `init()` function using it. This tool can be used for teleoperating all robots without changing the code.

Creating text input

The following is the HTML snippet that creates a textbox to enter the teleoperation topic and base frame ID inside the web application. When the button is pressed, the teleop object will start publishing Twist messages to the given input teleoperation topic.

```
<form >
  Teleop topic:<br>
  <input type="text" name="Teleop Topic" id='tele_topic'
value="/cmd_vel_mux/input/teleop">
  <br>
  Base frame:<br>
  <input type="text" name="Base frame" id='base_frame_name'
value="/odom">
  <br>

 <input type="button" onmousedown="submit_values()" value="Submit">

</form>
```

The following code tries to load the `init()` function when the web page is loaded, but we've coded it in a way that it will initialize only when the **Submit** button is pressed:

```
<body onload="init()">
```

The slider and 3D viewer are displayed in the following HTML:

```
<div id="speed-label"></div>
<div id="speed-slider"></div>
<div id="urdf"></div>
```

Running the web teleop application

Let's see how we can run this web application.

First, we have to start a robot simulation in Gazebo. Here, we are testing with a TurtleBot simulation. You can launch the TurtleBot simulation using the following command:

```
$ roslaunch turtlebot_gazebo turtlebot_world.launch
```

Now, we can set the parameter `use_gui` to `true`. The robot will only visualize on the browser if this parameter is set.

```
$ rosparam set use_gui true
```

After running this command, run `tf2_web_republisher` in another Terminal window, using the following command:

```
$ rosrun tf2_web_republisher tf2_web_republisher
```

After launching it, let's launch the rosbridge server to start WebSocket communication. You can start it using the following command:

```
$ roslaunch rosbridge_server rosbridge_websocket.launch
```

Congratulations; you are done with the commands that need to be executed from ROS; now, let's open `keyboardteleop.html` in Chrome or Firefox.

You will see the following window in the browser:

Web-browser keyboard teleoperation

Teleop topic:
/cmd_vel_mux/input/teleop
Base frame:
/odom
Submit

Run the following commands in the terminal then refresh this page. Check the JavaScript console for the output.

1. roslaunch turtlebot_gazebo turtlebot_world.launch
2. rosparam set use_gui true
3. rosrun tf2_web_republisher tf2_web_republisher
4. roslaunch rosbridge_server rosbridge_websocket.launch
5. Use your arrow keys on your keyboard to move the robot (must have this browser window focused).

Figure 4: Initial components in keyboard teleoperation

When you submit the teleop topic and base frame, you can see the 3D visualizer appear in the same window with the robot model. Now you can use keys such as W, S, A, and D to move the robot around the workspace. You can adjust the speed of the robot by moving the slider. Here is the window you will get when you press the **Submit** button:

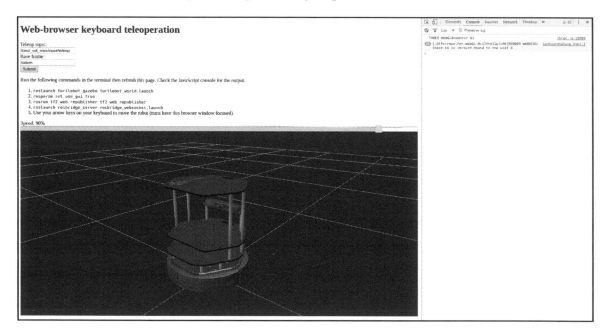

Figure 5: Web-based keyboard teleoperation

In the previous screenshot, you can see a JavaScript console window too. You can enable it by pressing *Ctrl + Shift + I* or right-clicking on the page and using the **Inspect** option. This window will be useful for debugging.

 If you keep on clicking on the **Submit** button, a new 3D viewer will be created. So refresh the page to change the teleop topic and base frame ID.

Controlling robot joints from a web browser

This is the second project we are going discuss in this chapter. The aim of this project is to control robot joints from the web browser itself.

Here is the block diagram of the working of a joint state publisher from the web browser:

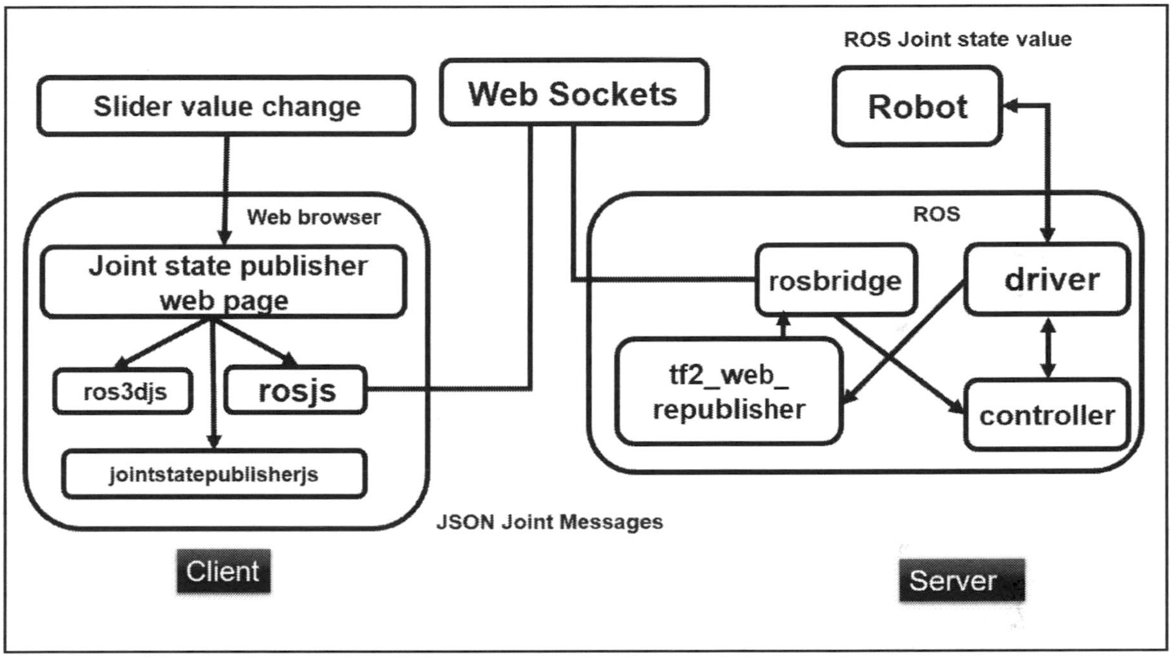

Figure 6: Block diagram of web-based joint state controller

From the block diagram, we can see that we are using another JavaScript module called
jointstatepublisherjs. This module has a class to create a joint state publisher for all
joints defined inside the URDF file.

Installing joint_state_publisher_js

To use this joint state control module, we need to clone the following package into the ROS
catkin workspace. Here is the command:

```
$ git clone https://github.com/DLu/joint_state_publisher_js
```

You can use catkin_make after executing the preceding command.

You can see the JavaScript module from the `joint_state_publisher_js/build` folder. You can copy this module and use it for your own applications.

You will get HTML code for the joint state publisher from `chapter_12_codes/ros_web_ws/joint_state_publisher.html`. The code is very similar to our first project, but you can see some new APIs inside this code. Let's look at the new code snippets that you can see in this code.

Including the joint state publisher module

As we have discussed, to enable sliders inside the web browser, we need to include some JavaScript modules. We can insert them from the `build` folder or directly from the Web itself.

Including from the `build` folder:

```
<script src="../build/jointstatepublisher.js"></script>
```

Including directly from the Web:

```
<script src="http://cdn.robotwebtools.org/
jointstatepublisherjs/current/jointstatepublisher.min.js">
</script>
```

Creating the joint state publisher object

Here is the code snippet for creating the joint state publisher. The sliders will be placed in the HTML `divID` called `sliders`.

```
var jsp = new JOINTSTATEPUBLISHER.JointStatePublisher({
    ros : ros,
    divID : 'sliders'
});
```

Creating an HTML division for sliders

Here is the definition of the HTML `div` element with an `id` of `sliders`.

```
<div id="sliders" style="float: right"></div>
```

That's all about the code. Now let's go through the procedure to run this project.

Running the web-based joint state publisher

First, start a robot simulation or load a robot description. Here, we are using the robot model of the PR2 robot. If you don't have this model, you can install it using the following command:

```
$ sudo apt-get install ros-kinetic-pr2-description
```

After installing, you can load the PR2 description using the following command:

```
$ roslaunch pr2_description upload_pr2.launch
```

After uploading the code, you can set the ROS parameter called `use_gui` to `true` using the following command:

```
$ rosparam set use_gui true
```

After doing this, you can start the `joint_state_publisher_js` node using the following command. This will launch joint state publisher, `rosbridge`, and `tf2_web_republisher` node in a single launch file.

```
$ roslaunch joint_state_publisher_js core.launch
```

Okay, you are done launching the ROS nodes; now, it's time to open the HTML code in a web browser. You can open `joint_state_publisher.html` from `chapter_12_codes/ros_web_ws`.

You will get the following window if everything works fine:

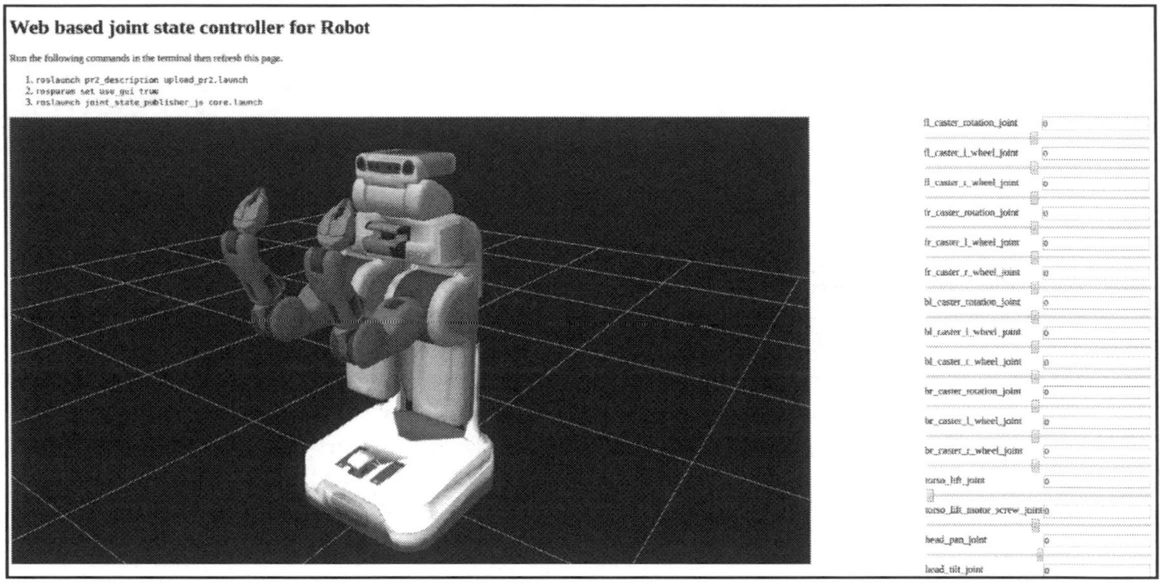

Figure 7: Web-based joint state publisher

Congratulations, you have successfully set up a joint state publisher inside a web browser. Now you can move robot joints by moving the sliders.

Robot surveillance application

This is another interesting web application, which can move a robot and display the camera view of the robot in a browser. This application is best used to teleoperate a robot for surveillance. Let's see how to set it up in ROS Kinetic.

Prerequisites

- `web_video_server`: This is a ROS package for the HTTP streaming of ROS images in multiple image formats. You can find the package from the following ROS wiki page: http://wiki.ros.org/web_video_server
- `mjpegcanvasjs`: This JavaScript module can display the MJPEG stream from `web_video_server` in an HTML canvas. You can get the code from the following link: http://wiki.ros.org/mjpegcanvasjs

- keyboardteleopjs: This JS module helps us teleoperate a robot from a web browser using a keyboard. We used this module in the first project. You can get it from here: http://wiki.ros.org/keyboardteleopjs

Installing prerequisites

Install the web_video_server package. Switch to your catkin workspace and clone the package code to the src folder:

```
$ git clone https://github.com/RobotWebTools/web_video_server.git
```

Build the package using the catkin_make command.

Download the mjpegcanvasjs module. You can simply use the following command:

```
$ git clone https://github.com/rctoris/mjpegcanvasjs
```

Okay, you are done with the packages and modules. Now you can check the code in chapter_12_codes/ros_web_ws/ws/Robot_Surveillance.html.

We'll now discuss the main parts of the code.

Explaining the code

Initially, we have to include the JS module, which is mjpegcanvas.js, to get streamer functionality inside the browser. The following code does this job:

```
<script src=" http://cdn.robotwebtools.org/
mjpegcanvasjs/current/mjpegcanvas.js">
</script>
```

The following is the function to start an MJPEG viewer inside the browser. You can set parameters such as width, height, and ROS image topic to display in the viewer.

```
var viewer = new MJPEGCANVAS.Viewer({
   divID : 'mjpeg',
   host : 'localhost',
   width : 640,
   height : 480,
   topic : '/camera/rgb/image_raw',
   interval : 200
 });
}
```

To visualize multiple camera views, we can use code like this. Here, you can add any number of image topics. We also need to mention the image label. In the viewer, we have a provision to select the desired view from the list:

```
var viewer = new MJPEGCANVAS.MultiStreamViewer({
  divID : 'mjpeg',
  host : 'localhost',
  width : 640,
  height : 480,
  topics : [ '/camera/rgb/image_raw', '/camera/rgb/image_raw',
      '/camera/rgb/image_raw' ],
   labels : [ 'Robot View', 'Left Arm View', 'Right Arm View' ]
});
```

Running the robot surveillance application

Okay, so we are ready to run the application. Let's begin.

You can run any robot simulation that has some sort of image topic or camera topic.

For a demo, we will launch the TurtleBot simulation using the following command:

```
$ roslaunch turtlebot_gazebo turtlebot_world.launch
```

After launch the simulation, run the HTTPS streamer node from `web_video_server`:

```
$ rosrun web_video_server web_video_server
```

After running `web_video_server`, launch `rosbridge_server` to send Twist messages to ROS from the keyboard teleoperation module:

```
$ roslaunch rosbridge_server rosbridge_websocket.launch
```

Now, open `Robot_Surveillance.html` to look at the output.

Here is the output you will get for the `Robot_Surveillance` application.

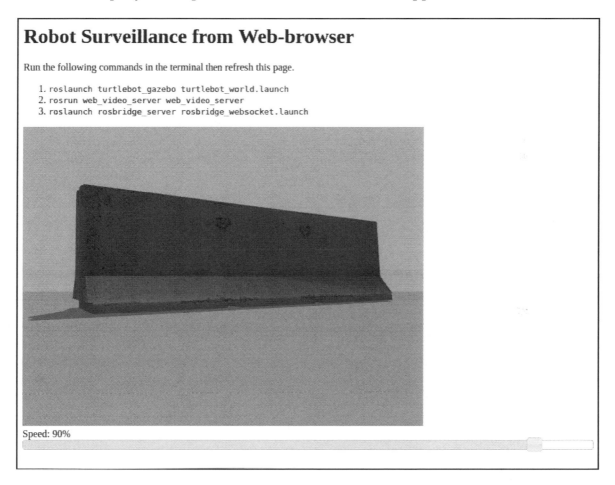

Robot Surveillance from Web-browser

Run the following commands in the terminal then refresh this page.

1. `roslaunch turtlebot_gazebo turtlebot_world.launch`
2. `rosrun web_video_server web_video_server`
3. `roslaunch rosbridge_server rosbridge_websocket.launch`

Speed: 90%

Figure 8: The robot surveillance application

Now you can move the robot and look at the camera view from inside the browser itself.

Web-based speech-controlled robot

The next project we will discuss is to control a robot from a web browser using speech commands. It enables teleoperation of the robot using a button interface and speech. If we are not interested in moving the robot with voice commands, we can try moving the robot using buttons.

We can assign a set of voice commands in this application, and when a voice command is given, the robot will perform the corresponding task.

In this application, we are using basic commands such as move forward, move backward, turn left, and turn right to move the mobile robot. We will demo this application using the TurtleBot simulation.

Prerequisites

We need a few things installed for the proper working of this application.

We need to install the apache2 webserver to run this application. We can install it using the following command:

```
$ sudo apt-get install apache2
```

This project is actually adapted from a project from roswebtools. The current project can send the command velocity to the robot, but there is no visualization to get feedback of robot motion. So we are adding a 3D viewer inside this application. Here is the existing project:

https://github.com/UbiquityRobotics/speech_commands

You can find the new application's code from chapter_12_codes/ros_web_ws/speech_commands/speechcommands.html. We'll now look at the new APIs and code you may need to customize to work with your own robot.

Enabling speech recognition in the web application

Speech recognition functionality is something we haven't discussed yet in any of our projects. Actually, performing speech recognition from a web browser is better than using offline speech recognizers. The reason is that web-based speech recognition uses Google's speech recognition system, which is one of the best speech recognition systems available today. So let's see how we can implement speech recognition in our application.

The web speech API specification
(https://dvcs.w3.org/hg/speech-api/raw-file/tip/speechapi.html) provides speech recognition and synthesis APIs for a web application, but the majority of web browsers don't support it anymore. Google introduced their own speech recognition and synthesis platform and integrated into these APIs. Now these APIs can work well with Google Chrome.

Let's look at the procedure to enable web-based speech recognition APIs.

The first step is to check whether the browser supports the speech APIs. We can check this using the following code:

```
if (!('webkitSpeechRecognition' in window)) {
    //Speech API not supported here...
} else { //Let's do some cool stuff :)
```

If the browser supports speech recognition, we can start the speech recognizer.

First, we have to create a speech recognizer object, which will be used throughout the code:

```
var recognition = new webkitSpeechRecognition();
```

Now we will configure the speech recognizer object. If we want to implement continuous recognition, we need to mark this as true. This is suitable for dictation.

```
recognition.continuous = true;
```

The following settings enable intermediate speech recognition results even if they are not final:

```
recognition.interimResults = true;
```

Now we configure the recognition language and accuracy of detection:

```
recognition.lang = "en-US";
recognition.maxAlternatives = 1;
```

After configuring the speech recognition object, we can fill in the callback functions. The callback functions handle each speech recognition object event. Let's look at the main callback of the speech recognition object.

The `start()` callback function calls when the recognition starts, and we may add some visual feedback, such as flashing a red light or something here to alert the user:

```
recognition.onstart = function() {

  ;
  };
```

Also, if the speech recognition is finished, the `onend()` callback will be called, and you can give some visual feedback here too:

```
recognition.onend = function() {

  };
```

The following callback, `onresult()`, give the final recognized results of speech recognition:

```
recognition.onresult = function(event) {

    if (typeof(event.results) === 'undefined') {
        recognition.stop();
        return;
    }
```

After getting the results, we have to iterate inside the result object to get the text output:

```
for (var i = event.resultIndex; i < event.results.length; ++i)      {
        if (event.results[i].isFinal) {
            console.log("final results: " +
event.results[i][0].transcript);

        }

else {
            console.log("interim results: " +
    event.results[i][0].transcript);
        }
    } };
```

Now we can start the speech recognition through a user-defined function called `startButton()`. Whenever this function is called, the recognition will start.

```
<div onclick="startButton(event);"></div>

function startButton(event) {
    recognition.start();
}
```

Running a speech-controlled robot application

To run the application, you have to copy the `chapter_12_codes/ros_web_ws/speech_commands` folder to `/var/www/html`. If you are in the `ros_web_ws` folder in Terminal, you can use the following command to do this:

```
$ sudo cp -r speech_commands /var/www/html
```

Now run the following ROS launch files to start the TurtleBot simulation, rosbridge, and `tf2_republisher` nodes:

```
$ roslaunch turtlebot_gazebo turtlebot_world.launch
```

Launch the rosbridge server:

```
$ roslaunch rosbridge_server rosbridge_websocket.launch
```

Now launch the `tf2_web_republisher` node using the following command:

```
$ rosun tf2_web_republisher tf2_web_republisher
```

Okay, you are done with launching all the ROS nodes. Now, let's open Chrome and enter the following address:

```
localhost/speech_commands/speechcommands.html
```

If everything works fine, you will get a window like this:

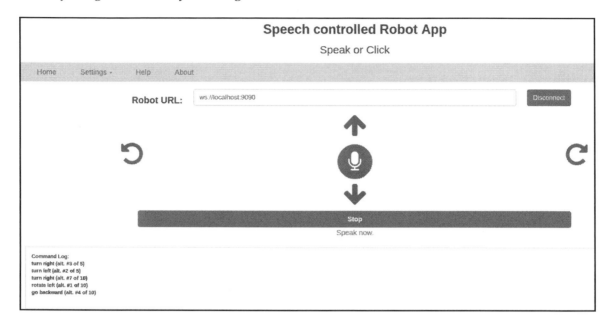

Figure 9: Speech controller Robot App screen

Here, find the **Robot URL** box, which has to be set to `ws://localhost:9090`, and click on the **Connect** button. If it connects, you'll get a confirmation, and the **Connect** button will become **Disconnect**. After connecting to rosbridge, you can see the 3D viewer inside the browser. Now you can click on the mic symbol. If the mic symbol turns green, then you are done. You can give it a command and the robot will start moving. If the mic did not turn green, you may need to check Chrome's mic settings to allow mic access to this app. The complete app will look like this:

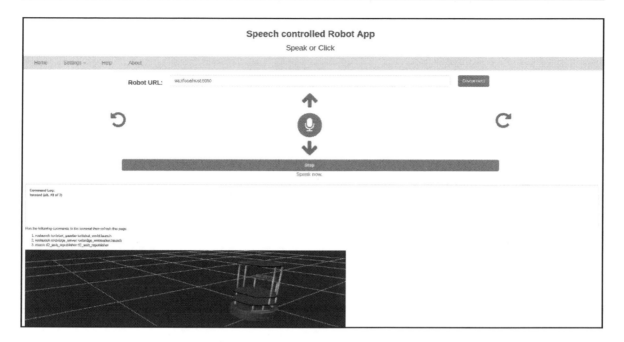

Figure 10: Speech controller Robot App screen

You can see the detected commands in the **Command Log** box. You can also move the robot using the arrow keys shown in the window.

Questions

- What is the main use of the `rosbridge_server` package?
- What is the use of `roslibjs` and `ros3djs`?
- What is the ROS package used to stream images from ROS to a web browser?
- How is the robot surveillance application used?

Summary

This chapter was about creating interactive web applications using ROS. The chapter was started with discussing basic ROS packages and JavaScript modules used for building a robot web application. After discussing the packages, we discussed how to install it them. After setting up all the packages, we started our first project, teleoperating the robot from a web browser. In that application, we controlled the robot using a keyboard and visualized the robot at the same time. The next project was about controlling the joint state of the robot. We created the application and tested it on the PR2 robot. The third project was about creating a robot surveillance application, which combines keyboard teleoperation and image streaming from the robot. The last project was about creating a cool speech recognition-based robot controller application.

Index